DHARMA FEAST COOKBOOK
RECIPES FOR A FRESH START

DHARMA FEAST COOKBOOK

RECIPES FOR A FRESH START

THERESA ROGERS AND TIKA ALTEMÖLLER

KALINDI PRESS
PRESCOTT, ARIZONA

Cover Design and Painting: Matt Sullivan

Interior Design and Layout: Tiia Antere

Library of Congress Cataloging-in-Publication Data

Rogers, Theresa (Courtney Theresa), 1969-
Dharma feast cookbook : recipes for a fresh start / Theresa Rogers and Tika Altemöller.
   p. cm.
Includes bibliographical references and index.
ISBN 978-1-935826-21-7 (trade paper)
1. Vegetarian cooking. 2. Cooking (Natural foods) 3. Cookbooks. I. Altemöller, Tika. II. Title.
TX837.R746 2012
641.5'636--dc23

                    2011041288

Kalindi Press
P.O. Box 1589
Prescott, AZ 86302
800-381-2700
http://www.kalindipress.com

This book was printed in the U.S.A. on recycled, acid-free paper using soy ink.

DISCLAIMER: The material in this book is intended for educational purposes only, and as such is not meant to be a substitute for professional medical intervention or used to treat or diagnose diseases. In any use of the recipes, diets or other recommendations or approaches discussed in this book, please apply common sense and as necessary consult a qualified, licensed health care professional.

For Lee Lozowick

who was the embodiment of both the essence
and form of the pages that follow.

This book is dedicated to his good name.

ACKNOWLEDGEMENTS

We would like to thank Purna Steinitz for his editorial and contextual contributions.

Suzanne Nestrud for her vast contribution to this book, which included overseeing the project, editing, and the testing of recipes.

Madeline Rains, Bhu Sullivan, and Fire Williams for photographs.

Matt Sullivan for the painting on the cover and cover design.

Khandro Kelly and Lisa Ratto who supported this entire project.

Tiia Antere for formatting and layout.

And our many friends who tested recipes.

Recipes and other information from *Intuitive Eating* by Humbart Santillo, N.D. used by generous permission of Hohm Press, Prescott, Arizona.

Recipes from *Hohm Cookin': Music for the Tastebuds* used by generous permission of Hohm Press, Prescott, Arizona.

Raw recipes from *Raw Soups, Salads, and Smoothies* by Frederic Patenaude used by generous permission of the author.

Quotes from the *Hohm Sahaj Mandir Study Manuals* used by generous permission of Hohm Press, Prescott, Arizona.

Information from *10 Essential Foods* by Lalitha Thomas used by generous permission of the Hohm Press.

Information from Health Coach Systems Intl. Inc. used by generous permission of Dr. Mark Percival.

CONTENTS

When wonderful things are ordinary and ordinary things are wonderful,
then at last God has been glimpsed.

– LEE LOZOWICK

People try to solve their problems in a therapist's office or in support groups when, in fact, many can be solved at the dining room table. It is possible that an emotional problem may very well just be a clogged liver or weak kidneys. If you want to change something in your life, start with a change in your diet.

– PURNA STEINITZ

Most of us in the West spend our days surrounded by a fast-paced, technological world that is not particularly nurturing. Western culture has evolved into a way of life in which we cram as many words, information, and activities as we can into our day. Eating is often what we do while we're busy doing something else. For the most part, grocery stores feed this lifestyle— they are filled with processed foods meant to be prepared and eaten as quickly as possible. Magazine, newspaper, radio, and television ads reinforce getting carried away by and becoming lost in unhealthy habits and food cravings.

We have lost our intuitive understanding of how to feed ourselves and our loved ones in a way that nourishes rather than one that does little more than placate the cravings of the less conscious part of ourselves. We crave concentrated foods— they are fast, easy, processed and often full of salt, fat, and sugar—like chips, power bars, and ready-made energy drinks and shakes. We think we don't have time—or energy—to cook.

So why, when it seems like we have less time in the day than ever, would we consider using a cookbook that asks us to make our meals from basic, natural ingredients? The answer is as simple as the recipes themselves. Within such an intentional diet are the seeds to bring sanity back into our lives.

If asked about our physical state, many of us would say "I feel pretty good." Maybe we're tired or irritable sometimes, or our stomachs occasionally hurt, or we have a skin rash, but overall we don't get sick very often and we unconsciously think this is an indication of robust health. What many of us consider to be "fine" or "normal" means we don't have a debilitating disease, which is not a good definition of "healthy." In fact, our concept of "health" changes considerably when we learn about what we are eating and how it affects us. Once we do, we may realize that we have not experienced the natural life force of our bodies other than on a camping trip, yoga class, or weekend seminar.

Our bodies can tolerate many toxic substances, until the point that these cause disease. In the meantime, the body compensates for the neuro-toxins (toxins that make the brain malfunction) found in processed food additives. It compensates for vitamin, mineral, and protein deficiencies. It compensates for lack of water and exercise. It adapts to overindulgence in sugars, salt, and fat. But a body in such a condition is not one that is healthy, whole, or balanced enough to function properly, and this can significantly impact every area of your life. If your brain is flooded with neurotoxins on a daily basis, for example, then your whole thought process is affected. Ideas, physical reactions, and even the depths you are capable of in relationships and life in general are all altered by the "fog" stealing through your mind. Indeed, eventually the body won't compensate anymore, and then acute or chronic disease will likely set in. The list of symptoms of physical crisis is long and includes, gas and other digestive problems, allergies, symptoms of arthritis, insomnia, depression, spaciness and emotional fixation on anger, fear, and drama.

Sanity begins with learning about food, preparing it properly, and eating it consciously. If we do this, we have the possibility of becoming healthy and free of the confusion and reactivity caused by toxic foods. The diet we recommend, which is based on plant-based whole foods, leaves fewer residues physically, mentally, and emotionally. It does not leave a coat of plaque on our intestines, tissues, brain, etc., so it does not alter our body or brain chemistry the way many animal-based and processed foods do. For example, when we eat a lot of sugar, whether we know it or not, we have chemically-induced emotional highs and lows. The same is true with eating too many artificial preservatives, which cause a feeling of ungrounded spaciness.

When we eat a clean diet these residues are naturally eliminated from our body, and this has a deep effect on our mind and emotions. We can start experiencing a more natural response to the world around us, instead of reacting to it as per the toxins in the foods we eat. But we can't know the impact these substances have until we get our bodies to a cleaner state and can experience the contrast.

As our diet changes, we become able to take care of ourselves and model for our children and others a relationship with food and life itself that is an expression of intention and sanity. Our premise is that a change in diet is the single most effective way to begin to move your attention away from psychological and physical problems so that you may dedicate that energy to your highest commitments.

Our recommendations are based on scientific findings as well as personal experience. *Dharma Feast Cookbook : Recipes for a Fresh Start* also draws on the way people have eaten for thousands of years from a wide range of cultures[1]. One of this book's strengths is that we have synthesized knowledge from these many different sources so that you don't need to. *Dharma Feast Cookbook* offers you enough of the basics to help you make informed food choices, and encourages you to seek out more information if interested.

The 3-Stage Diet

We understand it can be tough to change your diet. Where do you even start? That's why we've created the following 3-stage chart. It's based on the chart found in Humbart Santillo's book *Intuitive Eating* but we've modified it significantly to fit the Dharma Feast diet.

In each stage, we help you transition toward more healthy food choices.

By going a little bit at a time you have a much greater chance of making lasting change. And you get to decide which stage you want to stick with. Maybe you're a Stage 3 for beverages, a Stage 2 for Dairy, and a Stage 1 for nuts and seeds! That's great—you're still eating healthy! The point is to have intention with your diet.

Stage 1 is the first step. Here we replace more processed foods with healthier alternatives. We eliminate alcohol, processed white flour, refined white sugar, and many foods which contain these ingredients. We also begin to add the foods on the recommended diet.

[1]"Dharma" refers to the universal truths that underlie all of life. It is the intrinsic nature of things, the right order of things; life as it is—the natural condition and essence of everything.

Stage 2 contains a few foods, such as limited dairy products and eggs, which are eventually eliminated in Stage 3. We recommend that all dairy products in Stage 2 be raw and preferably goat (for example, raw goat milk, cheese, yogurt, etc.) When a dairy product is raw, it contains the enzymes that are needed for digestion.

The **Stage 3** diet we recommend is plant-based (with the exception of organic butter or organic ghee), and is composed of whole foods as close to their original form as possible. These foods include raw and cooked vegetables, greens, fruits, grains, nuts, seeds, beans, fermented foods, seaweeds, fresh-squeezed juices, good-quality organic butter or organic ghee, water, and certain supplements (see *Supplementation* in *Resources and Recommendations*, Chapter 8).

STAGE **1**	STAGE **2**	STAGE **3**
BEVERAGES	**BEVERAGES**	**BEVERAGES**
Strictly limit coffee and caffeinated tea.	Eliminate caffeinated coffee and tea. Drink herbal teas.	Same as Stage 2.
Eliminate alcohol. Substitute juice and herbal teas.	Increase fresh fruit and vegetable juices.	Same as Stage 2.
FLOUR	**FLOUR**	**FLOUR**
Eliminate white flour; use whole-grain or nut flours only.	Reduce use of flours.	Eliminate flours except for special occasions.
BREAD	**BREAD**	**BREAD**
Use whole-grain bread, or whole-grain sourdough bread, without additives or preservatives. No white flour.	Limit the use of whole-grain breads.	Only eat whole-grain breads for special occasions if we wish.
CEREALS	**CEREALS**	**CEREALS**
Use whole-grain cereals. (Don't substitute natural boxed cereal for boxed cereal except for our children if they're used to this kind of food.)	Same as Stage 1.	When you feel like you need grain in the morning, choose raw whole grains like oatmeal or 7-grain cereal. Soak them before cooking.
GRAINS	**GRAINS**	**GRAINS**
Add more whole grains to meals.	Use whole grains no more than one time each day.	Use whole grains for meals no more than three times a week. If you live in a cold climate, you may need grains more often than this.
BEANS	**BEANS**	**BEANS**
Add more beans to meals.	Use beans for meals no more than four times a week.	Use beans for meals no more than three times a week.

STAGE 1	STAGE 2	STAGE 3
PASTA	**PASTA**	**PASTA**
Use whole wheat or rice, etc., pastas. Eliminate white flour pasta.	Use whole-grain pastas no more than two times a week.	Occasional use of whole-grain pasta for special occasions if we wish.
SWEETENERS	**SWEETENERS**	**SWEETENERS**
Eliminate white sugar and sugar substitutes. Use real raw sugar, honey, maple syrup, Sunfood Organic Raw Agave syrup, stevia, or unsulfured molasses instead.	Use natural sweeteners (raw honey, Grade B maple syrup, Sunfood Organic Raw Agave syrup or stevia) in limited quantities.	Use as little sweetener as possible, training ourselves to appreciate the natural taste of food.
SPICES/ CONDIMENTS	**SPICES/ CONDIMENTS**	**SPICES/ CONDIMENTS**
Eliminate table salt, using sea salt instead. Eliminate all spice blends that include sugar, MSG, or other artificial ingredients.	Pay attention not to use too much salt. Limit the use of spices—see *Spices* in *Dharma Feast Diet* in *The Basics,* Chapter 3.	Use a small amount of sea salt daily because the body needs salt, not for taste purposes. Same as Stage 2 for spices.
Eliminate catsup, mustard, etc., made with additives or preservatives. This does not apply to condiments listed in *Dharma Feast Diet* (Chapter 3).	Limit condiments to once or twice a week.	Limit condiments to special occasions if we wish.
FATS AND OILS	**FATS AND OILS**	**FATS AND OILS**
Use raw unsalted organic butter or organic ghee (clarified butter) No margarine. If you live where raw butter is not available then substitute unsalted organic butter.	Same as Stage 1.	Same as Stage 1.
Use cold-pressed extra-virgin olive oil, coconut oil, sesame oil, grapeseed oil, and safflower oil. Palm oil can be used for sautéing. Do not use soy oil.	Same as Stage 1.	Same as Stage 1.
FRUITS	**FRUITS**	**FRUITS**
Increase intake of fresh fruits.	Fresh fruit should be 20% of diet.	Fresh fruit should be 30% of diet.
Eliminate canned fruits.	Same as Stage 1.	Same as Stage 1.
Use unsweetened, unsulfured dried fruits.	Use no more than a handful of dried fruits daily.	Same as Stage 2.
JUICES	**JUICES**	**JUICES**
Use freshly made or bottled, not-from-concentrate, unsweetened juices with no additives or preservatives.	Reduce use of all pre-packaged juices. Use primarily freshly-made fruit and vegetable juices.	Eliminate all prepackaged juices. Use freshly-made fruit and vegetable juices.

Adapted from Santillo, Humbart "Smokey," N.D., *Intuitive Eating: Everybody's Guide to Lifelong Health and Vitality Through Food* (Hohm Press: Prescott, Arizona, 1993),162-168. Used with permission.

STAGE 1	STAGE 2	STAGE 3
DAIRY	**DAIRY**	**DAIRY**
Switch to organic raw cheese.	Limit use of organic raw cheese to four times a week.	Eliminate cheese.
Use organic free-range eggs from grass-fed chickens.	Reduce use of eggs to three times a week.	Eliminate use of eggs.
Use organic raw cow or goat milk or use rice, oat, or nut milk.	Limit animal-based milk intake to three times a week.	Eliminate animal-based milk; use rice, oat, or nut milk.
MEAT, FISH, POULTRY	**MEAT, FISH, POULTRY**	**MEAT, FISH, POULTRY**
Use organic, grass-fed meat; organic, free-range poultry; and select fish either once a day or every other day.	Use organic, grass-fed meat; organic, free-range poultry; and select fish either once a day or every other day.	Eliminate meat, poultry, and fish except for special occasions.
NUTS AND SEEDS	**NUTS AND SEEDS**	**NUTS AND SEEDS**
Use unsalted nuts/seeds.	Use soaked raw nuts and seeds, toasted nuts and seeds, or nuts and seeds prepared according to recipes.	Use toasted nuts and seeds or soaked raw nuts and seeds.
VEGETABLES	**VEGETABLES**	**VEGETABLES**
Eliminate iceberg lettuce. Use romaine, green leaf, red leaf, spinach, etc.	Increase vegetables and salads to 25% of our diet.	Increase vegetables and salads to 30% to 40% of our diet.
Limit use of packaged, frozen, and canned vegetables. Please refer to *Canned or Jarred Foods* and *Frozen Foods* in *Dharma Feast Diet* (Chapter 3).Use primarily raw, sautéed, or steamed fresh vegetables.	Same as Stage 1.	Eliminate canned, jarred, and frozen foods. Limit potatoes to no more than twice a week. Limit sautéed and steamed vegetables. However, take into consideration what is needed in colder months, our personal needs, etc.
SALAD DRESSING	**SALAD DRESSING**	**SALAD DRESSING**
Use homemade or natural bottled dressings. Avoid those with "natural flavors" or other additives.	Use predominately homemade dressings. Limit the use of dressings containing sweeteners.	Use only simple, dairy-free homemade dressings that do not contain sweeteners.
SOUPS	**SOUPS**	**SOUPS**
Limit use of canned or pre-packaged soups.	Use only homemade soups.	Same as Stage 2. Use mostly during cold weather.
SWEETS & DESSERTS	**SWEETS & DESSERTS**	**SWEETS & DESSERTS**
Decrease amount of candy, desserts, etc. by 50%—buy health food varieties.	Use dark chocolate, homemade desserts, etc., no more than three times a week. Non-dairy frozen desserts and frozen fruit desserts can be used as treats.	Eliminate all candy, desserts, etc., except for special occasions. Occasionally have frozen bananas, strawberries, blueberries, etc., that have been blended.

The Essential Foundations

The way of eating introduced in *Dharma Feast Cookbook* is supported by three pillars:

1. Discipline and Commitment: For most of us, our relationship to food is unconscious. It is an expression of psychological need, self-indulgence, or avoidance, and changing it takes discipline and commitment.

2. Open Mind: For some of us what is contained here may be radical and provocative but if we are open to what we are reading, we just might jump in with both feet and make one of the most positive changes in our lifetime.

3. Conscious Experimentation: Eating on this diet means eating or moving towards primarily non-animal, plant-based whole foods (as close to their original state as possible)—raw and cooked vegetables, greens, fruits, grains, nuts, seeds, beans, fermented foods, seaweeds, raw organic butter or organic ghee (clarified butter), fresh-squeezed juices, water, and certain supplements (see *Supplementation* in *Resources and Recommendations*, Chapter 8). We call this the Stage 3 diet. But pay attention while experimenting with the Stages—make sure what you "crave" is something your body needs, not just something you want. The cleaner your body is, the easier it will be for you to feel what's working and what needs to be modified.

A Word About Our Differences

We understand that a sane relationship to food and eating comes easier to some due to our past efforts, or because of what was modeled for us as children. Others really struggle with establishing this type of "sanity." Being aware of and being "in one's body" gets a lot of press and air-time in magazines and workshops and following the recommendations in this book is a powerful and practical way to experience this possibility. However, we recognize that many people are not ready to eat exclusively at Stage 3, which is why we've also included a wide range of recipes for what we call the Stage 2 diet, which contains a few foods, such as limited dairy products and eggs, not found in Stage 3. Most important is that we choose a diet for ourselves and cultivate the discipline to follow it.

With this in mind, the material presented here is designed to put as much power as possible back in your hands when it comes to choices about your diet. We have found that making different decisions is much easier when we really know what it is we're choosing. We invite you to try eating this way for a month—it may take that long for your body and taste buds to adapt. But the goal should be to include as much healthy food in your everyday life as possible.

Ultimately, our bodies are all different, so what will work for one person may not work well for another. Please create your own relationship to what you find here. Give yourself space to experiment and have fun. But, let the ideas take root in you and see what sprouts. In our experience, the recipes and lifestyle changes suggested here can open the door to a healthier and more centered body and mind.

We hope this cookbook brings you a renewed sense of connection to the meals you create. Let's bring back the tradition of families and friends gathered around the table, sharing good food and good conversation. Here's to helping make sure that never goes out of style!

THE CONTEXT OF AN INTENTIONAL DIET

> You cannot experience wisdom if
> you refuse experience.
>
> — ARNAUD DESJARDINS

Coming home to fresh, simple, delicious food is one of the best ways to nurture ourselves and our families. One of the goals of *Dharma Feast Cookbook* is to inspire and educate so that the food you eat, and the way you eat it, grounds and strengthens you. But there is more to a nurturing meal than just the food on the table and we would be remiss if we didn't address this. Dr. M. Scott Peck hints at this "more" when he says, "Community is the salvation of the world."

People feel cared for when a meal is cooked and served with intention. We create that feeling when we prepare food for others with the particular aim of serving them (something that is often overlooked in our "me-driven" culture). When we also then take time to set the table and sit down to eat with people we care about, we get much closer to creating the relationships and community we long for. Eating together boils down to not being separate from others. So how about inviting friends over to eat more often?

Creating a nurturing meal begins with our mood. We are not trained to consider this when we prepare a meal, and yet whatever we're feeling is transferred directly into the food. This is not a "new age" idea—the impact of mood has been discussed for centuries in books like *How to Cook Your Life—From the Zen Kitchen to Enlightenment* by Zen Master Dogen and Kosho Uchiyama Roshi, and has even been explored in movies such as *Babette's Feast, Chocolat,* and *Like Water for Chocolate*.

Cooking and Eating

Cooking doesn't come easily to everyone. For some of us, even considering cooking a meal puts us in a bad mood. We might think, "Why do *I* always have to make dinner?" It can be challenging to be faced with this endless job, which for the most part is invisible to the people around us. It's easy to feel taken for granted, and for resentment to grow. Some of us unconsciously go out to eat a lot because of this. And yet what mood we bring to cooking a meal is fed to (and can be felt by, consciously or unconsciously) those we are feeding.

One way to work with mood is to remember the bond we have with the people we are cooking for. Maybe they have been busy all day and need a nurturing space to rest. A grounding, satisfying, healthy, and tasty meal is an opportunity to connect with each other away from whatever the challenges of the day have been. As the cook, part of your responsibility could be to stand for sanity during meals—no cell phones, pagers, or house phones on; no negative gossip, no complaining about the day, and a minimum of talking about logistics. You can invite your family into this way of being by speaking from the heart about such things. This, too, helps create a meal that feeds on all levels.

Whatever negative thoughts you may have during cooking, try drawing your present attention back to the cutting board, the knife, and the onion in front of you. It is a saving grace that the task before you is often simple and physical. You can use this to bring yourself out of your head— to feel the knife in your hands, your feet on the floor. Look at your surroundings. Find ways to ground yourself in the present moment, which will keep your mind on the task at hand, not the numerous tasks waiting for you after your meal.

There are many opportunities to bring intention and life to creating a meal, including how you prepare ingredients. For example, the simple task of chopping vegetables can be made intentional by following their natural shape while cutting them. Broccoli begs to be made into little trees. Carrots can be sliced into longish rounds that fit into the mouth. Little things like this make a mindless task into a conscious one.

When preparing a number of vegetables, try varying the size of the pieces—all one size tends to make the ingredients combine together in an unappetizing way. Also make sure that the various sizes work well together both for the eye and the mouth.

Consider textures. Pair a mashed or pureed food with a solid-textured dish like raw vegetables or salad. You might also want to pay attention to color combinations. In Germany they say, "The eye is eating, too." A meal of potatoes, cabbage salad, and cauliflower can look uninteresting because the colors are so similar.

Another way to bring life to a meal is to serve dishes at different temperatures—hot soup and a cool salad complement each other nicely. Serve hot foods *really* hot—make sure cold dishes are on the table first and bring hot foods out just before everyone takes their seats.

Create a beautiful meal from seasonal ingredients. This not only helps vary your diet but also brings the season alive—fresh peaches mean summer in the same way that pumpkins represent autumn. When choosing produce, try to buy food grown as locally as possible. Foods offered out of season have often been flown thousands of miles to the grocery shelves. They are not allowed to ripen on the plant and so contain less nutrients. (See *Farmers Markets* and *Gardens* in *Restoring a Culture of Food*, Chapter 7)

If you've had a long day and the thought of making a meal seems overwhelming, a salad with avocado, roasted nuts and olives, or a hearty soup can serve as a main dish. Or have two vegetables as a main dish—one hearty (like potatoes) and one that complements it (like asparagus)—with a fresh green salad. And as we're all busy people, the recipes in this book make use of readily-available ingredients, and are simple and easy to make. Each recipe is also delicious—as reported by our families and friends who have tested them.

Finding ways everyone can contribute to making a meal also creates the feeling of community. If you're creative and plan well, there are always enough tasks—from chopping to cooking to cleaning up. Young children can tear lettuce for a salad or cut soft vegetables with a butter knife. What children learn in the kitchen they may take with them through the rest of their lives.

It is equally important to pay attention to *how* we eat a meal. Everything in life is food that either feeds our souls or feeds our survival-based, automatic behavior. Observing our relationship to eating is an opportunity to view a microcosm of everything we do because who we are when we eat is who we are in our lives. If we can observe what we do as we eat we can gain valuable insight into issues that show up in all areas of our lives.

Socrates said, "Anyone can be angry. The trick is to be angry at the right person, for the right reason, in the right amount, at the right time, and in the right way." We can apply this to eating as well. "Anyone can eat. The trick is to be the right person, who eats for the right reason, in the right amount, at the right time, and in the right way."

"To be the right person" means that we are relaxed when we eat (i.e., not eating in a hurry, not using the food to suppress our feelings, not getting up from the table several times during the meal) and really paying attention to those we are eating with.

"For the right reason" means we remember we are sharing a meal not just to get eating out of the way but to have a sense of joy and communion with those at the table. We are also aware of the food, not distracted by the activities from our day or the latest story on the news.

"In the right amount" means we are sensitive and disciplined enough to stop eating before we have overeaten. This requires experimentation because it takes about twenty minutes for the brain to register how much food we have consumed. This is a call to slow down and savor our meal.

"At the right time" means we eat when we are hungry. Obviously, many of us need to eat according to a schedule at home or at work. So "at the right time" implies that we could sit with our family during a meal, and if we are not hungry, we might eat a small portion and then have a bit more later in the day or evening. This also means, ideally, that we don't eat at least three hours before going to sleep. If we have food in our stomachs, we have to work at digesting during the night, which doesn't give our bodies time to replenish energy.

"In the right way" means that we pay attention to taste, to chewing, to our pace, to our conversations, and, without being obvious, to the way we bring our fork to our mouth.

Chewing

Observe how you chew. When we understand the basic mechanics of what's going on in the mouth, we can begin to see how what we're doing reflects who we are.

Chewing begins the process of digestion with the release of saliva, which contains enzymes that begin the digestive process. When we take solid food and chew it, we are also breaking it down so that our body does not have to overwork itself in the upper and lower stomach. This saves a tremendous amount of energy. Ideally, food should be chewed until it is as close to liquid as possible.

Staying present to the moment means paying attention to the food that is in the mouth, not the food on the plate. When we focus on the food that hasn't been eaten this distracts us from chewing thoroughly. We also look at how much food we put in our mouths. Taking huge bites doesn't allow room to chew properly.

Conscious chewing requires us to slow down and experience eating. It requires us to take stock of what's really going on for us at the table. It can also be an invitation to reinvent ourselves if we consider how chewing may be a metaphor for other activities in our life:

- Do you chew everything with aggression? You may be pursuing everything you do with too much intensity.

- Do you not chew much at all? You may be afraid to truly engage your life, instead just skimming along the surface of your experiences.

- Are you rushing through your meal, maybe chewing only five or six times before swallowing, desperate for the next bite? Perhaps you are afraid to slow down, always running toward the next task, too stressed out to really enjoy the present moment.

- Do you continually take huge bites that make your cheeks bulge? You may be unconsciously trying to "eat" your emotions, to stuff them down with as much food as you can fit in your mouth.

• Do you eat constantly? This is often a nervous habit indicating an inability to deal with stress or emotion in another area of life.

Minimalism

It's common sense to be aware of how we're using resources. If we're trying not to waste gas or plastic or paper, why not food? We can figure out how we're doing by carrying a little pad and pen with us and writing down every bit of food we waste over a period of a month. Include the times you give your children too large a portion and don't save it to serve to them later. It may be a shock to discover how much food we're throwing away.

There are many other ways to be a minimalist with food. For example, some packaged breakfast cereals have minimal ingredients, while others have fifteen to twenty. While neither is a whole food, the first is a better choice.

A friend of ours told us she has about eight kinds of mustard in her refrigerator at her home. Many people have refrigerators, freezers, and pantries packed with food so they have every possible option available. If this is true for you, consider using up all those items that have been sitting on your shelves or, if you can't realistically use them in a few months, take unopened canned goods or packaged foods to a food bank or food drive. Then experience a kitchen that has a feeling of simplicity and space. Minimalism is the challenge to live first with what we *need*, and then choose what we *want*.

In terms of food preparation, the goal is to make an amount that will satiate everyone's hunger and have little or no food left over. (This does not apply to deliberately making extra food for future meals.) This idea also applies to how many items are prepared for one meal. Some people find it comforting to have many different dishes on the table. Three, or at most four, are generally enough. Take a risk and give your family the gift of a minimalist meal—like a simple rice stir-fry and salad—once a week.

You don't need too many different ingredients within each dish. Keeping ingredients lists small makes the food easier to digest. For example, you can prepare a satisfying salad with greens and three other vegetables. The same applies to spices. Use sauces and dressings sparingly to highlight the taste of the whole food you are serving. Let those natural flavors come to life! Many of us have over-stimulated taste buds so it may take time to appreciate food's natural flavors.

Take the time to observe how much you put on your plate and how you feel after eating. Some people pile large portions on their plates and eat only two-thirds, or overeat. It is an art to eat the right amount of food, but an art worth mastering.

Years ago we met a man who ate nothing but fruits and greens. He also ate only one food at each meal. For dinner one evening he only ate bananas while we ate pizza. He had been on this diet for fifteen or so years. We're not recommending his diet by any stretch of the imagination—just sharing an experience we had which gave us a new reference point for simplicity.

If we eat in restaurants regularly because our profession demands it, we might order a salad with a simple dressing, a baked potato, and some vegetarian soup, rather than a fancy shrimp dish, some kind of fried food appetizer, a soda or glass of wine, meat or fish, and dessert. There's something humble and noble in the first choice. At times, other people may think our eating habits are a bit out of the ordinary, but that's okay.

Different approaches can lead us to an intentional relationship with food. Some people choose to strictly follow a specific system, such as macrobiotics or raw food. Another approach is to draw information from different dietary regimes that support healthy eating. This is the approach we take in *Dharma Feast Cookbook*.

The following sections highlight the most important influences on our Dharma Feast diet. Our descriptions are meant to give you a sense of the context and content of each of these influences. If you resonate with one or more of them, many books about each one are available to guide you.

#1—The Vegetarian Diet

One argument for a vegetarian diet looks at our dental structure and digestive juices and concludes that these reflect the eating tools of herbivores. We aren't meant to eat meat or fish, some vegetarian proponents say, as our teeth aren't designed to tear it and our digestive juices aren't designed to digest it.

While health experts differ on that particular argument, it is commonly accepted that lighter proteins are easier to digest, and that digestion is one of the essential keys to health. For example, fish is easier to digest than meat, and in general, plant-based protein is easier to digest than animal-based protein because less hydrochloric acid is needed to break it down.

Also, eating animals and animal-based products (such as dairy) is scientifically linked to cancer, heart disease, obesity, diabetes, osteoporosis, and more. These conclusions are substantiated in the book *The China Study*, which was run jointly by Cornell University, Oxford University, and the Chinese Academy of Preventative Medicine. The researchers conducted their own studies and also referenced the findings of other respected researchers and clinicians over the past fifty years. All pointed to the recommendation of a plant-based diet over an animal-based one for optimal health. We recommend reading *The China Study*.

If we eat a typical American or even European diet, we are eating 70 to 100 grams of protein a day, most of which comes from animal products (meat, fish, dairy, eggs). This is up to ten times more protein than people eat in Asian countries, and these populations have significantly less degenerative disease than we do. For example, *The China Study* states that an animal protein-based diet leads to a 17-times higher incidence of death from heart disease in American men compared to Chinese men.

Our bodies need protein—we can't live without it. Proteins function as hormones and enzymes, and are a part of structural tissue. They have to be continually replaced. When we eat a protein, we break it down into its building blocks, called amino acids, and these are the building blocks we use to rebuild proteins we've lost.

The body itself is able to make many of the amino acids that are needed, but eight of them must come from the food we eat. Eating a variety of vegetables, fruits, nuts and seeds, and fermented foods gives us all the additional ones we need. Be careful, though—our body only recognizes whole food in its natural state. When food is processed we're basically taking nature apart. If we eat isolated proteins, for example in isolated protein powder, the body doesn't recognize it and it is much more difficult, and in some instances impossible, to assimilate.

Our vegetarian approach in *Dharma Feast Cookbook* is based on the fact that the closer we eat to the original source of energy—the sun—the more of that energy we get. All life gets its energy from the sun, but only plants can get it directly, through photosynthesis. We can't photosynthesize so our choices are to eat things that do (plants), or to eat things that eat things that do (plant-eating animals). Only 10 percent of the stored energy in plants makes it to the meat of the animals that eat them, so eating plants is the best and most efficient way to get the energy we need.

Finally, it's not that we never recommend the use of meat in your diet. If you are frail you may need to eat it to get enough protein for your muscles. Another instance where plant-based proteins may not be enough for a period of time is if a person is in a state of severe nutritional deficiency. Of course this needs to be determined by a health professional.

#2—A Raw Food Diet

"Raw" means foods in their whole, natural state. Any plant or animal food, when not heated over 110 degrees F (43 degrees C), canned, or frozen, is a raw food. Every food in this state has the enzymes it needs for digestion. The Eskimos eat raw meat and have no heart disease because raw meat contains high amounts of protease, the enzyme that helps digest protein. Raw nuts contain the appropriate amount of lipase, the enzyme that helps digest fats. This is a pristine example of the intelligence of life. Cooking, canning, and freezing destroys these enzymes. Vitamins, minerals, and proteins can also be either altered or destroyed when cooked.

The foundation of eating raw foods is that they contain everything our bodies need in order to break down, digest, and assimilate them easily. One might then ask why not eat a 100 percent raw food diet if this is the case. Our experience is that most people do not have the desire, discipline, constitution, or lifestyle to do so. While eating raw may be what's needed for a time, it is a difficult diet to maintain, especially if we add in the demands of family, professional life, and city life.

A good goal is a 50 percent to 75 percent raw food diet, combined with cooked beans and grains, steamed vegetables, roasted nuts and seeds, and fermented foods. At the same time, different people tend to function better with more or less of this amount of raw food, or with even a minimal amount of animal products, depending on one's profession, one's state of health, and the climate one lives in.

As we begin to eat a greater percentage raw, our overall calorie count declines. We may begin to crave carbohydrates such as pastas and breads to fill in for the "missing" calories. We can add beans and soaked raw nuts and seeds instead. While raw nuts and seeds give us the calories we need, they are difficult for the body to break down, so we soak or toast them and eat them in small quantities. To learn how to soak and toast nuts and seeds for optimal digestion, see *Soak and Toast Nuts and Seeds* in *How To*, Chapter 6.

Our protein and fat intake will also drop with a raw food diet. We may start craving foods that have high concentrations of these substances (meat, dairy products, sweets) because our bodies may have become inefficient at processing vegetarian and raw food. They have not had to work as they naturally should to get fats and proteins from food because we have overloaded them with foods that have these substances in highly concentrated amounts. It's similar to a student who cheats on tests at school. The longer they cheat, the more they lose their ability to study. If they begin studying again, at first it will be very difficult and the desire to cheat will feel overwhelming. Just as studying will become easier over time, the body will readjust itself over time and begin to take what it needs from vegetarian whole food sources and our cravings will ease.

#3—Macrobiotics

This diet is based on the ancient rural Japanese diet. It consists primarily of whole grains, vegetables, soups (especially miso), seaweed, beans, and minimal fruit. Condiments include nuts, seeds, typical Asian condiments like soy sauce, and fermented foods like pickles and sauerkraut. Because it relies so heavily on grains, it is very grounding.

Key to this diet is balance. It is maintained by making choices in five areas—the energy of food and how it is prepared, the balance of acid and alkaline (what the Japanese have long referred to as *yin* and *yang*[1]), the impact of foods on blood sugar levels, the ratio between sodium and potassium, and the preference for local, seasonal foods.

Macrobiotics emphasizes eating living foods. These are foods which can continue to grow even after they are harvested. For example, beans and grains will sprout, and greens, if put in water, will continue to live. Fermented foods contain living organisms.

According to this philosophy, the way food grows and how it is cooked influences its energy. Foods which grow vertically up—like greens—are believed to focus energy in the head and chest. Root vegetables grow down, which makes them more grounding. Vegetables like squash and potatoes grow out, spreading energy outward.

[1]In Asian philosophy, *yin* represents soft, yielding, slow, diffuse, feminine energy; *yang* represents hard, aggressive, fast, solid, masculine energy. *Yin-yang* is always portrayed together to show the interdependence, interconnection, and natural balance between what can appear to be contrary forces.

Horizontal foods, like cucumbers and zucchini, concentrate energy inward. At which stage these foods are harvested also has an energetic impact. Macrobiotic experts say that plants harvested early in their growing cycle provide us with energy for growth and expansion. Mature plants give us the energy needed to learn from our experiences and absorb wisdom.

Cooking techniques also affect the energy of the body, with much the same impact as the direction of growth. Steaming focuses energy up, while stewing moves it down. Sautéing moves it outward and boiling focuses it inward.

Of core importance in macrobiotic teaching is listening to the body, which tells us what to do when we lose our equilibrium. Using this system we learn to choose what foods to eat and how to prepare them based on what we need. And, on a day-to-day basis, we eat from a variety of growth and cooking styles. However, if we are feeling out of balance, we focus on the foods and styles that we know will balance us. For example, we can reduce a lack of clarity by eating steamed, upward-growing foods, as they focus energy in the head. If we are sick we may need to concentrate energy inward for healing, so we choose horizontal foods and boil them. If we need both upward and outward energy, we steam potatoes.

Keeping a balance between *yin* and *yang*, acid and alkaline, is important for health. Please see *The Acid/Alkaline Consideration* below (#5) for further information.

Another way the macrobiotic diet maintains balance in our health and emotions is by paying attention to blood-sugar levels. All foods impact blood sugar. The glycemic index (GI) number assigned to a food tells us how fast its carbohydrates turn into sugar. The higher the number the faster it happens and the more havoc it wreaks as our energy surges and then crashes.

Too many of these cycles for too long increase the risk of developing type 2 diabetes and also contribute to weight gain. None of us can afford emotional instability. It is difficult to function in a body unbalanced from intense blood sugar swings. The goal is to eat foods with a GI below 55. Almost all living foods fall into this category.

Along with GI we need to know a food's glycemic load (GL). This tells how much carbohydrate is in one serving. Foods with a GL of 10 or lower are best. A food can have a high GI but a low GL because of its density. For instance, pineapple has a GI of 66 but a GL of 6 because it isn't very dense. A good list of GI and GL numbers can be found at www.mendosa.com/gilists.htm.

#4—The Traditional Diet

The Traditional Diet is based on the work of Westin A. Price, a prominent dentist who studied the nutrition of indigenous cultures around the world to research the causes of dental decay and deformation as well as the physical degeneration he saw in America. He founded what became the Research Section of the American Dental Association. In general, but not across the board, these indigenous cultures eat meat and animal products. Therefore, except for the two specific aspects discussed below, we do not recommend this diet, although we know people who follow this regimen with great success.

1. The Traditional Diet advocates eating high-quality saturated fats. These fats ensure that we get enough fat-soluble vitamin A, which supports the immune system, cell structural integrity, and bone, eye, and heart health. One of the best saturated fats is organic, raw butter. Coconut oil and coconut milk also provide good fats, and many of our recipes will suggest these. We recommend that you use at least a tablespoon a day of high-quality saturated fats for cooking, or more in a smoothie. A good oil mix for cooking is equal parts olive, coconut, and sesame oils. A tablespoon or more of coconut oil or at least a quarter-cup of coconut milk can be a delicious addition to a smoothie.

2. The second aspect of the Traditional Diet that we incorporate is the use of fermented foods. They support healthy digestive-tract bacteria. These include sauerkraut, pickles, tempeh, soy sauce, and kimchi (a Korean sauerkraut). Mulkasan, a fermented whey drink, can be found in most health food stores, so this can be used in Stage 1 and Stage 2 of the diet.

#5—The Alkaline/Acid Consideration

The recipes in *Dharma Feast Cookbook* support healthy eating and healthy bodies. The discussions in *Our Main Influences* are designed to introduce different aspects of achieving this goal. And although acid/alkaline was touched on in *The Macrobiotic Diet*, this balance is so important we gave it its own section as well.

Keeping alkaline and acid balanced (pH) is essential for health. Almost every biological system requires an alkaline environment. The digestive system is the body's only acidic environment. It needs to have the right proportion of acids to digest food.

Every food is either alkaline or acid in nature. An **alkaline food** is one in which, after it is metabolized, there are leftover electrolytes. The body needs these surplus electrolytes to carry electrical impulses across cells in the nervous system, heart, and muscles. An **acid food** is one in which its electrolytes are insufficient to neutralize the acid it contains. Thus the body must pull electrolytes from cells, thus weakening or killing them.

In general, we eat considerably more acidic foods than alkaline foods. Dairy products, meat, most grains (not millet and quinoa), and most processed foods are acidic. If too much acidic food is eaten, the body is stripped of electrolytes. Physical symptoms can include fatigue, depression, headaches, mouth ulcers, muscle spasms, overall muscle weakness, twitching, convulsions, irregular heartbeat, blood pressure changes, and numbness. We may also develop nervous system or bone disorders. To regain balance and keep the blood at an alkaline level it extracts minerals from the bones. Natural medicine says that this is the main cause of arthritis. Other medical and common-sense arguments also support that an acidic environment in the blood and tissues is much more likely to breed disease. (*Read Cleanse and Purify Thyself: Book 1* by Richard Anderson and *The China Study* for further information on diseases caused by a body in an acid state.)

The way to assure proper pH balance is through diet. To maintain this balance some acidic foods are necessary. The goal is to eat within a range of 70 percent alkaline foods, 30 percent acidic foods. *Dharma Feast Cookbook* draws heavily from the alkaline side of the chart, as most of the foods recommended on this diet are alkaline. The chart below is a good introduction to foods from each category. If you are concerned about a food not on this list, there are many websites you can consult. One good one is www.rense.com/1.mpicons/acidalka.htm.

Alkaline Forming Foods

All fresh fruits
All fresh salad greens
All sprouts
All vegetables (raw or cooked)
Almonds (soaked)
Sunflower seeds (soaked)
Apple cider vinegar
Berries (fresh)
Corn on the cob* (fresh)
Dates
Dried fruits (unsulfured)
Fresh or dried herbs

Fresh raw fruit juice
Fresh raw vegetable juice
Garlic
Goat whey* (raw)
Grapefruit
Green foods (algae, spirulina, chlorella)
Herbal teas (caffeine free)
Honey (raw)
Lemons
Lima beans*
Melons
Millet*

Molasses
Potatoes*
Quinoa*
Raisins
Olive or flaxseed oils (raw, organic)
Sea salt
Sauerkraut (unsalted)
Sea vegetables (well rinsed)
Vegetable broth
Vegetable soups
Wheat grass juice

Acid Forming Foods

Alcohol**
Barley
Black or white pepper
Bread, baked
Canned or frozen fruits and vegetables
Cereals, all
Chocolate
Coffee
Dairy
Eggs

Foods cooked with oil
Grains, except quinoa and millet
Honey
Beans
Meat, fish, birds, shellfish
Nuts
Oatmeal
Oils
Pasta
Popcorn
Preservatives

Processed foods†
Salt, processed
Soda crackers
Soft drinks
Sugar, white and processed
Sweeteners, artificial
Tea, unless caffeine free
Vinegar, distilled
Wheat, all forms

*Eat foods from this group no more than three times a week
**Alcoholic beverages are highly acid forming and destroy friendly bacteria in the digestive system.
†Processed foods lack enzymes and minerals, making it difficult for the body to get the nutrients it needs.
Charts from the book *Cleanse and Purify Thyself, Book 1,* by Richard Anderson, and used with permission.

Everything changes when we overlay a sense of discipline on our lives.

—LEE LOZOWICK

The Dharma Feast Diet

The diet we recommend is composed primarily of grains, cooked and raw vegetables, greens, fruits, fresh-squeezed juices, nuts, seeds, beans, seaweeds, fermented foods, raw organic butter or organic ghee (clarified butter), water, and certain supplements (see *Supplementation* in *Resources and Recommendations*, Chapter 7).

The following lists will introduce you to the kinds of foods on this diet. We are not recommending that *every* kitchen have *all* of them:

Grains: The * items do not contain gluten. Short and long grain brown rice*, brown basmati rice*, millet*, quinoa*, bulgur, buckwheat*, oats (whole oat groats, steel-cut, or rolled), teff*, amaranth*, wild rice*, polenta*, barley, and sticky sushi rice* (naturally white). These grains can be bought in bulk from your local natural food grocery or food co-op.

The healthiest, least-processed rice is brown because only the first hull has been removed, leaving the bran and germ, which is where all the nutrients are. White rice ("unpolished rice") has had the bran and germ removed. Polished rice is white rice that has been buffed with glucose (sugar) or talc powder to make it bright and shiny. "Enriched rice" is polished rice that has been sprayed with synthetic vitamins and minerals. Converted or parboiled rice is white rice that has been boiled in the husk before milling (removing the outer hull).

Eat grains no more than three times per week because they are acidic. They should be soaked before cooking to remove phytic acid, which blocks the absorption of minerals. Pan-roast millet before cooking to bring out its flavor. Further instructions can be found in *Grains* in *Recipes,* Chapter 5.

Beans: Red and brown lentils, red kidney beans, black beans, great northern beans (navy beans), pinto beans, mung beans, garbanzo beans (chickpeas), split peas, black-eyed peas, and aduki beans (which are easy to digest). These can all be bought in bulk. Beans added to soups make them more filling.

Beans should be soaked. Further instructions can be found in *Cooking Beans* in *Recipes,* Chapter 5.

We recommend eating beans no more than three times a week on the Stage 3 diet (see *The 3-Stage Diet* in *To Begin With*, Chapter 1) because they are very acidic. The commitment in Stage 3 is gradually to be getting protein from lighter and more refined sources. Beans are heavy foods, heavier than soaked nuts and seeds. Someone with a clean body (meaning the liver and the large and small intestines are relatively clean of debris and toxins) can utilize protein from all kinds of vegetable sources, not just beans.

Cooking Oils: Extra virgin olive oil, coconut oil, sesame oil, grapeseed oil, palm oil, and safflower oil. Buy cold-*pressed* oils (not cold-*processed,* which involves chemical processing) to preserve nutrients inherent in the oil. Store oils in a dark or opaque bottle in the refrigerator for longest shelf-life—exposure to light, heat and oxygen spoils some oils quickly.

Choose extra virgin olive oil, as it is 100 percent olive oil. Virgin olive oil is 75 percent olive oil and pure olive oil is 50 percent olive oil at best. Olive oil can be stored on a shelf in a dark location. It does not lose its nutrients when heated, which is why it makes a good cooking oil.

Palm oil is good for sautéing because it has excellent stability at high temperatures. Buy red palm oil because it naturally contains red carotene, the substance that is found in carrots, but note that it will give the sautéed food a golden color. The white variety has been boiled so that the red carotene is removed. One good brand is Jungle Products Red Palm Oil. Do not use palm kernel oil.

Another good cooking oil is a mix of equal parts olive, coconut, and sesame oils. The coconut and sesame oils have strong flavors so make sure they are compatible with the flavors in your finished dish. Safflower oil is sometimes preferred over this mix of oils because it is a light, delicately-flavored oil.

If any oil is heated to the point that it begins smoking, it has broken down and now contains free radicals (molecules that, when they bond to molecules in our bodies, damage cells and DNA. They play a part in the aging process and some autoimmune diseases and are linked to the development of cancer.). Throw it out and start with fresh oil.

Other Cooking Liquids: Soy sauce, tamari, Tabasco, red wine vinegar, apple cider vinegar, balsamic vinegar, rice vinegar, and rice wine (cooking wine).

Condiments for the Table: Apple cider vinegar, extra virgin olive oil, Tabasco, cayenne, sea salt, pepper, gomasio (ground sesame seeds, see recipe), nutritional yeast, garlic and onion powder, Bragg Liquid Aminos (a low sodium soy sauce substitute), and tamari.

A word on salt: If your salt is white and doesn't clump together that means it is highly processed. Processing uses chemicals and high temperatures so that many of the minerals that naturally occur in salt are removed and other harmful substances are added. We suggest a high-quality salt (Himalayan www.saltworks.us/himalayan-salt.asp and Celtic www.healthfree.com/celtic_sea_salt.html are good choices) because it is not processed and its minerals are intact. Sea salt is also the only salt that is used in raw recipes because it is unprocessed. A word of caution—some salts are "saltier" than others. Until you get used to the sea salt you choose, add it to taste instead of in amounts suggested.

Canned or Jarred Foods: Used on Stages 1 and 2 of this diet. The process of canning destroys enzymes so use sparingly. Choose glass jars whenever possible. Black olives, green olives, dill pickles, sauerkraut, artichoke hearts, diced tomatoes, tomato sauce, tomato paste, coconut milk, tahini, pickled ginger, wasabi, Dijon mustard, and almond butter.

Dairy: Raw, organic butter, or organic ghee (clarified butter) see *Ghee* in *Recipes*, Chapter 5.

Dried Fruits: Raisins, Medjool dates (very sweet, so use sparingly), figs, bananas, mangoes, apricots (the dark ones are the least processed), cranberries (a few make a nice addition to a salad). Watch for added sweeteners and buy non-sweetened, unsulfured dried fruit. Dried fruits are concentrated sugar so eat them in small quantities.

Frozen Foods: Used on Stages 1 and 2 of the diet. The process of freezing food also destroys enzymes. Fresh is much better, but if we're using berries in a smoothie, fresh berries can be very expensive. If you have a choice between canned and frozen, choose frozen—these foods are picked and frozen right away, so they are riper and fresher. We recommend Cascadian Farm organic, Woodstock Farms organic, or any organic choice, preferably locally grown.

Flours: Baking is an example of processing food. Sometimes we need flour for a special meal or occasion. Whole wheat pastry flour can usually be substituted for all-purpose white flour. If not, use unbleached, organic wheat flour when all-purpose white flour is called for in a recipe. Garbanzo bean flour tastes great and gives a good texture to baked goods. Spelt offers a broader range of nutrients than wheat and has a delicious, nutty flavor. Teff flour isn't hulled before being ground into flour which preserves virtually all of the nutritional value of the whole grain. Teff is a good gluten-free alternative but makes baked goods drier. To avoid this, after baking, bring to room temperature, cover, and refrigerate overnight. Other flour options: cornmeal, rye flour, whole wheat flour, almond or other nut flours, or any unprocessed natural flour. See *Gluten* in *Resources and Recommendations*, Chapter 8, for a selection of gluten-free flours.

Grain or nut milk: Often a good replacement for milk in recipes such as soups. Eat with hot cereals and granola, use in smoothies, add to tea, or drink as a beverage. Choices include rice, oat, almond, hemp, and hazelnut. Buy unsweetened.

Vitamin D2 is not found naturally in humans and so is not used efficiently. There is evidence that it is toxic at higher levels. We are also generally unable to absorb "enriched" forms of vitamins and minerals, as they are synthetic (see *Supplementation* in *Resources and Recommendations*, Chapter 8, for further information). So when possible, buy unenriched. Only Rice Dream Original Classic doesn't have D2 and isn't enriched. However, many companies are switching from using vitamin D2 to D3, which is the form used by humans. The next best choices are Pacific Natural Foods Oatmilk, Pacific Natural Foods Hazelnut Milk, and Living Harvest Hemp Milk, but these contain D2.

Again, always check ingredients. As always, the fewer the better. You can also make your own grain or nut milk. See *Grain and Nut Milks* in *Recipes*, Chapter 5, for instructions.

Kitchari: A delicious dish made from a mix of spices, rice, and red lentils. If you're following a Stage 2 diet, kitchari can easily be an excellent staple food. See *Kitchari I* and *Kitchari II* in *Recipes*, Chapter 5.

Nuts/seeds: Almonds, pecans, walnuts, pine nuts, cashews, pistachios, sunflower seeds, flax seeds (must be ground), sesame seeds, and pumpkin seeds. These should be eaten in small quantities, because "nuts can make you nuts." Nuts and seeds contain oils, so it is possible for them to go rancid. Walnuts will need to be refrigerated because they are high in omega-3 but other nuts can be unrefrigerated. Men may wish to eat a handful of unsalted, hulled pumpkin seeds every day, as folklore says this can help prevent prostate cancer. **Important Note**—Nuts contain enzyme inhibitors which make them very difficult to digest. They are best eaten when soaked overnight in water or in water with a little pineapple juice added. Also, when nuts and seed are toasted, the enzymes are activated, so they are available for digestion. Instructions can be found in *Soaking and Toasting Nuts and Seeds* in *How To*, Chapter 6.

Seaweeds: The most popular varieties are dulse, kelp, and nori (the seaweed used in making sushi). Seaweed is the most nutrient-dense food we can eat. It contains more minerals in easily-absorbable forms than any other vegetable and is very high in protein. Spirulina (powdered seaweed) has more protein pound-for-pound than most meats. Spirulina is not used with meals, but rather is used as a food supplement and can be mixed in juice or water to create green drinks and smoothies. On a macrobiotic diet, seaweed is a part of every lunch and dinner.

Soy: Tofu (extra firm or firm tastes best, eat only once a week), natto (a fermented bean dish), tempeh (see entry below), miso. Miso has enzymes that are destroyed with boiling, so heat with care. Miso soup makes a fulfilling breakfast food in winter with the addition of a few vegetables. Miso can also be used in salad dressings. We recommend eating miso, natto, tempeh, and tofu (in limited quantities), but limiting or eliminating processed soy food intake (foods which contain processed soy protein, for example)—please read *Soy* in *Resources and Recommendations*, Chapter 8, for further information.

Spices: Dried spices are best used within one year from the time they are processed. Buy in small quantities as needed. Black and white pepper, cayenne pepper (rich in vitamins, minerals and enzymes; aids digestion), red paprika, dark and light mustard seeds, cumin, cardamom, coriander seeds, cinnamon, curry powder, garam masala powder, cloves, turmeric powder, caraway seeds, sage, thyme, rosemary, basil, oregano, dill, bay leaves, fresh herbs (chives, parsley, dill, oregano, basil, thyme, rosemary, mint), and salt (use sea salt, which has trace minerals and iodine. The more color the salt has, the less refined it is. See *Condiments for the Table* above for more information on salt.) or a salt substitute such as gomasio (See *Gomasio* in *Recipes*, Chapter 5). Another good salt mixture is equal parts sea salt, paprika, and kelp. This balances the sodium and potassium in a way that makes salt easiest to absorb.

Sweets: Sweet is one of the tastes we are genetically programmed to crave. It is not appropriate to remove all sweet tastes from our diet. If we try to do so we will naturally begin to crave them. The Dharma Feast diet allows for many sweets

that work, so check the chart in *The 3-Stage Diet* in *To Begin With,* Chapter 1, and eat these sweets in moderation. Fruits, both fresh and dried, are a good source of sweet, as well as fresh fruit juices. Sweeteners like Grade B maple syrup and honey can be added to foods to satisfy the need for sweet. Stevia is also good because it doesn't elevate blood sugar. Eating burdock, a root vegetable, can help reduce cravings for sweets. (See *Sweeteners* in *Resources and Recommendations*, Chapter 8)

Teeccino: Coffee is not recommended. The coffee substitute Teeccino is alkaline (coffee and chai are acidic).

Tempeh: An excellent fermented soy food. Because it is made from the whole bean, it has a high content of protein and vitamins. The fermentation process makes it more digestible and removes the health hazards of soy and tofu (see *Soy* above and in *Resources and Recommendations*, Chapter 8). Tempeh can be eaten as often as you wish. Steam first before sautéing so that it will absorb more flavors. There are instructions for making tempeh in *Wild Fermentation* by Sandor Ellix Katz, as tempeh is expensive. We recommend Turtle Island or Wildwood.

Please also see *The 3-stage Diet* in *To Begin With*, Chapter 1. The 3-stage chart has more information on foods appropriate for whichever stage you wish to pursue. One of the strengths of the Dharma Feast diet is its flexibility—you get to choose what you will and will not include and you can still be assured you're eating a healthy diet!

Food Combinations

Food combining guidelines are based on how slowly or quickly different foods go through the process of digestion. For example, sweet fruits digest more quickly than acidic fruits, and all fruits digest much faster than grains, proteins, and vegetables. We don't eat fruits with slower-digesting foods because they begin to ferment, causing gas and bloating. Pay attention also when combining starches and proteins.

The four fruit categories are:

ACID		SUB-ACID		SWEET	NEUTRAL
Carambola	Medlar	Apple	Litchi (fresh)	Apricot	All melons
Ceylon	Orange	Pear	Mango	Banana	
Cranberry	Pineapple	Blackberry	Mulberry	Carob	
Currant	Pitanga	Cactus fruit	Nectarine	Date	
Gooseberry	Pomegranate	Cherry	Plum	Fig	
Grapefruit	Shaddock	Elderberry	Paw Paw	Jakfruit	
Kumquat	Sour Apple	Grape	Peach	Litchi (dried)	
Kiwi	Strawberry	Guava	Persimmon	Prune	
Lemon	Tamarind	Huckleberry	Raspberry	Raisin	
Lime	Tangerine	Jujube	Soursop	Sapodilla	
Loganberry	Tomato	Juneberry	Papaya	Sapote	

Eat any fruits listed in the same category together. Mix from categories right next to each other: acid with sub-acid, or sub-acid with sweet, but not acid with sweet. Melons should not be mixed with any other category ("Eat them alone or leave them alone."). Citrus should also be eaten alone. (Citrus fruits are identified on the next page.)

Add mixed nuts, seeds, and raisins sparingly to a fruit salad.

(From *Infant Nutrition,* Canada, 1995: Health Coach Systems Intl. Inc. Canada, 3rd Ed. For further information, see both *Intuitive Eating* and *10 Essential Foods*, listed in *Recommended Reading*.)

Follow these guidelines for starches and proteins.

STARCHES (concentrated)	NON-STARCH VEGGIES (high water content)		PROTEINS (concentrated)	FRUITS	
Grains	Asparagus	Parsley, Radish	Beans	Apple	Pineapple
Pastas	Broccoli	Zucchini	Legumes	Apricot	Papaya
Rice	Brussels sprouts	Watercress	Fish	Banana	Peach
Corn	Cabbage	Green beans	Poultry	Berries	Pear
Potato (all)	Cauliflower	Artichoke	Wild game	Cherry	Plum
Turnip	Celery, Chives	Sea vegetables	Meat (all)	Date	Tomato*
Squash	Cucumber	Dandelion greens	Seafood	Lemon*	Fig
Parsnip	Kale, Kohlrabi	Endive, Orka	Seeds	Grape	Orange*
Beet	Leeks	Swiss chard	Nuts	Grapefruit*	
Carrot	Leafy greens		Dairy products	Melons (all)	
Eggplant	Onion			Mango	
Avocado	Peppers (all)			Nectarine	

Mix starches only with non-starch vegetables.
Mix non-starches with starches or proteins.
Mix proteins with non-starches.
Fruits do not mix well with anything else.
*Eat citrus fruits alone for optimal digestion.

(from *Infant Nutrition,* Health Coach Systems Int'l, Inc. Canada, 3rd Ed., 1995)

We realize that some of the combination or "non-combination" suggestions presented here may be a departure from the way you are used to eating. In the spirit of self-education and experimentation that we offer as one of our foundations for this diet, we urge you to explore what your body needs to function optimally. You get to decide how much you want to use these guidelines.

We also know that some recipes in this cookbook have "non-ideal" food combinations, as per this chart. We are convinced that sometimes it is more beneficial to vary from the purest diet in the spirit of enjoyment. What we have found to be most important is to choose and then stick with your choices until something else becomes more obvious. Know the facts and then make your choice.

Food Rotation

We need variety in our diet to get good nutrition. For those of you who want to embrace a right relationship to food and leave no stone unturned, varying your food choices gives you the best chance of getting all your nutritional needs met. For example, you might be in the habit of eating "regular" potatoes, but sweet potatoes (not the same as yams) are actually one of the most nutritious vegetables. They have almost twice the U.S. recommended daily allowance (RDA) of vitamin A, 42 percent of the recommendation for vitamin C, four times the RDA for beta carotene, and more fiber in the skin than oatmeal. Another example is greens—there are over a dozen types, so you may wish to go beyond spinach and lettuce and make a dish with kale or collards.

Eating a wide variety of food is also a way to practice being open to new experiences. And obviously we enjoy certain foods more than others. So the recommendation here is to open up and experiment, and try to include foods in our diet that are different than the foods we became accustomed to eating when we were children.

One simple way to bring variety into your meal plans is to eat in color. When you vary food colors you eat a wide range of fruits and veggies, from blueberries, to squash, to peppers, to cabbage. Had anything orange lately? How about red? Or purple? Each color represents a different group of phytochemicals.

Diet rotation involves individual foods as well as food groups. Food groups are foods that are so similar genetically that they are considered the same food. For instance broccoli and cabbage are the same genetically—the only reason they look different is because of selective breeding by humans. See *Food Rotation Chart* in *Appendix*.

It's easy to integrate variety into your diet. Buy Collard greens instead of spinach the next time you're at the store. Try bringing a new color of food into a meal two or three times a week. Think of your grocery cart as a rainbow—what colors do you see a lot, and which have you not seen for a while? Variety is the spice of life.

THE CANDLE CAFE COOKBOOK

PIERSON/POTENZA

 moosewood restaurant
celebrates

THE MOOSEWOOD COLLECTIVE

Keavy Smith   THE QUICK & EASY AYURVEDIC COOKBOOK

MOOSEWOOD RESTAURANT
COOKS AT HOME   THE MOOSEWOOD COLLECTIVE

GREEN FOR LIFE   BOUTENKO

 Ani's Raw Food Kitchen   Easy, Delectable Living Foods Recipes

shauna james ahern   gluten-free girl
HOW I FOUND THE FOOD THAT LOVES ME BACK... & HOW YOU CAN

Katz   wild fermentation   The Flavor, Nutrition, and Cra
of Live-Culture Foods

saran & lyness   indian home cooking

THE USBORNE INTERNET LINKED CHILDREN'S WORLD COOKBOOK

Quick & Easy   Sushi Cook Book

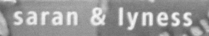 COLETTE ROSSANT
AND
MARIANNE MELENDEZ   VEGETABLES

A fork is a fork, of course, it is a simple implement of eating. But at the same time, the extension of your sanity and your dignity may depend upon how you use your fork.

—CHÖGYAM TRUNGPA RINPOCHE

It can be challenging to train ourselves to think differently about food and change our diet. A good way to begin is by choosing which dishes you will serve for a meal. For instance, for dinner the first step is choosing the main dish. Then group a vegetable, a salad, and if needed, a protein to match. It can be that easy.

Remember to keep in mind who will be eating—if your family has just spent the day hiking through snow, you'll want to provide a warm, filling meal. A hot summer day calls for lighter food.

We designed the following menus to give you an idea of how to transition into the Dharma Feast diet and what this could look like in daily life. Much time and attention have gone into these meal plans, in part because we understand that many of us don't usually have time to make elaborate meals.

The Benefits of Planning

It can be very helpful to plan menus for a week in advance. This may stretch us a bit at first, but doing so takes a lot of unnecessary stress out of our lives. If you create four weeks' worth of menus, then over time you can draw on these every weekend to plan your meals for the following week, which shortens the amount of time needed for planning.

We also recommend sometimes making a larger quantity than your family or guests can eat at one meal so that what is left over can be used for meals later in the week. We use this "strategy"

in the following Two-Week Menu Plan to give you a sense of what is possible. For example, next to "MONDAY" under "Dinner" you will see: "Millet (Cook enough to use in Parsley Garlic Millet for Wednesday lunch and Veggie Burgers for Thursday dinner)." This means that the millet you prepare Monday should be enough for Monday's dinner, the Parsley Garlic Millet for Wednesday's lunch, and the Veggie Burgers for Thursday's dinner.

Shopping is time consuming. Plan to buy most of your food for the week in one trip, although it may be necessary to shop for fresh produce more than once. When you get home from the store, plan to devote thirty minutes or so to washing and soaking and drying salad ingredients, vegetables, and fruits so it's done for the next few days. (Don't soak or wash vegetables and fruits that absorb water, like mushrooms or berries, until right before use or they will get soggy. Also, dry lettuce in a salad spinner before storing or it will turn to mush.)

Planning ahead also allows us to properly prepare foods. Grains and beans can soak on a counter overnight (see *Grains* in *Recipes*, Chapter 5). Beans can cook all day in a Crock Pot. (See *Cooking Beans* in *Recipes,* Chapter 5.)

Nuts can also be soaked overnight, then drained and put right onto a pan to be roasted, if you wish, and sprinkled on salads throughout the week or added to lunches. (See *Soak and Toast Nuts and Seeds* in *How To*, Chapter 6.)

Don't overlook simple meals. Cooking smart doesn't mean cooking more. Salad and reheated rice is an easy lunch or dinner. Add avocadoes, celery, and nuts for a more filling and interesting meal.

Other Ways To Cook "Smart":

- Cook a pot of beans and put what you don't need for that meal into different-sized containers to freeze—small amounts to add to a soup or larger amounts to be served as a main dish with rice and salad.

- Make two salad dressings on Sunday and use them throughout the week.

- Soups and stews can be made in larger quantities and can also be frozen in individual or family-sized portions. Or they can be heated in the morning and carried in a thermos for lunch.

- Adapt recipes—double them or be creative with ingredients. For instance, use the leftover baked potatoes from one dinner in a soup that calls for boiled potatoes two days later.

- Meal sharing is another way to eat well in a busy life. Get together with friends or one or two families in your neighborhood and plan a few dishes to make in larger quantity. If each family triples a soup recipe, everyone will have three different soups to choose from throughout the week.

We encourage you to use these ideas to help catalyze your own!

Special Occasion Meals

"Special Occasion Foods" are those that are generally not included in our simple everyday fare. These foods may contain sugar, white flour, or even meat. One of the reasons we refrain from eating these foods casually is because they alter our body chemistry and mental and emotional well-being. If we are eating them more than a couple of times a month, we need to understand that this is having an impact.

Special occasion meals are meant to mark occasions that are a part of our family tradition and our religious or personal life. For example, it's probably not a good idea to plan salad and rice for the meal that celebrates our child's graduation from high school. Then there are less obvious times where hospitality and elegance dictate being a bit looser with our diet. Like when you go out with your children and they want to eat pizza, they might not say that they want you to eat pizza, but they probably would appreciate it if you joined in the fun of the occasion. Enjoy a slice! Or eat a bowl of simple pasta.

The special occasion menus listed below include meals that we love. They can be used as alternatives to more common and richer foods. The recipes are all in this book and contain few ingredients that cause our body chemistry to change. They are considered "special" because of the use of dairy and/or dessert and also because they are more complex.

Menu Examples for Special Occasion Dinners at Home:

Indian
Daal with *Tarka*, Brown Basmati Rice, Indian Zucchini, Raita, Chai, and Cardamon Shortbread Cookies

European Gourmet
Warm Green French Lentil Salad with Shaved Raw Goat Cheese, Oven Roasted Rosemary Potatoes, Asparagus with Pine Nuts, Sparkling Water, and Tart Shell with Chocolate Filling topped with Toasted Sliced Almonds

Japanese Sushi Buffet
Miso Soup, Japanese Sushi Buffet (fish is included but optional), Seaweed Salad (Sunomono), Hot Green Tea, and Mango Sorbet

TWO-WEEK MENU PLAN FOR STAGE 2 DIET
Recipes for the following dishes are in this book

WEEK 1

DAY 1

Drink 3 to 4 liters of water
Breakfast Granola, Yogurt, Banana*
Lunch Tomato Coconut Soup, Arugula Salad
Dinner Roasted Beets (Roast enough to use in Potato, Beet, and Cabbage Salad for Thursday lunch), Millet (Cook enough to use in Parsley Garlic Millet for Wednesday lunch and Veggie Burgers for Thursday dinner), Warm Broccoli Salad, Green Salad and Dressing of your choice, Rosemary Cashews.
* A banana is actually a nut, not a fruit, so it combines well with foods.

DAY 2

Drink 3 to 4 liters of water
Breakfast Fruit Salad, Toasted Almonds
Lunch Asian Stir-Fry, Sticky Sushi Rice (Cook enough for Veggie Burgers for Thursday dinner)
Dinner Tempeh Shepherd's Pie, Green Salad* with Raw Vegetables and Dressing of your choice
* Green Salads are eaten almost every day. Use different greens, vegetables, and dressings for variety.

DAY 3

Drink 3 to 4 liters of water
Breakfast Oatmeal (Make enough for Buddha Gruel for Friday breakfast) with Maple Syrup
Lunch Garlic Parsley Millet, Cucumber Tomato Salad
Dinner Lentil Soup (Make enough for Friday lunch), Greens, Green Salad and Dressing of your choice

DAY 4

Drink 3 to 4 liters of water
Breakfast Raw Smoothie of your choice
Lunch Potato, Beet, and Cabbage Salad; 2 Hard Boiled Eggs
Dinner "Too Good" Veggie Burgers, Lettuce, Tomato Slices, Red Onion Slices, Mustard, Green Salad and Dressing of your choice

DAY 5

Drink 3 to 4 liters of water
Breakfast Buddha Gruel
Lunch Lentil Soup
Dinner Polenta (Make enough for Saturday lunch), Goulange, Spinach Salad (Wash enough spinach for soup for Saturday dinner and frittata for Sunday brunch), Toasted Sunflower Seeds (Make enough for Carrot Salad for Monday dinner)

DAY 6

Drink 3 to 4 liters of water
Breakfast Vegan Pancakes with Maple Syrup
Lunch Fried Polenta with Tomato, Olive Oil, and Garlic; Green Salad with Dressing of choice; Olives
Dinner Yam and Chickpea Soup (Cook enough chickpeas for Fluffy Hummus for Monday lunch and make enough soup for Tuesday lunch), Green Salad and Dressing of your choice

DAY 7

Drink 3 to 4 liters of water
Breakfast Smoothie of your choice
Brunch Tomato, Onion, and Spinach Frittata
Dinner Daal with Tarka, Brown Basmati Rice, Aloo Gobi (Potatoes and Cauliflower) (Wash and cut enough cauliflower for Monday lunch), Raita (optional)

WEEK 2

DAY 1

Drink 3 to 4 liters of water
Breakfast Millet-Almond Cereal (make enough for Thursday breakfast)
Lunch Fluffy Hummus with Raw Vegetables (carrots, celery, broccoli, cauliflower, others of your choice)
Dinner Quinoa (Make enough for Quinoa Tabouleh for Wednesday lunch), Scrambled Tofu, Carrot Salad, Baked Brussels Sprouts

DAY 2

Drink 3 to 4 liters of water
Breakfast Brown Rice Cereal with Honey
Lunch Yam and Chickpea Soup
Dinner Asparagus, Mushroom, and Bok Choy in Coconut Lime Sauce; Brown Basmati Rice, Green Salad and Dressing of your choice

DAY 3

Drink 3 to 4 liters of water
Breakfast Granola with Almond Milk
Lunch Quinoa Tabouleh, Green Salad and Dressing of your choice
Dinner Baked Potatoes with Butter and/or Tahini Sauce (Bake enough potatoes for Breakfast Burritos for Saturday brunch), Green Salad with Dressing

DAY 4

Drink 3 to 4 liters of water
Breakfast Millet-Almond Cereal
Lunch Carrot Potato Soup (Make enough soup for Friday lunch), Green Salad and Dressing of your choice
Dinner Mexican Buffet (Cook enough beans for Bean Salad for Friday dinner) with Fresh Tomato Salsa (Make enough salsa for Saturday brunch)

DAY 5

Drink 3 to 4 liters of water
Breakfast Fruit Salad
Lunch Carrot and Potato Soup, Green Salad, Roasted Almonds (Make enough for Sunday lunch)
Dinner Bean Salad, Brown Rice (Make enough for Winter Rice Breakfast on Sunday), Oven Roasted Carrots

DAY 6

Drink 3 to 4 liters of water
Breakfast Smoothie of your choice
Brunch Breakfast Burritos with Fresh Tomato Salsa, Sliced Avocados
Dinner Whole-grain or Rice Noodles with Pesto, Baked Portobello Mushrooms, Fennel Salad

DAY 7

Drink 3 to 4 liters of water
Breakfast Winter Rice Breakfast
Lunch Fruit Salad with Roasted Almonds
Dinner Spaghetti Squash, Hot Salad

DAY 1

Drink 3 to 4 liters of water
Breakfast Fruit Salad
Lunch Baked Potatoes, Avocado Mayonnaise, Green Salad with Raw Vegetables and Vegan Thousand Island Dressing
Dinner Millet, Carrot Almond Soup (Make enough soup for Tuesday lunch), Purple Cabbage and Basil Salad

DAY 2

Drink 3 to 4 liters of water
Breakfast Day Starter Smoothie
Lunch Carrot Almond Soup, Arugula Salad
Dinner Spaghetti Squash, Green Salad with Raw Vegetables and Vinaigrette of choice, Toasted Sunflower Seeds

DAY 3

Drink 3 to 4 liters of water
Breakfast Miso Soup
Lunch Fruit Salad, Coconut-Date-Apricot Paté
Dinner Lentil Soup (Make enough for Friday lunch); Marinated Potatoes, Artichoke Hearts, and Asparagus

DAY 4

Drink 3 to 4 liters of water
Breakfast Tropical Smoothie
Lunch Green Salad with Miso Date Dressing, Raw Vegetables, Soaked Nuts
Dinner Baked Yams with Butter, Baked Brussels Sprouts, Cabbage Salad, Green Salad with Vinaigrette

DAY 5

Drink 3 to 4 liters of water
Breakfast Fruit Salad
Lunch Lentil Soup, Spinach Salad
Dinner Brown Rice, Tahini Sauce, Greens, Carrot Salad

DAY 6

Drink 3 to 4 liters of water
Breakfast Mango-Coconut-Pineapple Smoothie
Lunch Steamed Broccoli with White Miso Sauce, Green Salad with choice of Dressing, Olives
Dinner Soba Noodles with Asian Sauce, Asian Stir-Fry

DAY 7

Drink 3 to 4 liters of water
Breakfast Oatmeal with Almond Milk, Banana
Lunch Fruit Salad
Dinner White Bean Stew with Tomatoes, Garlic, and Sage; Italian Tomatoes; Fennel Salad

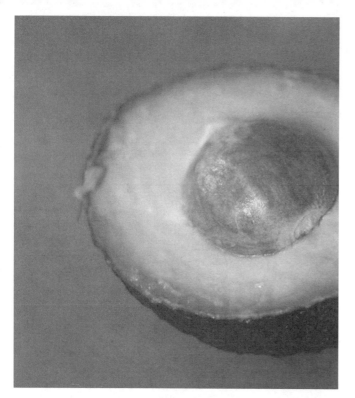

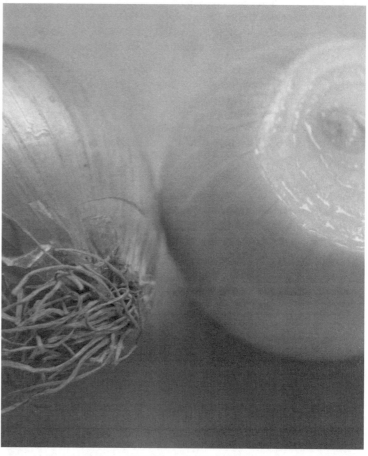

RECIPES

It's not so much the ingredients that you put into a recipe,

it's who you are when you prepare the food.

— MAMA SITA'S SISTER

Important information regarding how the recipes are categorized:

② = Stage 2 Diet — See page 3

③ = Stage 3 Diet — See page 3

RAW = Raw Food Recipe

Note–For more information on Stages 1, 2, and 3, see Chapter 1, *To Begin With*.

BREAKFAST

Breakfast is exactly that—it breaks the fast that has occurred overnight because the body cleanses during the night. If we want to continue that cleanse until lunch, then it's a good idea to pay attention to what we eat in the morning. Fruit salad, fresh fruits, and smoothies, all easy to digest, are good choices.

Pay attention to what you need in terms of what season of the year it is. Fruit salads and smoothies are preferable in warmer months—hot cereals, grain cereals, and heavier dishes may be needed in winter. Miso soup is great, particularly in the winter, if you prefer something savory. Add vegetables to miso for a hearty breakfast or simply drink it as a nurturing broth.

Eat foods from Stage 2 on special occasions or for one of your weekend breakfasts. These include baked goods, potato dishes, frittata, granola, and pancakes.

Smoothies

The four-year-old daughter of one of our German friends used to call it "Schmusie." The way this word sounds describes it perfectly—something very, very soft and pleasant. Choose from these different recipes what kind of "Schmusie" you like: filling, fresh, fruity, rich, sweet, or packed with Vitamin C. The first seven recipes, which are raw, are from Frederic Patenaude's book, *Raw Soups, Salads, and Smoothies*. These are indicated with an asterisk. The final two recipes are not raw because they contain canned coconut milk.

Add one or all of the following supplements to any smoothie recipe to make your smoothie a nutritional powerhouse. As you experiment more and more, you may discover other liquid or powder food supplements that are appropriate for you. (The supplements listed below are not raw ingredients.)

- 2 tablespoons green powder—100% absorbable vitamins, minerals, and protein

- 2 tablespoons Udo's Oil—Essential fatty acids

- 1 capful of Majestic Earth liquid minerals—Highly absorbable minerals

- 1 tablespoon cod liver oil—Essential fatty acids

- 1 heaping tablespoon NutriBiotic brown rice protein powder or organic hemp protein powder—Highly absorbable forms of non-animal and non-dairy protein

Papaya Pudding Smoothie *

SERVES 2

PREP TIME 10 MINUTES

1 medium papaya,
about 2 cups

2 oranges

3 dates

¼ cup water

Peel and seed fruits. Blend all ingredients until dates disintegrate. This is a very filling smoothie.

Tropical Smoothie *

SERVES 3–4

PREP TIME 15 MINUTES

¼ cup water

1 papaya

½ pineapple

1 mango

Peel and seed the fruits. Blend papaya and water first. Add mango and pineapple a few chunks at a time while blender is running. Blend until smooth. Add additional water to desired thickness.

Nut-Fruit Smoothie *

SERVES 2

PREP TIME 8 MINUTES

1 centimeter of real vanilla
bean or 3–4 drops of vanilla
extract (optional)

12 almonds

1 cup water

5 dates, pitted

2 bananas

Put the vanilla, almonds, and enough water to cover them in a food processor. Blend until relatively smooth. If using a regular blender, use raw almond butter or soaked almonds (see *How To—Soak and Toast Nuts and Seeds* in Chapter 6). Add dates and blend. Blend in bananas. This smoothie is very sweet!

DAY STARTER SMOOTHIE *

SERVES 2

PREP TIME 12 MINUTES

1 cup water

2 oranges

1 apple

3 dates

Peel oranges. Core apple and cut into chunks. Blend water and oranges first. Add apple, then dates. Blend until smooth.

PEAR-MANGO-BANANA SMOOTHIE *

SERVES 2

PREP TIME 8 MINUTES

2 bananas

1 mango

water

1 pear

Peel banana and mango and seed fruits. Blend banana, mango, and water until smooth. Add pear in chunks. Blend and add water to desired thickness.

MANGO-COCONUT-PINEAPPLE SMOOTHIE *

SERVES 1–2

PREP TIME 8 MINUTES

1 cup coconut water

1 big mango

3-inch slice of fresh pineapple

Peel and seed the fruits and cut them into chunks. Add coconut water and mango to blender. Blend until smooth. Add pineapple and then blend again.

You can substitute 1 cup of water and 2 dates for coconut water. Blend water and mango until smooth, then add dates and blend until dates are finely chopped, then add pineapple and blend until smooth.

GREEN SPIRULINA SMOOTHIE *

SERVES 1–2

PREP TIME 10 MINUTES

1 cup water

1 cup papaya

1 large mango

1–2 teaspoons spirulina powder or other green powder

1 teaspoon olive oil or coconut butter

Peel and seed the fruits. Cut into chunks. Blend water, papaya, and mango until smooth. Add green powder and oil or coconut butter and blend again.

BASIC SMOOTHIE

SERVES 1

PREP TIME 5-10 MINUTES

BASE

In addition to this base, you can add one of the following

1/3 cup unsweetened (canned) coconut milk

1 peach, pitted and cut into pieces

½ cup blueberries

1½ cups unsweetened rice or almond milk—more or less for desired thickness

1 cup fresh pineapple chunks

1 banana

Also add:

Any or all of the liquid or powder supplements listed at the beginning of the *Smoothie* section. Combine all ingredients in blender. Blend.

FRUIT EVERYTHING SMOOTHIE

SERVES 2

PREP TIME 15 MINUTES

¼ cup unsweetened (canned) coconut milk

1½ cup unsweetened rice milk

2 spears pineapple (1 inch wide by 5 inches long)

6 strawberries, cut into quarters

10 grapes

7 cherries, pitted and stemmed

1 banana, broken into pieces

lemon juice to taste (optional)

Put all ingredients in blender and blend.

FRUIT SALAD

Fruit Salad is especially good when in-season fruits are used. You may wish to make the effort and find out if there is a local orchard that allows you to pick your own fruit. If not, buy fruit grown as locally as possible. These will be more nutritious because the fruit has had time to ripen on the plant. Fruit salads can also be made with only one or two fruits if that is all you can get locally in season. Avoid using melons, or make a fruit salad with melons only, as they should not be eaten with other fruits or foods for best digestion (see *Food Combinations* in Chapter 3, *The Basics*). When possible, buy organic grapes, strawberries, and apples. The pesticides on these are particularly toxic and are more likely to be absorbed (see *Organics* in Chapter 8, *Resources and Recommendations*).

If using banana, add it last. Drizzle the slices with lemon or lime juice to keep them from turning brown and mushy.

Add nuts, seeds, and/or coconut to make it more filling. Add immediately before serving so they don't get soggy. Lightly toast the coconut for extra flavor.

Prepare a bigger portion than you will eat and freeze the remainder for future smoothies. Freeze flat, in a single layer, so that you can break off chunks. This is a great way to store summer fruits, which can rot quickly.

Regular Fruit Salad

We call this our "regular" fruit salad because it can be made in any season. These fruits are available in most grocery stores. Buy organic apples so the peels can be left on, adding color and texture.

Add any other in-season fruit—for instance, in Montana in July, add fresh, pitted cherries or raspberries. In Arkansas, add fresh local peaches in July and August. California and Florida residents will have many fresh local fruits to choose from. Peeled, diced mangoes can also be added when they are in season. Raisins or chopped dried figs provide additional sweetness and texture for every season.

SERVES 4

PREP TIME 30 MINUTES

2 apples, cored and cut into half-inch pieces

2 pears, cored and cut into half-inch pieces

2 bananas, peeled and sliced

2 oranges, peeled and cut into half-inch pieces

2 cups grapes, halved, seeds removed

1 cup toasted walnut pieces or toasted sliced almonds

Fresh-squeezed lemon juice

Put fruits in a bowl. Drizzle with lemon juice. Add nuts; gently mix.

Summer Fruit Salad

We only make this one in the summer when these fruits are in season. With its beautiful color and full flavor, it's a treat any morning for breakfast. Or bring it to a barbeque potluck.

Serves 4

Prep Time 30 Minutes

2 peaches, pitted and cut into half-inch pieces

2 nectarines, pitted and cut into half-inch pieces

1 pint blueberries

1 pint raspberries

1 pint strawberries, cut into quarters

2 bananas, peeled, halved, and then sliced

Fresh-squeezed lemon juice

Drizzle lemon juice over bananas. Combine all ingredients in bowl.

OATMEAL

Some people are oat lovers and some are not. Oats are usually not something that get us out of bed in the morning, but this simple recipe starts your day on the right foot. We ate oats cooked this way for the first time in New York City when a friend made them for breakfast with lots of butter. This dish is so nurturing and filling that it has become one of our favorite breakfast recipes. Soaking the oats in warm water with a squeeze of lemon juice overnight makes them more easily digestible. And don't forget to add the butter.

SERVES 4–6

3 cups rolled oats (not quick-cook oats)

3 cups warm water

A squeeze of fresh lemon juice

2½–2¾ cups water

As much butter as you wish

Pinch of sea salt

PREP TIME 20 MINUTES

Put oats and warm water in a glass bowl. Add a squeeze of lemon juice. Stir together. Cover and let sit overnight.

Put oats in a saucepan. Add 2½–2¾ cups water and a dash of salt. Bring to a boil, then immediately turn heat down. Stir and let simmer for about 10 minutes or until oatmeal has the desired consistency. Cover with lid and let it sit for 1–2 minutes.

Serve with a healthy portion of organic butter. You can also top it with:

rice milk	almond milk	almonds
walnuts	cashews	sesame seeds
raisins	dates	honey
		Grade B maple syrup

If reheating, add water/rice milk to desired thickness.
Stir while it heats.

Note–To make this recipe appropriate for Stage 3, do not use honey or Grade B maple syrup.

BROWN RICE CEREAL

Another friend invented this cereal out of necessity to bring variety to our Sunday brunches. It's easy to prepare, inexpensive, and gluten-free. It has become a much-loved standard dish in our diet.

SERVES 7

PREP TIME 20 MINUTES

1 cup brown rice

4 cups water (or more if needed)

Sea salt to taste

Heat rice in unoiled skillet until it starts to turn brown and begins to have a nutty aroma. Put rice in blender and grind to flour texture.

Combine rice and water in saucepan. Bring to boil. Reduce heat, stirring. Cook for 3–5 minutes. Add a pinch of salt to taste.

MILLET-ALMOND CEREAL

A friend from Germany invented this recipe. Millet is one of the few alkaline grains, and this is a great way to include more of it in your diet. Cooked by itself millet makes for a heavy, dry breakfast. Ground millet and almonds together make a substantial cereal that also has a delicious nutty flavor. It is even better if you dry roast the ground millet and almonds before cooking. If you don't want to mix fruits and grains, leave out the apricots.

SERVES 1–2

2 tablespoons ghee or organic butter

Vanilla extract to taste

¼ cup dried apricots, soaked and chopped

2 cups hot water or oat, almond, or rice milk

¾ cup millet, ground in coffee grinder

¼ cup almonds, ground in coffee grinder

Butter (optional)

PREP TIME 50 MINUTES

Melt ghee or butter in a medium-sized pot. Add vanilla, apricots, and boiling water or milk. Cook long enough to sweeten the liquid, about 10 minutes.

Slowly add almonds and millet, stirring frequently until cereal gets thick, about 30 minutes. In the last 15 minutes the cereal burns easily, so be ready to stir more frequently. If it gets too thick add more liquid to fully cook the grain.

The cereal can be made thick or thin according to preference by adding more or less water.

Serve with butter on the side.

Note–For Stage 2, serve with maple syrup, if desired.

BUDDHA GRUEL

This is called Buddha Gruel because Buddha includes everything. You can add just about anything you can think of that goes nicely with gruel. Everything except the oats and water is optional. This can also be prepared using leftover oats.

SERVES 8

3 cups rolled oats

6 cups water

½ teaspoon salt

1 cup chopped or slivered almonds

½ cup sunflower seeds

1 cup raisins or dried apricots or goji berries

1 cup fresh, chopped apple

Cinnamon

Honey

Rice or almond milk, heated

PREP TIME 25 MINUTES TOTAL IF OATS ARE SOAKED OVERNIGHT; 50 MINUTES IF OATS ARE COOKED THE SAME DAY

Combine oats and water. Cover and soak overnight (this gives them a creamy and digestible consistency). In the morning put in saucepan, add salt and bring to a boil. Or omit soaking—combine oats, salt, and water in saucepan and bring to a boil.

Add almonds and sunflower seeds and dried fruit. Let simmer for 10 minutes, checking thickness. If needed add more boiling water. After 5 minutes or so, add the chopped apple and cinnamon. When cereal is done, you can add hot rice or almond milk and honey to taste.

Note–For Stage 3, omit honey.

WINTER RICE BREAKFAST

Another one of our German friends gave us this delicious breakfast recipe. Cardamom gives it a unique flavor that is a nice change from other hot cereals. If you start your day with this dish, you will feel warm, nurtured, and grounded, especially in the winter, and you might not have anything to worry about for the rest of the day. It's also a great way to use leftover brown rice.

SERVES 3

4 cups cooked short grain brown rice

1¼ cups chopped dry-roasted nuts and seeds (walnuts, hazelnuts, almonds, pecans, and/or sunflower seeds— any combination you like)

2 tablespoons olive oil

¾ cup raisins

½ teaspoon cinnamon

¼ teaspoon freshly ground cardamom or to taste

Pinch of sea salt

1 apple, leave peel on, remove core, cut into cubes

1 pear, leave peel on, remove core, cut into cubes (optional)

PREP TIME 35 MINUTES WITH ALREADY-COOKED RICE

Cook (see introduction in *Grains* section) or reheat rice.

Roast nuts in a dry skillet until they begin to turn dark, about 5–7 minutes. Remove and set aside.

Heat olive oil in skillet. Add raisins and stir until coated. Add cinnamon, cardamom, and salt. Stir to mix. Sauté at medium heat, stirring occasionally, for 30–60 seconds until raisins start to expand.

Add apples and/or pears and sauté, covered, for 3 minutes.

Put cooked rice, roasted nuts, and fruit mixture into a large bowl and mix well.

ABOVE THE LINE GRANOLA

"Above the Line" means taking responsibility for something. We call this "Above the Line Granola" because one time I (Tika) was preparing this granola and it burned. Somebody else came into the kitchen and asked, "What happened to the granola?" I responded, "It came out dark." The other person replied, "What? It came out dark? Are you saying that the granola is responsible for how it turned out?" Once they put it that way, I took responsibility for the fact that I had actually burned the granola. We still remember this story with a twinkle in our eyes.

Adjust the amounts of the ingredients or add or leave them out to taste. Serve with yogurt, almond milk, or rice milk.

16 cups raw oats

5 cups almonds, sliced

4 cups walnut halves (or chopped pecans)

1½ cups safflower oil (use organic, cold-pressed oil)

1½ cups water

2 cups honey or Grade B maple syrup

4 cups unsweetened coconut

PREP TIME 1 HOUR 45 MINUTES

Preheat oven to 325°F.

Mix oats, almonds, and walnuts or pecans together. Set aside. Mix oil, water, and honey together in a saucepan and warm over low heat until the honey is liquid.

Make a hole in the middle of the dry ingredients and pour in the liquid. Mix with hands until everything is coated.

Don't add coconut until the last 30 minutes of baking.

Lightly oil pans. Bake granola for about 1 hour and 15 minutes total, but watch closely so that it doesn't get too brown. *It may be necessary to decrease baking time.* If using deep dish pans, put in oven and stir after 15 minutes and again after another 15 minutes, then every 10 minutes after that. If pans are shallower, stir more often so granola doesn't burn. If using two pans, move the top one to the bottom and vice versa after each stir. Remove from oven. Cool. Store in an air-tight container.

BREAKFAST POTATOES

My (Tika's) grandfather would have been very happy about Breakfast Potatoes because he used to eat potatoes every single day. His wife served him potatoes by pouring them out of the pot right onto his plate. This recipe would have been a nice variation for him. You can also prepare this with cubed baked sweet potatoes (omit the onion). Often called "home fries" in a diner, they are great served with eggs but also reputable with kale sautéed in butter and garlic. Or if you want to go the Mexican route, serve them with guacamole and salsa. Buenos Días!

SERVES 4

3 large russet baking potatoes

3 tablespoons olive oil

1 medium onion, diced

Sea salt to taste

Pepper to taste (optional)

Preheat oven to 350°F.

PREP TIME 2 HOURS

Wash potatoes. Poke each potato several times with fork. Put potatoes on oven rack with poked side facing up. Bake for an hour or until potato is soft when squeezed. Let potatoes cool enough that they can be handled. Or use leftover baked potatoes that have been refrigerated.

Cut potatoes into bite-sized pieces.

Pour olive oil into large skillet. Heat oil. Add onion and sauté until translucent. Add potato cubes. Cook over medium heat. When potato begins to brown, turn with spatula. Add salt and pepper, if using. Continue cooking and turning potatoes until they have browned on each side.

Serve hot. To keep potatoes hot until serving, spread on a baking sheet and put in a 200°F oven for up to 20 minutes.

VEGAN PANCAKES

Mmmm. On the day of our friends' marriage, we made a big batch of these for a festive and healthy brunch. Nobody would have guessed that they were made without eggs. You might think that pancakes without eggs and cow milk would equal flat and dry cardboard, but these are surprisingly fluffy and light. They're great with butter and maple syrup of course, or a generous serving of fresh berries.

MAKES 10–12 PANCAKES

PREP TIME 1 HOUR

2 cups whole wheat pastry flour

2 tablespoons baking powder

1/8 teaspoon salt

2 cups almond or rice milk

1 tablespoon raw honey

2 tablespoons safflower oil

Additional oil

Combine flour, baking powder, and salt in a bowl. Combine almond or rice milk, honey, and oil in small bowl. Add to dry ingredients. Mix until smooth.

Put a little oil in skillet or griddle on medium heat. When hot, spoon about ¼ cup of pancake batter into the pan. Then flip carefully when you see bubbles in the middle of the pancake or if the edges are looking stiffened. Cook second side until golden brown. Repeat until the batter is gone. Serve hot with maple syrup.

Tomato, Onion, Spinach Frittata

If you're serving brunch to a large group, a frittata is a good choice. The great thing about frittatas is that once you prepare the ingredients, you only need a few minutes to combine them before the frittata goes in the oven and it doesn't need your attention again until it's done. This gives you time to prepare the other items on your menu. When it is done, you just pull the frittata out of the oven, put it on the table, take a seat with your guests, and enjoy their company.

A frittata is also great because the vegetables and herbs that are used can be varied according to personal taste or to what is available seasonally. Use mushrooms, marjoram, and tarragon instead of tomato, spinach, basil, and thyme. Or use any vegetables that you would use in a sauté—for instance, mushrooms, zucchini, and potato.

Serves 6–8

Prep time 1 hour 10 minutes for both stovetop and oven methods

6–8 eggs

Rice milk or water

Salt and pepper

1 yellow onion, sliced

2 tablespoons organic butter

¼ cup fresh basil, some chopped, other leaves whole for garnish

1 teaspoon dried or 2 tablespoons fresh thyme

¼ cup chopped fresh parsley

4 cups spinach, washed and loosely chopped

2 tomatoes, sliced

Put eggs, milk or water, salt, and pepper in bowl. Beat to combine. Set aside.

Sauté onion in butter in a cast iron skillet. Add herbs and spinach, and sauté until spinach is wilted.

Stove top method—Pour egg mixture into cast iron skillet over sautéed vegetables, and let set for about 1 or 2 minutes. Cover pan tightly with lid and turn heat down as low as possible. It may take 30–45 minutes to cook and set completely. About half way through, place sliced tomato and basil leaves on top. Cover again and cook until egg has set completely.

Oven method—Preheat oven to 325°F. Heat glass or ceramic baking pan; add sautéed onion, herbs, and spinach. Pour egg mixture over sautéed vegetables. Cover with aluminum foil and bake for about 25 minutes or until eggs are set. Add sliced tomato and basil to top halfway through baking time.

BREAKFAST BURRITOS

A friend makes this dish when her college-aged children come home for a visit. It was their favorite brunch dish when they lived at home. Now they sometimes invite their friends over for this delight from Mexico. You might want to make enough so that you have leftovers to take to work the next day, or for the children's lunch or snack. We can't get too much of a good thing. Salsa provides extra flavor, color, and spice; and guacamole is always a welcome accompaniment.

SERVES 4

PREP TIME 1 HOUR 45 MINUTES (SALSA ACCOUNTS FOR 1 HOUR)

4 large whole wheat
or rice tortillas

Olive or safflower oil

2 large baked potatoes, well
chilled

Sea salt

8 eggs

2 tablespoons butter

Sea salt and pepper to taste

8 ounces raw cheddar cheese,
grated

Sliced green onion (optional)

Fresh Tomato Salsa (optional)
(see recipe in *Sauces,
Spreads, and Dips*)

Preheat oven to 250°F.

Wrap whole wheat tortillas in aluminum foil and put in oven. For rice tortillas, steam until soft.

Grate baked potatoes. Pour enough oil into large skillet to lightly cover bottom and heat. Sprinkle grated potato evenly in skillet and lightly salt. Cook until bottom of potatoes is golden brown. Using a spatula, divide the potatoes into pie-shaped fourths and turn each section. Cook until golden brown. Put on very lightly oiled baking sheet in 250°F oven to keep warm.

While potatoes are cooking, beat eggs in a medium-size bowl until thoroughly combined. Melt butter in large skillet over medium to low heat. Add eggs and scramble. Do not overcook.

Remove warm tortillas from oven or steamer. Turn oven temperature up to 350°F.

Sprinkle a few tablespoons of grated cheese down middle of tortilla in about a 2-inch wide strip. Spread ¼ of the potatoes over it. Top with ¼ of the scrambled eggs, then salt and pepper to taste. Roll tortilla up and lay it seam-side down in glass baking dish. Repeat for remaining tortillas.

Sprinkle top of tortillas with remaining cheese and green onion if desired. Cover with foil but do not let foil touch cheese. Return to oven for about 10 minutes or until cheese is melted.

Serve with our *Fresh Tomato Salsa* on the top or on the side, if you wish.

TOFU BACON

If you like savory food for breakfast this is a good option. It provides plenty of protein so you'll have the energy to rake your entire yard. It can also be used for lunch or dinner. Try this: Cut the tofu in small pieces and serve it with *Soba Noodles in Asian Sauce* and steamed greens like kale. Or add it to *Spinach Salad* and serve as a main dish.

1 or more blocks extra firm tofu

Olive oil

Low sodium soy sauce or tamari

PREP TIME 50 MINUTES

Preheat oven to 500°F. Move oven rack to the topmost position.

Cut the tofu into ¼-inch slices. Thicker slices won't be crispy, but are still good.

Lightly oil a cookie sheet and lay slices on it. Brush on (with a food brush) a mixture of olive oil and soy sauce. (More soy sauce = saltier.)

Place cookie sheet on top oven rack. Leave the oven door cracked to keep an eye on the tofu bacon. Broil for 20–25 minutes on the first side, 5–10 minutes on the second side. It should be crispy when it's done.

Note—Works best in a gas oven. We've had mixed results with an electric oven.

SALADS AND DRESSINGS

Salads are good all year, but especially in the spring and summer. As a meal unto themselves they're a great way to get a fresh start after eating heavy meals or off-diet foods.

When making a salad, first choose which type of leafy green will form the base (romaine, spinach, mixed greens, etc.) before deciding which other ingredients to add. For example, it's best not to put heavy chopped vegetables on delicate spring lettuce.

Salad-making provides an excellent opportunity to work with color and texture. Add cut fresh peppers, roasted sunflower seeds, and tomatoes to a mixed green salad, but keep it simple; we recommend using at most five ingredients. Pay attention that all ingredients are raw if your goal is to have a raw salad.

We usually tear lettuce by hand because it gives a different feel to the salad. But sometimes we chop everything, including the leafy greens, into approximately the same size as a way to balance different flavors.

Consider choosing one ingredient from each of the following five categories to make a good salad.

Sweet—Tomatoes, red bell pepper, sun-dried tomatoes, fresh corn, beets, carrots, jicama, apples, pears (sweet tree fruits are a good mix with greens) and sun-dried fruits. Sun-dried fruits and vegetables are raw. You can also make your own raw dried fruits if you have a dehydrator that allows you to keep the temperature below 110°F.

Spicy—Green onion, garlic (chopped fine), regular or red onion (chopped fine). Pepper (the spice) is not raw unless the peppercorns were picked, dried naturally, and then ground.

Oily—Avocado, nuts, oils, olives. They make a salad more filling as the fat content helps the body register "full." Olives soaked in vinegar brine are not raw. The best raw olives are vacuum-sealed Peruvian olives. They can be ordered online through www.livingtreecommunity.com, which is a great source for many raw ingredients.

If using olive oil on a salad or in a dressing, the best choice is extra-virgin stone-crushed cold-pressed olive oil in dark green bottles. Sometimes even cold-pressed oils are exposed to temperatures above 160°F, so buy them from a trustworthy source.

Salty—Celery, tomatoes, seaweed, sea salt, tamari. The only raw soy sauce currently available in the U.S. is Nama Soya, which is unpasteurized. Braggs Liquid Aminos is a good raw, wheat-free alternative to soy sauce. It is not fermented or heated.

Tangy—Lemon, lime, grapefruit or orange juice (in small quantities), tomatoes, vinegar. Vinegars labeled "naturally fermented, unpasteurized" are raw.

The point of a dressing is to complement a salad. If using delicate greens, choose a vinaigrette or an oil-based dressing. Heavier salads pair well with creamy dressings like the *Pine Nut/Cashew Dressing*. Be careful not to overdress—you should still be able to taste the greens and other ingredients.

Dress a small amount of salad immediately before serving a meal. Dress more only if it's needed as dressed salad wilts quickly and sometimes ends up getting thrown away. If serving dressing on the side, make sure you have enough, as people tend to use more of it than if the entire salad is dressed ahead of time.

ARUGULA SALAD

This is a clean and satisfying salad. Full of avocados, tomatoes, and scallions. It feels healthy—like a spring breeze. The taste of arugula is often described as peppery and pungent so it's a nice complement to milder-tasting greens such as romaine and leaf lettuce. Don't forget to top the salad with small pieces of dulse, a sea vegetable that adds a mildly spicy, salty sea flavor and contains lots of minerals, vitamins, and protein.

SERVES 12–14

PREP TIME 45 MINUTES

¼ cup lemon juice

¼ cup olive oil

1 head romaine lettuce, torn into bite-sized pieces

1 head green leaf lettuce, torn into bite-sized pieces

1 (5 ounce) box or 4 large handfuls arugula, chopped

6 Roma tomatoes, cut in large dice

4 avocadoes, diced

6 scallions, thinly sliced

Dulse flakes to taste

Combine lemon juice and olive oil in small bowl.

In large salad bowl, combine romaine and leaf lettuce, arugula, tomatoes, avocado, and scallions. Add lemon-juice / olive oil dressing and gently toss. Sprinkle dulse flakes on top.

RAW RED BEET SALAD

One of our German friends created this salad, and it's always a winner. This hearty salad comes alive through the combination of raw beets, apples, onions, and horseradish. This recipe proves that it is a good idea to eat beets raw. The grated beets soften in the balsamic vinaigrette. It's a beautiful and tasty accompaniment to a simple green salad.

SERVES 4

1 medium red beet, peeled and coarsely grated according to preference

1 medium apple, cored but not peeled, coarsely grated (see Notes below)

¼ cup very finely minced onion

DRESSING

5 tablespoons apple juice

2 tablespoons balsamic vinegar

1 heaping teaspoon horseradish, freshly grated or from jar (use more or less according to spiciness and taste)

1 teaspoon sea salt

2 tablespoons olive oil

5 heaping tablespoons sesame seeds

PREP TIME 50 MINUTES

Combine beets, apples, and onions in a bowl.

Combine apple juice, vinegar, horseradish, salt, and olive oil for dressing.

In a frying pan, dry roast the sesame seeds.

Pour dressing over beet mixture. Add sesame seeds. Stir. Serve at room temperature.

Notes–For Stage 3, use freshly grated horseradish.

WARM BROCCOLI SALAD

You might wonder how broccoli can be made intriguing. The secret is the garlic-balsamic vinaigrette that is drizzled over the top—it opens heaven's doors. Serve hot, warm, or at room temperature.

<small>SERVES 4</small>

1 head of broccoli

4 tablespoons balsamic vinegar

1 tablespoon Dijon mustard

1–2 garlic cloves, finely minced or pressed

Sea salt

Pepper

8 tablespoons olive oil

<small>PREP TIME 25 MINUTES</small>

Cut florets off broccoli. Peel the stem (see *How To—Peel Broccoli Stalks* in Chapter 6) and slice into small slices. Cut florets into bite-sized pieces.

Lightly steam broccoli, around 5 minutes. It should not be too raw but not cooked all the way.

Remove from steamer and let water drain off.

To make dressing, combine balsamic vinegar, Dijon mustard, garlic, salt, and pepper in a small bowl. Slowly pour in olive oil, whisking continuously until creamy.

Arrange broccoli on a platter and pour dressing over it. Serve.

CABBAGE SALAD

This is the much-loved cabbage salad recipe we've been using for years. It is simple and hearty. Make it a few hours ahead of time so the flavors blend and the cabbage softens in the lemon juice and salt.

SERVES 6–8

PREP TIME 1 HOUR 20 MINUTES

1 medium white cabbage

¼ cup fresh lemon juice

½ cup olive oil

1 clove garlic, pressed

Sea salt

Remove outer leaves from cabbage. Cut out stalk. Slice half the cabbage very thinly. Cut slices in half.

Mix remaining ingredients together to make dressing. Pour over cabbage and stir. Let sit for ½ hour then stir and let sit another ½ hour. Can be served immediately, but tastes better when allowed to sit.

Purple Cabbage and Basil Salad

If you're a painter, this is your opportunity to paint yourself a salad. Purple cabbage is one of nature's gifts. Have you ever cut open a head of cabbage and looked at the incredible stained-glass-like pattern? Imagine combining slices of purple with the green of fresh basil. A painter couldn't do a better job. Tip: Slice the cabbage first and let it sit in the dressing so it can soften. Right before serving, add the basil so it doesn't wilt.

SERVES 8

1 medium-sized purple cabbage, sliced thinly

½ bunch basil, sliced thinly

¼ cup sesame seeds, lightly toasted

DRESSING

2 tablespoons low sodium soy sauce

2 tablespoons sesame oil

1 tablespoon apple cider vinegar

1 tablespoon honey

PREP TIME 30 MINUTES

Put cabbage in a large bowl, combine ingredients for dressing, and pour over cabbage. Toss.

Just before serving, add basil and sprinkle with sesame seeds. Serve.

Note–All stages of this diet have gradients. If you are just beginning to eat Stage 3, this recipe is appropriate for occasional use. If you are eating a pure Stage 3 diet, omit the honey.

CAESAR SALAD

This salad is called Caesar Salad because Caesar used to make it for his wife, Pompeia, on a regular basis. She loved it, especially the croutons. This is how that busy man served his wife and it made a big difference for their relationship. (Just kidding.)

Many people love Caesar Salad, especially when it comes with crunchy homemade croutons. It's considered elegant enough for special occasions and can be served either as a main dish or side salad. To make it even more special, toss or top with freshly grated Parmesan cheese. Because this recipe uses hardboiled eggs in the dressing, we don't have to be concerned with the hazards of eating raw eggs.

SERVES 4–6

1 large or 2 small heads of romaine, torn into bite-sized pieces, and spun dry

DRESSING

1 hardboiled egg, peeled and quartered, plus 1 hardboiled egg yolk

2 tablespoons fresh lemon juice

½ teaspoon Dijon mustard or more to taste

½ teaspoon tamari or more to taste

1 clove garlic, pressed

½ teaspoon sea salt or to taste

Fresh finely-ground pepper to taste (optional)

¼ cup olive oil

CROUTONS

½ loaf whole grain French or sourdough bread, cut into ¾-inch cubes (about 3 cups)

3 tablespoons olive oil

2 cloves garlic, pressed

Sea salt to taste

Fresh ground pepper to taste (optional)

PREP TIME 1 HOUR 55 MINUTES (30 MINUTES FOR DRESSING, 1 HOUR FOR CROUTONS, 25 MINUTES FOR LETTUCE AND SALAD PREP)

Put romaine lettuce in a large bowl. Cover with lightly moist towel. Put in refrigerator until just before serving.

For dressing—Put all dressing ingredients except olive oil into a blender. Blend until smooth. Slowly add olive oil with blender running. Refrigerate until ready to use.

For croutons—Preheat oven to 350°F. Put bread cubes in a bowl. Pour olive oil into a small bowl and add garlic, salt, and pepper, if using. Drizzle over bread crumbs. Toss to evenly distribute. Spread on baking sheet in one layer. Bake, stirring occasionally, until bread cubes are toasted and crunchy. Cool. Store in an airtight container.

To prepare salad just before serving, put romaine lettuce in a salad bowl. Pour desired amount of dressing over lettuce and toss. If serving from bowl, add croutons and toss, if desired, or serve croutons in a small bowl on the side. If using individual salad plates, put salad on plate and top with croutons.

Note—You can prepare croutons and dressing earlier in the day or the day before serving.

CARROT SALAD

Usually when we make this carrot salad we get the question, "What's in this?!" The answer is always, "Just olive oil, lemon juice, garlic, mustard, pepper, and salt." For some reason the simplicity of the ingredients surprises people. The secret is pepper and salt. What makes it even better: toasted sunflower seeds on top. Here we go.

SERVES 4

PREP TIME 30 MINUTES

6–8 medium carrots, peeled and grated

2/3 cup olive oil

1/3 cup fresh lemon juice

2 teaspoons Dijon mustard

1 clove garlic, minced

1 teaspoon sea salt

Black pepper (optional)

Toasted sunflower seeds (see *Nuts and Seeds)*

Put grated carrots in a bowl.

In a small bowl, combine olive oil, lemon juice, Dijon mustard, garlic, salt, and pepper, if using. Pour over carrots.

Sprinkle with toasted sunflower seeds. Serve.

CUCUMBER SALAD

Our friend from Russia makes this salad often. It only takes ten minutes to put together. Dill is a common herb in Russia, and this salad brings the garden right onto your dinner plate. It goes well with baked potatoes, corn on the cob, and baked eggplant or zucchini.

SERVES 4

4 small cucumbers

1 tablespoon fresh dill
or 1 teaspoon dried dill

½ small red onion, finely diced

DRESSING

2 tablespoons apple cider vinegar

¼ cup high-quality cold-pressed olive oil

½ teaspoon sea salt
to taste

PREP TIME 25 MINUTES

Peel cucumbers. Cut in half. Scoop out seeds. Slice.

Put cucumber in a bowl, add dill and onions. Combine ingredients for dressing and pour over cucumbers. Stir and serve.

CUCUMBER-TOMATO SALAD

There's a time in the summer when an abundance of fresh juicy garden tomatoes is available. Nothing like eating a tomato straight from the garden! As children we would pick them and eat them like apples. As adults, sometimes we enjoy them sliced with nothing added and other times we like to jazz them up a bit with ingredients that don't overpower their fresh taste. This salad is one of our favorite ways to eat garden tomatoes. Tip: Never refrigerate tomatoes. They lose flavor and the texture can become mealy.

SERVES 4

PREP TIME 20 MINUTES

3 medium cucumbers, peeled and sliced

2–3 medium tomatoes, cut into bite-sized pieces

½ medium red onion, chopped

DRESSING

1 clove garlic, minced

4 tablespoons olive oil

1 tablespoon lemon juice

Sea salt to taste

Put cucumbers, tomatoes, and red onion in a bowl.

Combine garlic, olive oil, lemon juice, and salt. Pour over vegetables. Serve at room temperature.

FENNEL SALAD

Try this salad on a picnic in a meadow with your family. It's a welcome variation from the usual green salad. The avocado and olive oil combine to make a dressing that's as green as blades of grass. The salad is light and fresh but filling at the same time. If you have children, you might want to serve them raw slices of fennel on the side.

SERVER 6

PREP TIME 30 MINUTES (WITHOUT SOAKING TOMATOES)

3 cups fennel, thinly sliced

¼ cup chopped parsley

1 yellow pepper, seeds removed, diced

1 rib celery, diced

½ avocado, peeled and diced

2 tablespoons olive oil

6–8 sun-dried tomatoes, soaked for at least an hour and chopped

Combine all ingredients in a large bowl. Toss.

(from *Raw Soups, Salads, and Smoothies* by Frederic Patenaude)

Green Salad

We serve some type of green salad with most lunches and dinners. Sometimes we use only one type of leafy green and other times we combine two or more. Adding a handful or two of fresh spinach is a good choice because it's high in nutrients. Use any or all of the ingredients listed below, in the amounts you prefer. (This is more of a guide than an exact recipe.) Vary your choices so that you're not eating the same salad each time.

SERVES 4-5 PEOPLE (DEPENDING ON OTHER ADDED INGREDIENTS)

Red leaf and/or green leaf lettuce

Romaine

Spinach

Carrot, shredded

Cucumber

Avocado

Vinaigrette

PREP TIME 20-30 MINUTES

Combine all ingredients in a large bowl.

Dress with vinaigrette. Toss gently.

HEARTY SALAD

This beautiful salad can be served as part of a special meal or as the main course. It is substantial enough to fill everyone up, yet it's simple. The avocado, feta cheese, and sunflower seeds give it weight, and the dried cranberries and basil give it a wonderful fresh taste. It's delicious dressed with *Simple Vinaigrette*.

SERVES 4 AS A MAIN DISH,
4–6 AS A SIDE

½ medium head green leaf lettuce—tear lettuces and spinach by hand

½ medium head red leaf lettuce

1 cup raw spinach

½ bunch basil, torn by hand

3 medium avocados, cut into bite-sized chunks

1 cup roasted sunflower seeds

1 cup dried cranberries

½ cup feta cheese

PREP TIME 45 MINUTES

In a salad bowl, lay down a layer of lettuce and spinach followed by a layer of basil, avocado, sunflower seeds, cranberries, and feta. Continue layering until all ingredients are used. Layering the ingredients helps the salad mix and keeps the heavier pieces from all ending up on the bottom.

Dress salad to taste with dressing of choice. Toss salad gently and serve.

HOT SALAD

This is a good salad to serve to a large group. We once served it at a dinner for 80! It can be made with romaine and bok choy, or with bolted lettuce from a garden, or with another hearty green. Don't use leaf lettuce or it will end up mushy.

SERVES 20

PREP TIME 1 ½ HOURS (WITHOUT OPTIONAL INGREDIENTS)

2 cups safflower oil

2 cloves garlic, finely minced

1½ cups toasted sunflower seeds (see *Nuts and Seeds*)

¼ cup balsamic vinegar

2 teaspoons raw honey

Tamari to taste

Sesame oil to taste

Umeboshi plum vinegar to taste (optional)

Gomasio to taste (optional)

Grilled portobello mushrooms to taste (optional)

1 onion

Oil

Organic butter

Greens—2 heads romaine and 6 heads bok choy

In a cast iron skillet, heat safflower oil. Add garlic and toasted sunflower seeds. When these are hot, add balsamic vinegar (it'll sizzle—stand back). Add honey, tamari, sesame oil, and any other ingredients desired.

Cut onion into thick rounds and caramelize (cook slowly until onion is golden brown) in oil and a bit of butter. Keep them hot.

Pour dressing and hot onions over greens. Cover and let sit for 15 minutes. Serve warm.

Kohlrabi Salad

Kohlrabi isn't as well known in the U.S. as it is in Europe. It is a mild cabbage with a light green peel and a white interior. The taste and texture are similar to those of a broccoli stem. Steamed, it is a slightly sweet vegetable that children often like. The basil and cilantro add a distinctive flavor to this refreshing raw summer salad. Make only what will be eaten at a meal because kohlrabi turns brown in the refrigerator overnight.

Serves 3

2 cups peeled and shredded kohlrabi

2 tablespoons minced fresh basil

¼ cup chopped fresh cilantro

Dressing

¼ cup water

Juice of ½ lemon

1 avocado

2 ribs celery, chopped

Sea salt to taste

Prep time 30 minutes

Put kohlrabi, basil, and cilantro in bowl.

Blend ingredients for dressing. Pour over kohlrabi salad. Toss and serve.

(from *Raw Soups, Salads, and Smoothies* by Frederic Patenaude)

POTATO, BEET, AND CABBAGE SALAD

This is a popular dish from Russia with the typical combination of potatoes, beets, and cabbage. Give the flavors enough time to blend before serving. For even more Russian flavor, sprinkle fresh dill over the top.

SERVES 8-10

2 medium potatoes, not peeled

2 medium carrots, peeled

1 small beet

½ medium white cabbage

1/3 cup fresh lemon juice

½ cup olive oil

1 clove garlic, pressed

Sea salt

Pepper

Red onion, chopped

Olive oil

PREP TIME 1 HOUR 15 MINUTES

Boil the potatoes until tender. Simmer carrots in small amount of water. Remove from water and cool.

Pierce beet with fork twice so it can vent while cooking. Place on a baking sheet lined with aluminum foil and bake at 400°F for 1hour. Cool, then peel off outer skin. For further information, see *How To—Work with Beets* in Chapter 6.

Chop potatoes, carrots, and beet into small pieces. The pieces should be the same size and small enough so that several pieces make up one bite.

Thinly slice cabbage and then cut slices into pieces that are about 1 inch in length. Place in bowl. Combine lemon juice, olive oil, garlic, salt and pepper, and pour over sliced cabbage. Add potatoes, carrots, beet, and onion.

Dress with olive oil and salt to taste. Chill and serve cold.

SEAWEED SALAD (SUNOMONO)

To serve this seaweed salad appropriately, first go to the ocean and collect algae at the beach. Bring it home, drape it over the couches, and hang it over the lamps as a welcoming decoration for your family when they arrive home. When they walk in, say, "Surprise!" Then offer them a drink of seashell water chilled with an ice cube. Seriously, this salad goes great with any kind of Asian dinner. It can also be made with hijiki seaweed, though hijiki takes longer to soak.

SERVES 4

½ cup dried wakame seaweed

2 tablespoons toasted sesame seeds

DRESSING

3 tablespoons seasoned rice vinegar (the kind without corn syrup)

1 teaspoon soy sauce

PREP TIME 20 MINUTES

Rinse wakame in a strainer. Reconstitute the seaweed by covering it with water and soaking for 5–15 minutes. It should expand to approximately four times its volume. (Be sure there's enough water in the bowl for it to do this and remain completely submerged.) Rinse again and strain, squeezing the seaweed to extract as much moisture as you can.

Mix the dressing and add to the wakame. Sprinkle in toasted sesame seeds and toss, or save the seeds for the top.

Note–You can substitute 3 tablespoons unseasoned rice vinegar and 1 tablespoon honey for seasoned rice vinegar.

Spinach Salad

Popeye loved spinach. (Popeye was a favorite cartoon character from the 1950s and 60s in the U.S.) It was his secret to unimaginable powers. Try this spinach salad and it might do the same for you. Tip: This salad is good all year round, but extra special in the spring when the spinach is young and fresh.

Serves 4

8 cups spinach leaves, torn

10 mushrooms, sliced

1 ripe avocado, thinly sliced

Dressing

¼ cup olive oil

2 tablespoons red wine vinegar

2 teaspoons Dijon mustard

1 tablespoon honey

1 avocado, sliced

Prep time 30 minutes

Put spinach and mushrooms into a salad bowl.

Whisk olive oil, vinegar, mustard, and honey in small bowl. Pour onto salad. Toss well. Top with avocado.

Note–All stages of this diet have gradients. If you are still easing into Stage 3 this recipe is appropriate for occasional use. If you are eating a pure Stage 3 diet, omit the honey.

ITALIAN TOMATOES

If you want to bring the taste of Italy home and still eat raw, this is a good way to go, particularly with fresh tomatoes and basil in the summertime. Because of the sunflower seeds, sun-dried tomatoes, and olives, this is a light but filling dish that's easy to make. It can also be served with an elegant dinner. People tend to love it and eat a lot so make more rather than less.

SERVES 4

PREP TIME 30 MINUTES (ONCE SOAKING IS ACCOMPLISHED)

3 cups sunflower seeds, soaked for at least 6 hours

1 cup chopped sun-dried tomatoes, soaked for at least 6 hours

½ teaspoon paprika

½ cup chopped fresh basil or 1 tablespoon dried basil

1 clove garlic

5 raw pitted black olives

Sea salt

4 large fresh tomatoes, cut into thick slices

Fresh basil for garnish

Combine sunflower seeds, sun-dried tomatoes and the water used to soak them, paprika, basil, garlic, black olives, and sea salt in a food processor. Blend until smooth. Spread the resulting paste on the tomato slices and garnish with fresh basil.

SIMPLE VINAIGRETTE DRESSING

This is a basic vinaigrette. We recommend experimenting with different vinegars and oils. Some options are red wine vinegar, balsamic vinegar, white balsamic vinegar, champagne vinegar (for special occasions), walnut oil, safflower oil, or toasted sesame oil (if more of an Asian flavor is desired).

MAKES ABOUT 1 CUP

PREP TIME 10 MINUTES

1/3 cup (or more to taste) apple cider or other vinegar or fresh lemon juice

2 teaspoons Dijon mustard

1 clove garlic, minced

1 teaspoon sea salt

Black pepper (optional)

2/3 cup olive oil

Combine all ingredients except olive oil. Whisk in olive oil. Refrigerate unused portion.

BALSAMIC VINAIGRETTE DRESSING

This is a classic Italian Vinaigrette. You can buy different qualities of balsamic vinegar. Aged balsamic is the best but also the most expensive. Most grocery stores carry a variety of high-quality balsamic vinegars.

MAKES ABOUT ¾ CUP

PREP TIME 12 MINUTES

4 tablespoons balsamic vinegar or more to taste

1 tablespoon Dijon mustard

1–2 cloves garlic, pressed

Sea salt

Pepper

8 tablespoons olive oil

Whisk together vinegar, mustard, garlic, salt, and pepper. Gradually add olive oil, whisking until creamy. Refrigerate unused portion.

HONEY MUSTARD VINAIGRETTE DRESSING

Children often like this sweet vinaigrette. It is a welcome variation to basic vinaigrette but isn't for daily use even on the Stage 2 diet because of the high quantity of honey.

MAKES 2 CUPS

1/3 cup apple cider vinegar

1/3 cup Dijon mustard

1/3 cup honey

1 cup safflower oil

½ teaspoon sea salt

PREP TIME 10 MINUTES

In a small mixing bowl, whisk together the vinegar and mustard. Continue to whisk while drizzling in the honey and then the oil until well-blended. Add salt. Refrigerate unused portion.

HERB DRESSING

This is another everyday salad dressing. It has enhanced flavor due to the combination of dried and fresh herbs. Feel free to use other herbs such as fresh chives, dill, basil, or oregano.

MAKES ABOUT 1 CUP

½ cup olive oil

4 basil leaves, chopped

3 tablespoons wine vinegar

1 tablespoon finely chopped onion

1 tablespoon water

1 tablespoon finely chopped fresh parsley

½ teaspoon salt

1/8 teaspoon dried thyme (rub between fingers into dressing)

1/8 teaspoon dried marjoram (rub between fingers into dressing)

PREP TIME 30 MINUTES

Combine all ingredients in a container that has a lid that won't leak. Shake hard. Let sit for 10 minutes so flavors blend. Shake again before using. Or strain out herbs to use in other cooking. Refrigerate unused portion.

PINE NUT-CASHEW DRESSING

This is a creamy dressing that looks like it has dairy in it because of the nut base. You can substitute almonds, macadamia nuts, or Brazil nuts.

MAKES 2 1/3 CUPS

PREP TIME 15 MINUTES

1 cup pine nuts or cashew nuts

Juice of ½ lemon

1½ cups olive oil

½ cup water

3 cloves garlic, squeezed through press

Sea salt and black pepper to taste

Cayenne pepper to taste

Blend the nuts first in food processor or blender. Then add other ingredients and blend until creamy. Refrigerate unused portion.

"GODDESS DRESSING"

This dressing is really green. Just looking at it will make your mouth water. The color comes from blended parsley and chives.

MAKES ABOUT 5 CUPS

PREP TIME 30 MINUTES

½–¾ cup olive oil

1¼ cups cold water

3 tablespoons tahini (see Note below)

½ cup lemon juice

1 teaspoon salt

3 tablespoons tamari

3 heaping teaspoons garlic

3 teaspoons toasted sesame seeds

½ cup chopped parsley

1½ cups chopped chives or green onions (optional—steam them)

Blend all ingredients until smooth. Refrigerate unused portion.

Note–If you are eating a pure Stage 3 diet, use homemade tahini (see recipe in *Nuts and Seeds*) or a good-quality tahini from a natural food store.

Sesame-Tamari Salad Dressing

This one goes well with any food that is Asian-oriented. You can also drizzle this dressing over steamed vegetables. It becomes even more "Asian" if you use toasted sesame oil instead of plain sesame oil.

MAKES 1½ CUPS

PREP TIME 10 MINUTES

¾ cup unrefined sesame oil

1/3 cup orange juice (about the juice of one orange)

1 tablespoon tamari

1 heaping tablespoon roasted tahini (see Note below)

Blend all ingredients. If oil separates, blend in one tablespoon of cold water. Refrigerate unused portion.

Note–For Stage 3, use homemade *Tahini* (see recipe in *Nuts and Seeds*) or a good-quality tahini from a natural food store.

Miso-Date Dressing

This unusual dressing is very tasty. The dried dates bring sweetness and the saltiness comes from the miso. Try it.

MAKES ABOUT 1½ CUP

PREP TIME 15 MINUTES

1 cup olive oil

3 tablespoons light-colored miso

3 tablespoons apple cider vinegar

2–3 garlic cloves

4 large dates, pitted

Blend all ingredients until creamy. If it is too thick, add more water. Refrigerate unused portion.

VEGAN THOUSAND ISLAND DRESSING

This is a nut-based Thousand Island Dressing (no mayonnaise!). Instead of ketchup, we're using fresh chopped tomatoes. The creamy pink color of the dressing looks very appetizing. It's also a great dip for raw vegetables.

MAKES 1 CUP (SERVES 4)

½ cup cashews

1 roma tomato, chopped

3 tablespoons apple cider vinegar

½ cup water

1 clove garlic, squeezed

1 teaspoon sea salt

½ teaspoon black pepper

PREP TIME 8 MINUTES

Put the cashews in blender; blend into cashew flour. Add remaining ingredients and blend until it becomes creamy. Refrigerate unused portion.

SWEET ONION DRESSING

This dressing takes a little bit more time to prepare than other dressings because you have to sauté the onions and the garlic first, but the effort is worthwhile. Another savory alternative to a regular basic vinaigrette.

MAKES ABOUT 3 CUPS

1 medium sweet onion, sautéed

6 cloves garlic, minced, sautéed

¼ cup chopped parsley

2 tablespoons honey or Grade B maple syrup

¼ cup Dijon mustard

¼ cup white wine vinegar

¼ cup water

Sea salt and pepper

2 cups olive oil

PREP TIME 20 MINUTES

Put ingredients in food processor or blender. Pulse or blend until smooth. Slowly add oil.

Note–All stages of this diet have gradients. If you are easing into Stage 3 this recipe is appropriate for occasional use. If you are eating a pure Stage 3 diet, omit the honey or maple syrup.

Main Dishes

These dishes are more substantial as many of them contain heavier proteins such as beans or tofu. They can be served either for lunch or dinner. Because they may be more elaborate than some of the other dishes in this cookbook, plan on a little extra time to make them.

Main dishes constitute the central part of a meal. Usually we make more than is actually needed because we think of this dish as the primary source of satisfaction. Take a walk on the wild side and make less. Let people enjoy eating salads, vegetables, seaweeds and the other delicious dishes you make!

There are several food cultures represented in this section. Many of us eat only the special-occasion food from other cultures (tamales or lasagna, anyone?), which are often filled with dairy and other foods not recommended for this diet. The recipes listed here are just as delicious and can be eaten in Stages 2 and 3. Try some of these cultural recipes to expand what you are used to eating. Take a tour of Asia and India with us and know that you are still eating healthy food!

Leftover main dishes can be used for lunch the next day or incorporated into a new dish for the next night's dinner. The ingredients of the Mexican Tortilla Buffet, for example, can be used in a stir-fry or soup.

In general, we recommend eating tofu no more than once a week because it's not fermented and the negative health impact of soy is not entirely removed. You can use tempeh more often because it's a fermented food and does not have the adverse effects of soy (see *Soy* in Chapter 8). On Stage 3, beans and lentils can be eaten three times a week. Rice noodles and whole grain pasta are processed, so are used for special occasions on Stage 3.

Japanese Sushi Buffet

It's difficult to make good sushi at home and going out for sushi is expensive. So a few years ago we invented this sushi buffet. People put their own rolls together and everyone loves it. This recipe is intended for special occasion meals. Usually it's served as a vegetarian buffet, but for really celebratory occasions we add sushi-grade tuna or yellowtail. *Seaweed Salad* is also a good addition to this meal.

SERVES 4

PREP TIME 1 ½ HOURS

2 cups sticky sushi rice–available in health food store or Asian market

3½ cups water

1–2 packages of firm tofu

1–2 tablespoons toasted sesame oil

1 cup low-sodium soy sauce

1 bag frozen edamame in the shell–available in most supermarkets

Coarse sea salt

1 container powdered wasabi (or 1 tube–available in health food store or Asian market)

2 carrots, cut into thin, 2-inch strips

2 cucumbers, cut into thin, 2-inch strips

12 seaweed sheets (Nori)–available in health food store or Asian market

3 avocados, cut into medium-thick, long slices

½ pound sushi grade tuna or yellowtail, (about ½ inch thick) cut approximately 1 inch wide, 2 inches long (optional)

Lemon slices for garnish

1 jar pickled ginger–available in health food store or Asian market

1 bottle Japanese mayonnaise–available in Asian market

Put rice and water in a pot and bring to a boil. Stir, cover the pot, and turn the heat down as low as possible. Let simmer for about 20 minutes, then stir and put the lid back on. Let it simmer for another 20 minutes. If rice begins to stick to bottom of the pot, turn the heat off and let the rice sit and steam.

Cut tofu into cubes. In skillet, heat 1 tablespoon toasted sesame oil per package of tofu. Add tofu cubes; sauté at a high temperature for 20–30 minutes, stirring often. The tofu will release water. Let the water completely cook off. After it has browned to the desired state, add 1 tablespoon soy sauce per package of tofu and sauté for another 5–10 minutes. If you like, add black pepper to taste.

Prepare edamame according to directions on bag. Before serving, sprinkle with coarse sea salt. Remember to put out bowls for the shells.

If using powdered wasabi, follow directions on container to make paste.

Everything should be put out on platters and in bowls. Serve the tuna and/or yellowtail on a platter garnished with lemon and other vegetables. Carrots and cucumbers can be nicely arranged on another platter. The nori sheets and avocados should each have their own platter and everything else can go in bowls.

Note–If you are eating a Stage 3 diet, omit the Japanese mayonnaise and tuna or yellowtail. Wasabi and pickled ginger are special occasion foods.

SOBA NOODLES WITH ASIAN SAUCE

If you're looking for a simple way to bring Japan to your dinner table this recipe is the right one. Make the sauce first so you have it handy. Soba noodles are made from buckwheat flour, which is gluten-free, but some Japanese soba noodles also contain whole-wheat flour so check the content if you're on a gluten-free diet. Rinse the soba noodles after boiling and immediately add the sauce and gently stir. This is crucial so that the soba noodles don't stick to each other. We have served this for many years for a nurturing dinner and for more special occasions.

SERVES 8

1/3 cup low sodium soy or tamari sauce

1/3 cup safflower oil

2 tablespoons toasted sesame oil

2 cloves garlic, mashed and minced

1 small piece of fresh ginger, very finely minced (about 1 tablespoon)

2 packages soba noodles

PREP TIME 30 MINUTES

Combine all ingredients except soba noodles and whisk together.

Cook and drain noodles. Rinse quickly in cold water. Put in a bowl and pour marinade over them to prevent sticking. Toss. Cover so that it stays hot. Serve right away.

CURRY COCONUT TOFU VEGETABLES

This has been our all-time favorite recipe for over thirteen years. Some of our friends who are passionate meat-eaters head straight for the kitchen when they step through the front door and smell the scent of cumin, mango, and coconut. This recipe works with any kind of vegetables but those included here are the ones that work the best for us. This dish is particularly tasty the next day once the flavors have blended thoroughly. About once a month we receive a phone call from someone asking for this recipe so now here it is in cookbook form.

SERVES 6–8 PEOPLE

For Tofu

2 packages firm tofu

2 teaspoons vegetable oil

2 tablespoons low sodium soy sauce

Dash of Tabasco

For Vegetables and Sauce

½ red onion, minced

2 tablespoons safflower oil

1½ tablespoons curry powder

¼ teaspoon red chiles, crushed

1 cauliflower, cut into small heads

10 carrots, peeled and cut into small, long strips

1½–2 pounds mushrooms, sliced

4 cloves garlic, crushed or minced

2 cans coconut milk

4 heaping tablespoons mango chutney (sweet, not spicy)

3–4 tablespoons low sodium soy sauce

Sea salt to taste

Black pepper to taste

PREP TIME 1 HOUR

Tofu–Preheat oven to 400°F. Drain tofu, cut into slices. Put slices onto oiled baking trays. Combine ingredients for marinade in small bowl. Brush tofu slices with marinade and pour the rest of the marinade over the slices.

Bake for about 40 minutes until tofu is crispy but not hard. Cut into small strips.

For vegetables and sauce–Sauté onion in safflower oil. Add curry powder and red chiles. Cook for a couple of minutes with onions. Add cauliflower and carrots, and then add mushrooms. Add a little water and continue to cook.

Add garlic, tofu, coconut milk, and mango chutney; stir. Add soy sauce, salt, and black pepper to taste; stir. Let simmer for a few minutes. Serve.

ASIAN STIR-FRY

This recipe includes fresh green vegetables, ginger, tamari, and toasted sesame oil. The best way to prepare this is in a wok but a frying pan is fine. Heat the wok first, add the oil, and then proceed with the recipe.

SERVES 6

45 MINUTES (WITHOUT OPTIONAL INGREDIENTS)

¼ cup toasted sesame oil

2 cloves garlic, peeled and minced

½-inch piece of ginger, peeled and minced

2 cups mushrooms, sliced (optional)

3 tablespoons soy sauce or more according to taste

1 bunch green onions, white and light green parts cut into 1½-inch diagonal pieces

1 head bok choy, cut into strips

1 red pepper, cut in half, seeds removed, and cut into 2½-inch-long thin strips (optional)

2 carrots, peeled, cut in half, and cut into 2-inch-long diagonal strips (optional)

2 cups broccoli florets (optional)

1/3 cup water

4 cups raw fresh spinach

Sea salt to taste

Pepper to taste

Soy sauce to taste

Tabasco to taste

Heat toasted sesame oil in wok or large skillet. Add ginger and garlic and sauté for 2 minutes.

Add mushrooms (if using) and stir. Sauté 3 minutes. Add soy sauce, then green onion and bok choy. Sauté for 3 minutes, stirring occasionally. Add pepper, carrots, and broccoli (if using), continue sautéing. Add water and cover with lid. Steam until vegetables are slightly tender.

Add spinach and replace lid. Allow spinach to shrink down a bit. Uncover and stir mixture together. Sauté for a few more minutes until spinach is done.

Season with salt, pepper, soy sauce, and Tabasco according to taste.

Serve alone or over rice.

ASPARAGUS, MUSHROOM, AND BOK CHOY IN COCONUT LIME SAUCE

We are grateful to God for lime. There are few flavors on this earth better than lime (perhaps garlic). The coconut-lime sauce gives this dish a slightly Thai flavor.

SERVES 3
(MAKES ABOUT 4 CUPS)

1 (about 14 ounce) can coconut milk

2 cloves garlic, minced

½ teaspoon lemon zest (finely-grated lemon peel)

½ teaspoon lime zest

2 cups sliced asparagus, cut into 1-inch pieces

2 cups sliced mushrooms

1 small red pepper, large diced

1 small head bok choy, sliced or chopped

½ teaspoon red pepper flakes

1 tablespoon soy sauce

1 tablespoon lime juice

1 tablespoon lemon juice

¼ cup chopped fresh basil

PREP TIME 30 MINUTES

Put coconut milk, garlic, and zest in blender or food processor. Blend until garlic is pureed. Pour into skillet and cook over medium heat for 2 minutes or until it begins to simmer.

Add the rest of the ingredients, stir, and simmer for 10 minutes, stirring frequently. Serve over rice.

KITCHARI I

According to the Indian teaching of Ayurvedic Medicine, kitchari is a healing and cleansing dish, and on top of this, it tastes fantastic. We eat it every week. It is deeply nourishing, grounding, and balancing. Tip: Make a bigger batch of it and you can re-heat it anytime. We don't recommend freezing it as it doesn't taste very good after it is frozen.

SERVES 4–6

1 cup basmati rice, soaked (see *Grains*)

½ cup red or orange lentils

3 tablespoons ghee

1 1-inch piece of ginger, minced

1 teaspoon ground fennel

1 teaspoon ground cumin

1 teaspoon ground coriander

1 teaspoon turmeric

Sea salt

PREP TIME 1 HOUR 45 MINUTES

Rinse basmati rice and lentils separately until the water is no longer foamy. Drain.

In a large, thick-bottomed pot, melt ghee on medium or low heat, add ginger and lentils, and fry lentils for about 5 minutes. Then add all spices except for salt. Fry for a few more minutes.

Add enough water that beans and spices are covered, at least 3 inches, and bring to a boil. When beans are boiling, turn down heat but keep lightly boiling until beans are well broken down, for about 45 minutes. Stir frequently. If necessary, add water to keep beans from sticking to the bottom.

Add soaked rice. Add more water so rice is covered and bring to a boil.

Cover and cook over low heat for about 45 minutes. Stir frequently. If needed, add water.

When done, the beans and rice will look like a porridge in which neither the rice nor the beans are distinguishable. Add salt to taste.

Note–When increasing this recipe to make more servings, be conservative with the amount of spices used or they will dominate the flavor. Add only a third more if doubling or even tripling the ingredients and then adjust the spices later if needed. Turmeric is added mostly for color and usually doesn't have to be increased.

This recipe is Stage 2 because it uses white basmati rice. We've included it because it has very healing and balancing effect on the body. It is also a good breakfast food.

KITCHARI II

This is our other favorite Kitchari recipe. This version has a bit more spice to it because of the red chiles. It also is made with brown basmati rice so it's appropriate for someone eating a Stage 3 diet. When doubling or tripling this recipe, be conservative with the amount of spices used or they will dominate the dish too much. Turmeric is added mostly for color so don't increase it. For the other spices, add only a third more and then adjust the spices later if needed.

SERVES 4–6

PREP TIME 1 ½ HOURS

1 ¼ cups red or orange lentils (see *Cooking Beans* on page 109), rinsed and drained

¾ cup brown basmati rice

¼ cup ghee or butter

3 whole dried red chiles

1 ½ teaspoons cumin seeds

2 bay leaves

8 whole cloves

4 black peppercorns

½ teaspoon turmeric

¼ teaspoon ground black pepper

2 medium onions, cut into approximately ¼ x ½-inch pieces

5¾ cups water

1 ½ teaspoon sea salt or to taste

¼ teaspoon garam masala

Combine the lentils and rice in a bowl and add cold water to cover; let soak 20 minutes. Drain and set aside.

Combine the ghee or butter, red chiles, cumin seeds, bay leaves, cloves, peppercorns, turmeric, and black pepper in a large, heavy-bottomed pot over medium-high heat. Cook, stirring, for 2 minutes.

Add onions and cook, stirring, until they begin to wilt, about 3 minutes. Add rice and lentil mixture and sauté, stirring gently so as not to break the rice, about 1 minute.

Add water, salt, and garam masala and stir gently to mix. Bring to a boil, turn heat down to low, cover, and simmer very gently for 45 minutes. Stir gently every 10 minutes or so. Then continue cooking, uncovered, until rice and lentils are tender and the mixture is still wet, like a very thick porridge, about 25 more minutes. Remove cloves, peppercorns, and bay leaves and discard. Adjust salt to taste. Serve hot.

DAAL

This daal recipe is from our good friend from Pakistan. Since she introduced this to us it has been our standard daal recipe, and everybody who eats it loves it. What makes it so distinct, so true to its roots, is the tarka—browned onions and garlic in oil stirred into the daal right before serving. In Pakistan, most families have their traditional tarka recipe that is handed down within their family from generation to generation. The onions and garlic need to be browned to the point that you worry they're getting too dark and maybe even burnt. At medium heat, you keep scraping the onions from the bottom of the pan over and over for about 20 to 30 minutes. You can also use other spices in the tarka such as bay leaves, curry leaves, lemon, coriander powder, green chiles, and mustard seeds.

SERVES 3–5

1 cup red lentils

3 cups water

1 medium tomato, chopped

1–3 teaspoons sea salt to taste (If the daal lacks flavor, add more salt.)

½ teaspoon cayenne pepper

¼ teaspoon turmeric

1 dried red chile

FOR TARKA

Half a small onion

4–5 tablespoons safflower oil, enough to cover bottom of pan, onions, and garlic

1 teaspoon cumin seeds

3 cloves garlic, sliced into thin rounds

2–3 tablespoons lemon juice

PREP TIME 40 MINUTES (INCLUDES PREPARATION TIME FOR TARKA)

For Daal—In a saucepan, combine red lentils and water and bring to a boil on medium heat. As it begins to boil, skim off lentil residue so water is clear.

While lentils are boiling, add tomato, sea salt, cayenne pepper, turmeric, and chile. Let spices boil for about a minute and then turn heat down to medium low and cover saucepan.

Keep at a low boil for the next 10–15 minutes. For the last 5 minutes, uncover saucepan and let excess water boil away. Prepare Tarka (below) during this time.

Turn heat off and cover saucepan. Daal should be fairly thick. If thinner daal is desired, add water. Boil uncovered if thicker daal is desired.

For Tarka—While daal is slowly boiling, cut onion in half lengthwise. With cut side facing down, slice it thinly, starting from side, not top or bottom.

Put oil in a small frying pan. Turn heat to medium and add cumin seeds. When they begin to sizzle and the scent of the cumin is obvious, add onions.

Add garlic to frying pan. As garlic and onion begin to brown, add lemon juice. (Stand back—oil will sizzle.) Continue to let the onions and garlic brown, but keep them from turning black or burning. Sauté until onions and garlic are nicely brown all over.

Uncover daal and pour in tarka. Don't mix. Immediately cover daal so flavors of tarka stay in saucepan and don't evaporate. Be careful—the tarka will sizzle very loudly when it is added. After about a minute, uncover saucepan and mix daal and tarka together. Serve hot over brown basmati rice.

GREEN LENTIL CURRY

Our same friend from Pakistan (see previous recipe) made Green Lentil Curry for us on a Sunday night in the winter when we were all too tired to cook. We picked up the huge pot at her house and brought it home in the back of the car. We were so grateful to eat this nurturing and slightly spicy dish. It's wonderful served with *Aromatic Indian Rice* (Recipe in *Grains*.) If you double or triple this recipe for a large group be conservative with the spices.

SERVES 4–6

2 tablespoons oil

1 teaspoon cumin seeds

1 medium red onion, cut in half lengthwise and then finely sliced lengthwise

2 cloves garlic, finely minced

1 inch ginger, finely minced

1 heaping teaspoon garam masala powder

2–4 small or medium roma tomatoes, coarsely chopped

½ teaspoon cayenne powder for a spicy dish or less to taste

¾ teaspoon coriander powder

¼ teaspoon turmeric

1 teaspoon sea salt

2 large red potatoes, halved or quartered

1½ cups green lentils

3 cups water

PREP TIME 1 HOUR 10 MINUTES

Add oil to saucepan, set on medium heat, and put in cumin seeds. When cumin seeds begin to sizzle, add onion. Fry onion until it begins to turn transparent, then add garlic and ginger. Keep frying until garlic begins to brown at which time onion should also start to brown. Add garam masala and mix in with onions so that the mixture has a brownish color. Fry for a few minutes.

Add tomatoes, cayenne, coriander, turmeric, and salt; fry until spices begin to melt into the sauce as tomatoes are cooked and the oil in the pan begins to separate, about 5–10 minutes.

Add the potatoes and fry well in the mixture of spices for 2 minutes. Add the lentils and stir well for about 2–4 minutes so that they are mixed well with the spices.

Add water and bring to a boil. Turn heat down to medium-low and cook, covered, for about 30–40 minutes, until potatoes are cooked through and lentils are done. Add more boiling water if lentils are drying out. Or if lentils are done and water remains, turn heat back up to boil excess water away.

Yellow Rice with Potato and Cumin

A good alternative to plain brown rice that goes well with Indian vegetable dishes (see *Vegetables*). The potato and onion give this dish a hearty foundation. Again, when doubling or tripling this recipe, be conservative with the amount of spices used or they will dominate the flavor. Add only a third more if doubling or even tripling the ingredients and then adjust the spices later if needed. Turmeric is added mostly for color and usually doesn't have to be increased.

SERVES 4

1½ cups brown basmati rice

3 tablespoons vegetable oil

½ teaspoon cumin seeds

½ onion, finely chopped

1 small potato, boiled, cooled, peeled, and cut into 3/8-inch cubes

½ teaspoon turmeric

¾ teaspoon salt

2¼ cups water

PREP TIME 1 HOUR 10 MINUTES

Wash rice several times. Drain. Cover rice with water and soak for 30 minutes. Drain thoroughly.

Heat oil in a small, heavy saucepan over medium-high heat. When hot, add cumin seeds and let them sizzle for 10 seconds. Add onion; stir and cook until it starts to brown.

Add potato and stir until it is lightly brown. Add rice, turmeric, and salt.

Turn heat to medium and stir rice gently for 2 minutes. Add water and bring to a boil. Cover tightly, turn heat to very low, and cook for 35 minutes or until rice is done.

YAM AND POTATO CASSEROLE

This is an excellent dish for the winter when you're looking for a way to warm up and feel good. You can use sweet potatoes instead of yams.

SERVES 4 AS A MAIN DISH

PREP TIME 1 HOUR 15 MINUTES

½ cup chopped onion

2 cloves garlic, minced

2 tablespoons water

2 cups diced yams

4 medium to large potatoes, diced

½ teaspoon ground oregano

2 tablespoons tahini, increase for thicker sauce (see Note below)

1 tablespoon tamari

½ cup water, increase for more sauce—make sure to increase tahini and tamari as well

Preheat oven to 350°F. Sauté garlic and onion in water over medium heat for 1 minute.

Stir in yams and potatoes and continue cooking for 5 minutes. Add oregano and sauté for 2 more minutes.

Combine tahini, tamari, and water and blend well. Transfer vegetables to lightly-oiled 2-quart casserole dish, cover with sauce.

Cover dish, bake 35–40 minutes.

(from *Intuitive Eating* by Humbart "Smokey" Santillo, N.D.)

Note–For Stage 3, use homemade *Tahini* (see recipe in *Nuts and Seeds*) or a good- quality tahini from a natural food store.

SPAGHETTI SQUASH

We've always wondered why the person who invented spaghetti never received a medal of honor. Visit any country and spaghetti is on the menu. In Germany, Italian ice cream parlors offer spaghetti ice cream. Of course we do not want to deprive any of our readers of a spaghetti recipe, but for this recipe we only use spaghetti squash. After the squash is baked, use a fork to separate the strands so that it looks like spaghetti. In this recipe it's topped with a sauce of mushrooms, green onions, and tomatoes. Or top it with *Marinara Sauce*—you might think you're sitting at the Piazza Navona in Rome.

SERVES 6–7

1 medium spaghetti squash

8 ounces mushrooms, sliced

1 bunch green onion, chopped

3 small to medium (on-the-vine type) tomatoes, diced

Olive oil

1½ tablespoons low sodium soy sauce or tamari or to taste

Salt and pepper to taste

PREP TIME 1 HOUR 5 MINUTES

Using a paring knife, cut a triangular hole in the squash. The sides of the triangle should be the width of the knife blade.

Place squash on a rack in oven so that the triangle is on top. Put a pan on the lower rack underneath the squash to catch juices that leak out. Bake at 350°F for 45–50 minutes.

5 minutes before squash is done, begin sautéing mushrooms, green onion, and tomato in oil and soy sauce to taste.

When squash is done, cut in half and remove seeds, scoop out pulp, and separate strands with a fork. Add it to mushrooms, green onion, and tomato mixture and sauté for another 10 minutes. Add salt and pepper to taste. Serve.

MARINARA SAUCE

I (Tika) had my first date with Marinara Sauce in a restaurant in Florence, Italy in 1988. It's been a mutual love affair ever since. Key ingredients: tomatoes, olive oil, oregano, and basil. Everything else is up to the cook. You can add other fresh herbs, olives, and capers. Here's our version.

SERVES 6

1 (28 ounce) can diced or whole tomatoes (or fresh)

1 teaspoon honey

2–3 bay leaves

Olive oil

4 or more cloves garlic, minced or put through a press

2 tablespoons dried oregano

1–2 tablespoons dried basil

2 tablespoons dried parsley

2 (6 ounce) cans tomato paste

4 tomato paste cans water

Fresh or dried herbs; if fresh use lots more. Add in several times and at the end

½ cup nutritional yeast (optional)

½ teaspoon cinnamon or curry to taste

1 teaspoon ground fennel or to taste

1 tablespoon crushed red pepper or to taste

Salt

PREP TIME 2 ½ HOURS

Put tomatoes and honey in blender and blend. Pour into large pot, add bay leaves, and bring to boil. Lower heat and simmer.

In sauté pan, warm olive oil and add garlic. Let it cook but not brown. Add oregano, basil, and parsley and let them sizzle for a moment.

Add tomato paste, scraping sides of can well. Let the paste fry in the herbs for about 3 minutes, moving it around. Then add 4 tomato paste cans of water. Stir slowly with spoon or whisk and let simmer. Add more herbs.

When this sauce has cooked for 10 minutes or more, add to the simmering tomato sauce pot. Add nutritional yeast if desired to increase thickness. Add more herbs, salt, cinnamon or curry, ground fennel, and crushed red pepper.

Let sauce simmer for at least 1½ hours and let it rest for about 30 minutes before serving. Remove bay leaves. Reheat 5 minutes before serving.

Note–This recipe is Stage 2 because it uses canned tomatoes and canned tomato paste. It could be adapted to a Stage 3 recipe by replacing the canned tomatoes with fresh tomatoes.

POLENTA

Our Italian friends used to fight over who had the best polenta recipe. We can't remember who won. Traditionally the secret to making good polenta is long, slow cooking while regularly stirring with a wooden spoon. The secret with this recipe is it's made in the oven with almost no stirring. Serve topped with *Marinara Sauce, Goulange*, any sauce or stew, or with grated raw cheese.

SERVES 4

1 cup polenta

4 cups water

1½ teaspoon sea salt

1 teaspoon organic butter or olive oil

PREP TIME 1 HOUR

Mix all ingredients and put in a large oven-proof or cast iron skillet. Put skillet in a 350°F oven for 40 minutes (do not cover). Remove and stir. Put it back in the oven for 10 more minutes. Remove from oven.

Variations–When polenta is cooked, spread it on a wooden cutting board that has been rinsed with cold water. Or spread it in a sheet pan and chill it. Either way, it will solidify when it cools. Then cut it into pieces. Fry polenta pieces in a skillet with olive oil until lightly browned. Put one slice of tomato on each piece of polenta. Squeeze a clove of garlic and mix with olive oil, then brush on tomato slices.

Or use 2 cups water and 2 cups rice milk instead of 4 cups of water to cook polenta. Or use 4 cups vegetable broth instead of water.

Or add spices such as curry, marjoram, garlic, and ground coriander to polenta and water mixture before it is cooked.

FUSILLI RICE NOODLES

Traditionally this recipe includes a lot of cream and cheese. We left out the dairy and added olive oil which makes it a delicious, healthy pasta dish. Rice noodles are great for people who want or need to eat gluten-free. These noodles are a little tricky to cook as they can come out sticky if you don't watch them. They're not the white flour pasta we grew up on and are used to, but we like them and have lots of friends who do too.

SERVES 4

½ cup olive oil

1 tablespoon minced garlic (2 cloves)

1 lemon, zest and juice

2 teaspoons kosher salt

1 teaspoon black pepper

1 pound rice fusilli noodles

½ pound baby arugula

1 pint grape or cherry tomatoes, halved

PREP TIME 35 MINUTES

Heat olive oil in medium saucepan over medium heat. Add garlic and cook for 1 minute. Then add the zest and juice of lemon, salt, and pepper.

Cook rice noodles according to instructions on package. Drain and return to pot.

Immediately add olive oil mixture to pasta and cook over medium low heat for 3 minutes. Pour hot pasta into large bowl. Add arugula and tomatoes. Toss well. Season to taste and serve hot.

Variations–Substitute whole grain pasta for rice noodles.

Or add finely grated raw cheese to top of pasta after tossing or serve in a small bowl on the side.

DELICATA SQUASH

The delicata squash is an oblong-shaped squash, not to be confused with a football, a pale watermelon, or a small stranded whale. (We thought we'd give you some clues to make the search for it at the grocery store easier.) It has a cream-colored, green-striped, thick outer skin and a golden, fine-textured inner flesh. When delicata squash aren't available, we substitute acorn squash and have equally good results. Bake it and enjoy.

SERVES 2

2 delicata squash

1–2 oranges, juiced

2 tablespoons miso or to taste

3–4 drops toasted sesame oil

½ inch ginger, grated

1 pinch cinnamon

1 pinch Chinese Five Spices (this spice blend can be found in Asian markets and most grocery stores)

PREP TIME 50 MINUTES

Preheat oven to 425°F. Cut squash in half lengthwise and scoop out seeds. With a fork, stab the inside of each half of the squash twice.

To make marinade, squeeze oranges and collect juice in a bowl. Add miso and mix thoroughly. Mix in toasted sesame oil, ginger, cinnamon, and Chinese 5 Spices.

Baste squash with marinade, making sure to coat the inside.

Place the squash in a baking dish with ½ inch of water so that the squash skin is in the water and the marinated inside of the squash is facing up. Bake for ½ hour for thin squash, longer for thicker squash. Halfway through baking, re-baste with marinade.

Squash is done when you poke it with a fork and it is soft.

BAKED TOFU

Tofu is like a blank check. It comes to life through how you fill it out. Baking, for example, makes it crispy and tasty. To make it spicier, add a few dashes of Tabasco, pressed garlic, and/or minced ginger to the marinade. Make sure you use extra firm tofu. Other kinds such as silken tofu are too soft and will fall apart. We recommend that people not eat tofu more than once or so a week, because of the health effects of non-fermented soy (See *Soy* in Chapter 8, *Resources and Recommendations*).

SERVES 3

1 (¾ pound) package tofu

2 teaspoons safflower oil

2 tablespoons low sodium soy sauce

3–4 drops sesame oil

PREP TIME 1 HOUR 5 MINUTES

Preheat oven to 400°F.

To get extra liquid out of tofu, lay a plate on top of it and put something that weighs 2–3 pounds on top of the plate. Leave for 10 minutes.

Mix oil, soy sauce, and sesame oil. Cut tofu into slices of desired thickness and put them on a baking sheet. Pour mixture over slices and bake for 45 minutes to 1 hour and 15 minutes, depending on thickness of slices and according to the desired crispness.

SCRAMBLED TOFU

If you're looking for an excellent substitute for your daily scrambled eggs, this might be it. The ginger, cumin, coriander, and garlic add the right spice to wake you up in the morning. Or serve this for dinner as we do. Tip: For a more interesting texture, sauté the tofu until crispy and add a pinch of turmeric to create an appetizing yellow color.

SERVES 6–8

Olive oil

2 onions, finely chopped

3 cloves garlic, peeled and minced

2–3-inch piece of fresh ginger, peeled and minced

1 teaspoon ground cumin

1 teaspoon ground coriander

Soy sauce to taste

2 packages extra-firm tofu, crumbled by hand into pieces

PREP TIME 45 MINUTES

Heat olive oil in a skillet. Sauté onion until translucent. Add garlic, ginger, spices, and soy sauce and fry for a minute or two, being careful not to burn garlic and spices.

Add tofu and fry at medium to medium-high temperature. As tofu begins to brown, turn tofu to brown on all sides. Continue frying and turning until tofu is crispy, which takes about 45 minutes.

BAKED HONEY MUSTARD TEMPEH

At first glance, tempeh appears to be an inedible item like a fermented sponge or a counter-top trivet. By itself, it doesn't have a lot of taste, but we make it taste really good. The honey-mustard sauce gives a lot of flavor, and when the tempeh is baked and a little bit crispy even vegetarian-adverse people often take seconds. Tempeh is made from the whole soybean so it has a high content of protein and vitamins. The fermentation process makes it more digestible and removes the health hazards of soy and tofu (see *Soy* in Chapter 8), so it can be eaten as often as you wish. In the U.S. we buy Turtle Island or Wildwood brands. You can also make your own using instructions in *Wild Fermentation: The Flavor, Nutrition, and Craft of Live-Culture Foods* by Sandor Ellix Katz (Chelsea Green Publishing: White River Junction, Vermont, 2003).

SERVES 6–8

PREP TIME 1 HOUR 35 MINUTES

3 tablespoons honey

3 tablespoons Dijon mustard

1 clove garlic, minced

1 tablespoon safflower oil

½ teaspoon soy sauce

¼ teaspoon sea salt

2 packages tempeh, cut into 1-inch cubes.

Preheat oven to 400°F.

Whisk together honey, Dijon mustard, garlic, oil, soy sauce, and sea salt.

Put tempeh cubes on a baking sheet. Pour sauce over and toss to evenly coat. Bake, turning occasionally to prevent burning, for 45–60 minutes, until crispy and browned.

Serve with rice, salad, and vegetable.

Note–All stages of this diet have gradients. If you are easing into Stage 3 this recipe is appropriate for occasional use. It is not appropriate for a pure Stage 3 diet because it contains honey.

TEMPEH SHEPHERD'S PIE

Shepherd's Pie was originally created to use leftovers from a roast lamb and potato dinner. This version, made with tempeh, is perfect on a cold winter night. One of our friends first encountered Shepherd's Pie in a South American Restaurant in San Francisco twenty-four years ago. The crispy sweet crust and the chunky steaming inside were unforgettable. You don't have to be a shepherd to love this.

SERVES 6

5–6 medium potatoes

2 tablespoons butter (optional)

Oat, rice, or almond milk

Olive oil

1 package tempeh, cut into ½-inch cubes

3 medium onions, chopped

2 cloves garlic, minced

2 cups fresh green peas

3 tablespoons tamari or low sodium soy sauce

¼ cup hand-chopped parsley (if using food processor, use less)

1 teaspoon pepper

1 teaspoon sea salt

PREP TIME 1 HOUR 15 MINUTES

Preheat oven to 350°F. Boil potatoes until tender. Mash, adding butter (if you wish), and milk to get desired consistency.

Pour ¼-inch olive oil into heavy skillet. Add tempeh and cook until well browned. Remove from oil with a slotted spoon. Add onions and sauté 5 minutes. Add garlic and sauté until onions are transparent.

Briefly steam peas. Drain liquid from peas (set peas aside) and add to onion mixture. Add tamari (or soy sauce) and tempeh to onion mixture and stir to combine.

Add the parsley, pepper, and salt to the potatoes.

In a large buttered or oiled casserole dish, layer as follows:

On the bottom, put tempeh and onion mixture.

Next add half of the parsley and potato mixture.

Next add peas.

On top, add the rest of the potatoes.

Bake, covered, for 35–45 minutes, or until potatoes are browned.

MEXICAN TORTILLA BUFFET

When we sit down to our Mexican Tortilla Buffet a great sigh of relief goes around the table. This colorful, festive buffet will please just about anyone. At the sight of the tortillas, beans, guacamole, and salsa, we are home again.

SERVES 4

PREP TIME 2 HOURS TOTAL (1½ HOURS FOR BEANS, 35 MINUTES FOR RICE, 15 MINUTES FOR GUACAMOLE, 45 MINUTES FOR PICO DE GALLO, 15 MINUTES FOR TORTILLAS, 10 MINUTES FOR VEGGIE PREP)

1 1/3 cups dried pinto or black beans

Ground cumin to taste

1 cup brown basmati rice

½ medium red onion, diced

2 tomatoes, diced

½ head romaine lettuce, cut into thin strips

8 ounces plain yogurt

1 jar pitted black olives, sliced

8–12 whole wheat flour, rice, or corn tortillas, depending on size

GUACAMOLE

3 ripe avocadoes

1½ tablespoons finely minced red onion

1½ tablespoons lemon or lime juice

1 large clove garlic, pressed or minced

Salt and pepper to taste

PICO DE GALLO

(or substitute *Fresh Tomato Salsa* in *Sauces, Spreads, and Dips*)

5–6 fresh, ripe tomatoes, seeded and diced (about 2 cups)

½ cup very finely chopped white, yellow, or red onion

2 tablespoons very finely chopped green bell pepper or more to taste

2 tablespoons very finely chopped red or yellow bell pepper or more to taste

1–2 finely minced fresh green jalapeno pepper(s) (about 2 tablespoons)

2 tablespoons chopped cilantro, plus extra for garnish

1 clove garlic, pressed or finely minced (optional)

Juice of 2 limes

Salt and pepper to taste

Beans–Soak beans overnight (See *Cooking Beans* on page 109), drain, and rinse. Put beans in pan and cover with water, add ground cumin to taste. Make sure beans stay covered with water while they are cooking. Bring water to boil, lower heat, and simmer for 60–90 minutes, to desired texture.

Rice–Rinse and soak rice overnight (See *Grains*). Drain and rinse. Put rice in pan, add 1 ½ cups water (1 ¼ cups in high altitudes). Bring to a boil, then cover and turn heat to low and cook until the water is almost completely gone, about 35 minutes. Turn the stove off, keep the cover on, and allow the remaining water to steam away (around 5 minutes).

Guacamole–Mash avocadoes. Add remaining ingredients. Stir to combine.

Pico de Gallo–Combine all ingredients. Mix. Season to taste.

30 minutes before serving, preheat oven to 250°F. Layer tortillas on baking sheet and cover with aluminum foil. Once the oven has reached 250°F, put tortillas in oven for about 15 minutes. If using rice tortillas, steam them until they are soft. Serve on platter.

Serve onion, tomato, lettuce, and black olives in separate small bowls.

Drain beans. Put beans, cooked rice, and yogurt into separate serving bowls.

Adjust amounts according to your preference.

Note–For pure Stage 3, omit olives, yogurt, and tortillas. Serve on lettuce leaves. Or serve beans over rice with toppings.

"Too Good" Veggie Burgers

This is an excellent way to use leftovers you have in your fridge. The secrets to a perfect veggie burger are to make sure the ingredients taste good before you bake them and also to have the burger not fall apart. Adding squeezed garlic makes it even better. You can top these with any and all kinds of burger fixings and eat them on a whole-grain bun (sorry, no bun on Stage 3 diet) or just plain.

Any leftover grains (millet is especially good because it sticks together well)

Oats (ground and whole)

Nuts and seeds—like almonds, walnuts, sunflower seeds

Grated carrot

Tomato (chunked up)

Onion (chunked up)

Spinach

Bragg Liquid Aminos

Water

Wheat flour, frozen peas, any leftover cooked veggies, grated potato (optional)

PREP TIME 45 MINUTES

Grind nuts and combine with grains and grated carrot in a large mixing bowl.

In a blender or food processor combine tomato, onion, Bragg, and a small amount of water; blend until smooth (can add other cooked veggies too).

Add blended ingredients to the grain-nut mixture. Combine just enough so that your burger mix is thick and evenly wet. You want the right texture to make burger patties. (Ideally that is the exact amount of wet mixture you have.)

Heat a non-stick skillet with a little oil in it (or an iron skillet with more oil in it).

Shape patties and brown on both sides in the skillet (optional—you could bake them.) Serve them up and eat them up.

(from *Hohm Cookin': Music for the Tastebuds*)

Veggie Burgers

This cousin of the "Too Good" Veggie Burger requires that you have specific ingredients on hand rather than just using whatever you have in the fridge. Serve these with mustard, sliced red onions, sliced tomatoes, and lettuce to provide the whole burger experience.

MAKES 10 (½ CUP) PATTIES

1 1/3 cups millet

3 cups water

1 cup rolled oats (use gluten-free if needed; some oats are gluten-contaminated, so check packaging for "gluten-free" label.)

½ cup raw sunflower seeds

2 large carrots, finely grated

1 small tomato, cut into pieces

½ small onion, cut into pieces

1 clove garlic, minced

1 large handful fresh spinach

2 tablespoons Bragg Liquid Aminos or tamari

2 tablespoons water

Sea salt and pepper to taste

Olive oil

PREP TIME 1 ½ HOURS

Toast millet in dry skillet. Combine millet and water in saucepan. Bring to boil. Once boiling, cover and reduce heat to lowest temperature. Cook about 40–45 minutes until millet is done. Or use 4 cups leftover millet. Put in large bowl.

Make oats and sunflower seeds into flour with a food processor or blender. Add to cooked millet, along with grated carrots; mix well.

Blend tomato, onion, garlic, spinach, Bragg, and water in blender. Add to millet mixture. Stir until evenly combined. Add salt to taste. Mix well.

Measure ½ cup portions of mixture; form into patties. Mixture should stick together. If it doesn't, adjust ingredients accordingly.

Heat olive oil in skillet over medium heat. Brown patties on both sides. Put on baking sheet into 250°F oven until ready to serve.

These can be frozen after cooking. Reheat in oven, on grill, or in a skillet with a small amount of oil. They can also be placed frozen in a toaster oven and baked at 350°F for about 30–45 minutes or until heated throughout.

Serve on a whole grain bun (Stage 2) or without a bun. Good with mustard or with whatever you like on your burger.

GOULANGE

Theresa, who has a love for playfully speaking with a French accent, came up with this one. You can quickly prepare this after picking up the children from school, doing the laundry, and making three phone calls. It tastes great and is nourishing. Especially recommended in the summer when zucchini and squash are in season. If you're in the mood for Italian, add fresh minced garlic, chopped basil, and a medium diced tomato. Or if you prefer a Mexican twist, substitute black beans for the garbanzo beans, add a cup of corn, and chopped cilantro and minced garlic to taste.

SERVES 2

PREP TIME 30 MINUTES (DOES NOT INCLUDE COOKING TIME FOR GARBANZO BEANS)

3 tablespoons olive oil

1 medium onion, chopped

1 medium zucchini, diced

1 yellow squash, diced

1½ cups cooked garbanzo beans

Salt to taste

Heat olive oil in a pan. Add onions; cook until transparent. Add zucchini and yellow squash. Cook until soft. Add garbanzo beans and simmer for 7–10 minutes. Serve over millet or rice.

Warm French Lentil Salad

These benign little lentils steal your heart like a Frenchman in Paris. The good thing is they barely take any time to cook and you can put this elegant dish together in the blink of an eye after coming home from a museum or a long day at work. You can serve this as a simple dinner with a salad or make it elegant with goat cheese and roasted asparagus. Then go all the way and invite Gérard Depardieu over for a tête-á-tête.

Serves 4

1 cup French green lentils (also called *lentilles du puy*)

2 cloves garlic, peeled

2 teaspoons dried tarragon

Sea salt

Pepper

2 cups water

½ cup finely chopped, jarred, marinated artichoke hearts

Dressing

¼ cup olive oil

1½ tablespoons red wine vinegar

½ teaspoon Dijon mustard

½ teaspoon salt

¼ teaspoon black pepper

Prep time 1 hour

Combine lentils, whole garlic cloves, tarragon, salt, pepper, and water in a pan and bring to a boil. Reduce heat and cover tightly with a lid. Simmer gently for 30–40 minutes until lentils are tender. Remove garlic and reserve for use in vinaigrette. Drain. Put in a mixing bowl.

Add chopped marinated artichoke hearts.

Combine ingredients for vinaigrette. Using a fork, mash cloves of cooked garlic. Add to vinaigrette and mix well. Pour vinaigrette over lentils. Toss. Serve warm or at room temperature.

Note–For Stage 3, substitute fresh artichoke hearts for jarred. Chop and marinate in dressing while lentils cook.

Bean Salad

We like to serve beans as a way to provide protein, but bean soup three times a week can be a little bit much. So out of necessity we invented this bean salad recipe as a creative way to serve legumes. You can use any kind of beans. Our favorites are great northern beans, pinto beans, black beans, and kidney beans. This bean salad is a satisfying and light dish for summer. You can experiment with variations; for example, add avocado, fresh tomatoes, onions, and summer cilantro from the garden to black beans for a Mexican version.

SERVES 8 AS A MAIN DISH, 12–16 AS A SIDE DISH

2 cups dried black beans, kidney beans, pinto beans or white Navy beans, or 5–6 cups cooked beans

½ medium red onion, diced

5 stalks celery, chopped

1 red pepper, diced

6 medium Kosher dill pickles, diced

DRESSING

2/3 cup olive oil

1/3 cup apple cider vinegar

1 tablespoon Dijon mustard

2 cloves garlic, minced

1 tablespoon honey

1 teaspoon sea salt

Black pepper (optional)

1 tablespoon chopped fresh dill (optional)

PREP TIME 1 ½ HOURS

Soak and cook beans (see *Cooking Beans*, page 109). Drain beans.

Combine beans, onion, celery, pepper, and pickles.

Make dressing. Pour over vegetables. Mix.

Let sit 30 minutes or longer to allow flavors to combine. Serve at room temperature.

Serve with rice, a green salad, and a side vegetable.

Note–For Stage 3, omit honey and use fermented pickles.

COOKING BEANS

Some beans (and some rice, too) come with little pebbles mixed in. Generally the pebbles are a lot smaller than the beans and the rice so put the beans in a big colander under running water and swirl them. This washes the little stones out and the beans or rice remain in the colander. Scoop out the beans or the rice and use the pebbles to re-pave your driveway.

Most beans and nuts have enzyme inhibitors. Soaking them for 24 hours gives the beans a chance to sprout, which removes the inhibitors and produces enzymes for digestion. Lentils, split peas, mung beans, aduki beans, and butterbeans should not be soaked because it ruins them.

Soaking also cleans the beans. Beans are covered in "field dust," which can contain anything from pesticides to rodent droppings to bacteria to insect larva (which aren't on the Stage 3 diet). This is why we don't use the water the beans soaked in for anything else and why we rinse the beans one more time after soaking.

Soak dried beans for 24 hours in a jar or pot on your kitchen counter (or 48 hours in the refrigerator) in water mixed with a few tablespoons of whey for 24 hours on the counter or 48 hours in the refrigerator before cooking. Whey helps the beans be less gas-producing and it also helps neutralize enzyme inhibitors. Dried beans will double or triple in size, so make sure to put them in a large container and cover with three times the amount of cold water as beans.

For a "quick soak," boil them in water for 3 minutes and then let sit, covered, for at least 2 hours (or up to 6). Remember to pour out the water they've been soaking in and rinse them again. While this works, the best method still is to soak them for 24 hours on the counter.

Make sure beans stay covered with water while they are cooking. After bringing water to a boil, lower heat and simmer for the remaining cooking time (60–90 minutes for soaked beans, depending on the texture desired). Soaking translates into less cooking time. Also, beans which have been soaked first cook more evenly.

Another method for producing less gassy beans is to add a 1" x 4" piece of kombu (a seaweed) to the beans as they cook.

Consider saving the water the beans cooked in (not soaked in) to use in other dishes—it's full of nutrients.

Store cooked beans in the freezer in an airtight container.

In general:

⅓ cup dry beans	=	1 cup cooked beans
½ cup dry beans	=	1 ½ cups cooked beans
⅔ cup dry beans	=	2 cups cooked beans
1 cup dry beans	=	3 cups cooked beans
2 cups dry beans	=	6 cups cooked beans

VEGETABLES

Vegetables come straight from Mother Earth. There are hundreds of varieties but most of us stay within the same range of choices. One way to increase variety is by eating with the seasons—asparagus and artichokes in spring, bell peppers and that barbeque staple, corn on the cob, for summer. Although available year-round, cauliflower and potatoes taste best when harvested in their rightful season—fall. And there is a whole category of squash, such as pumpkin and butternut, that are best in winter.

Another way to expand your range of choices is to be adventurous and try new vegetables. If you've never eaten fennel, try *Oven-Roasted Fennel.* Or explore the world of vegetables used in Indian cooking zucchini, cauliflower, or potatoes and spinach. Or work your way through the many suggestions for baked vegetables contained here.

Vegetables also bring balance to a meal with their different textures and colors. Instead of serving a main dish, try centering a meal on two well-prepared vegetables matched with a small salad, rice, and a sauce that brings the flavor of the vegetables to life.

Having a simple meal occasionally, such as steamed broccoli and rice with a sauce or dressing, can be a nice break from heavier meals. Light steaming is fine as it preserves the enzymes needed for complete digestion and absorption of nutrients; just make sure the vegetables are still a bit crunchy.

BAKED VEGETABLES

Baking brings out the sweetness of vegetables and getting them a little bit crispy makes them even better. A lot of children we know love baked Brussels sprouts which, in itself, is a miracle. Also, if you're as sick of your computer as we are, stick it in the oven and bake it with a little olive oil and then there'll be no conflict about buying the latest model.

Any vegetable, cut into medium pieces

Olive oil

Sea salt

Black pepper (optional)

PREP TIME 45 MINUTES TO 1 HOUR, DEPENDING ON VEGGIES

Spread vegetables one layer deep on a baking sheet. Add salt and pepper to olive oil and pour over vegetables. Toss the vegetables until coated with oil. Bake at 400°F. See baking times below.

Bake whole asparagus spears for about 15 minutes.

Cut carrots and bake for 30 minutes, turning when they begin to brown.

For pumpkin, squash, and beets, peel, cut into pieces, prepare as described above, and bake for about 45 minutes or until done.

For Brussels sprouts, wash the sprouts, cut off stems, and remove outer leaves; prepare as described above and bake for at least 30 minutes, turning when they begin to brown. Continue baking until crisp on the outside and tender on the inside.

For whole baked potatoes, wash and dry potatoes, rub with butter or olive oil, and bake at 400°F for 30 minutes. Pierce several times with a fork. Return to oven and bake 30–45 minutes, until potato is tender inside. Alternately, pierce potatoes before baking. Potatoes must be pierced or they will explode while baking.

ASPARAGUS WITH PINE NUTS

Many people think that thin spears of asparagus are younger and more tender than thicker spears. It's actually the variety that determines the thickness. The fat ones are more succulent and work best for roasting or grilling. Any thickness works in this recipe so choose what you prefer. Snap off and discard the tough ends before cooking. Asparagus is a refined vegetable that doesn't require anything added. But serving it with roasted pine nuts in melted butter and a hint of balsamic vinegar makes this dish just right for a special occasion.

SERVES 3–4

PREP TIME 35 MINUTES

1 pound fresh green asparagus, tough ends snapped off and discarded

1½ tablespoons pine nuts

2 tablespoons melted butter

2 teaspoons balsamic vinegar

Steam asparagus or cook them in a small amount of boiling water for 3–6 minutes until bright green and just tender. Cooking time varies depending on thickness of the spears.

Dry roast the pine nuts in a skillet.

In a small bowl, combine melted butter and vinegar; stir.

When the asparagus are tender, drain and arrange on serving platter. Drizzle butter sauce on top and sprinkle with roasted pine nuts. Serve immediately.

GREEN BEANS WITH GINGER

We made up this recipe at the last moment right before a meal. Tika was dealing with a big bag of frozen green beans that had been in the freezer for several months and had freezer burn. Steamed, the beans were tasteless, but that was the vegetable that was available, and she didn't want to waste them. This was one of those situations we as cooks are often faced with—invention in the moment. So she stuck her head into the pantry, saw a jar of pickled ginger, mixed it into the beans, added a dash of toasted sesame oil, and voilá! During the meal we quietly observed everyone's enjoyment as they ate the beans, and we were relieved.

SERVES 4

¾ pound green beans

3 ounces natural pickled sushi ginger

½ tablespoon toasted sesame oil

Sea salt

PREP TIME 30 MINUTES

Steam green beans (see *How To—Steam Vegetables* in Chapter 6) for about 20 minutes until tender but not soft. Drain beans and put in a bowl.

Pour sesame oil over beans. Sprinkle with salt. Add the pickled ginger. Mix everything together. Serve immediately.

Note—All stages of this diet have gradients. If you are beginning the Stage 3 diet, this recipe is appropriate for occasional use. It is not on a pure Stage 3 diet because of the pickled ginger.

ROASTED BEETS

We love beets. We love the color and the pattern inside when they are cut. Beets are a vegetable that has often been overlooked. Most of us only know the beet as pickled beet slices. Get to know beets by roasting them. You can cube the roasted beets and serve as a salad with any kind of dressing. Or try a salad with beets and mint leaves. To learn more about working with beets, please read about them in the *How To—Work With Beets* section in Chapter 6.

PREP TIME 1 HOUR

Buy beets with greens still attached. Wash to remove dirt. Cut greens off. Steam greens and serve them with beets.

Preheat oven to 450°F.

Pierce each beet twice with a fork so it can vent while cooking. Put beets on aluminum foil on a baking sheet.

Bake for 45 minutes to 1 hour for medium- to large-size beets.

Cool, then peel off outer skin.

Broccoli with Garlic and Mustard Seeds

The mustard seeds distinguish this broccoli dish. They take on a nutty aroma after being roasted in oil and bring the fragrance of Indian cooking.

SERVES 6

5 tablespoons mustard oil or extra-virgin safflower oil

1 teaspoon brown mustard seeds

2–3 garlic cloves, finely minced

2 pounds broccoli, trimmed and cut into spears

½–¾ teaspoon sea salt

¼ cup vegetable broth or stock

2 fresh long hot green chiles, cut crossways into 2 to 3 parts

PREP TIME 35 MINUTES

Heat oil in a wok or a large, wide skillet over medium-high heat. When hot, put in mustard seeds. As soon as mustard seeds begin to pop—just a few seconds—add garlic.

Stir once or twice, then add broccoli. Stir a few times and then add salt and vegetable broth or stock. Stir and cover.

Cook over medium heat for 2 minutes. Add chiles and cook for another minute or so. Remove cover. If there is liquid left, turn heat up to boil it away. Stir gently a few times as it boils.

GOLDEN INDIAN CABBAGE

This cabbage melts in your mouth (due to the butter!) and its warm golden color (from the turmeric) feeds the senses. Krishna from India would love this because of its buttery sweetness. That's why it is sometimes called "Krishna Cabbage."

SERVES 6

2 tablespoons brown mustard seeds

1/3 stick butter

1 tablespoon ground turmeric

2 teaspoons salt

1 medium head of green or white cabbage, sliced

¼ cup water

PREP TIME 2 HOURS 10 MINUTES

Preheat oven to 350°F.

Dry roast the mustard seeds in a small skillet for a few minutes.

Melt butter and add mustard seeds, turmeric, and salt. Put in a large baking dish. Add cabbage and water. Mix well. Cover with a lid or aluminum foil. Bake for 2 hours.

HEARTY WINTER CABBAGE

The red wine vinegar and the honey in this recipe give a slightly sweet and sour aroma to the combination of sautéed cabbage and tomatoes. Serve with oven-roasted potatoes and salad as a hearty winter meal.

SERVES 4–6

3 tablespoons olive oil

2 yellow onions, chopped

1 (15 ounce) can petite diced tomatoes with juice, or 9 roma tomatoes, finely diced

¼ cup red wine vinegar

¼ cup honey or Grade B maple syrup or more to taste

1½ teaspoons sea salt

¾ teaspoon ground black pepper

1 large head green cabbage

2 additional tablespoons olive oil

PREP TIME 40 MINUTES

Heat 3 tablespoons olive oil in a skillet. Add the onions and cook over medium-low heat for 8 minutes, until onions are translucent. Add tomatoes, vinegar, honey or maple syrup, salt, and pepper. Bring to a boil then lower the heat and simmer uncovered for 20–30 minutes, stirring occasionally, or until consistency of a thick sauce.

To prepare cabbage, cut it in half, then cut halves in half. Remove core. Then cut each quarter into slices from top down.

While the sauce is simmering, heat 2 tablespoons olive oil in a large stock pot or wok. Add sliced cabbage. Cover and sauté for about 25 minutes over medium heat, until tender. Add water as needed so cabbage doesn't burn.

Once cabbage is tender, add tomato sauce. Combine well. Heat for another 5 minutes to blend flavors.

Newberg-Style Carrots

Canned carrots and peas are of course always an option, but if you're looking for a healthier, interesting way to serve carrots, try them Newberg-style. They are served in a sauce flavored with parsley, onions, bell peppers, and a bit of honey.

Serves 4

Prep time 25 minutes

4 cups sliced carrots

1 teaspoon sea salt

1 teaspoon honey

2 tablespoons safflower oil

2 tablespoons whole wheat flour

¾ cup water

¼ cup oat or rice milk

½ teaspoon parsley, chopped

2 teaspoons onions, chopped

2 teaspoons any color peppers, chopped

Place carrots, salt, and honey into 1 inch of boiling water in a medium-sized saucepan. Cover and cook 12–15 minutes or until just crisp-tender.

Put oil in another pan. Blend in flour. Add water, oat or rice milk, parsley, onion, and green pepper. Stir, cook 5 minutes or until thickened. Add carrots. Serve hot.

(from *Intuitive Eating* by Humbart "Smokey" Santillo, N.D.)

OVEN-ROASTED FENNEL

In Europe, fennel is a commonly used vegetable either raw in salads or baked in casseroles. In the United States fennel is less used and remains a hidden treasure in the vegetable family. Because of the licorice taste many children love it. This dish combines the sweetness of the fennel with the savoriness of the olives and the tart juiciness of the cherry tomatoes. Be sure to make enough of this because the amount that people will eat is sometimes underestimated.

SERVES 3

5 tablespoons olive oil

3 cloves garlic, thinly sliced

1 heaping teaspoon sea salt

1 tablespoon fresh thyme or 1 teaspoon dried thyme

2 pounds fennel (core, stalks, and leaves discarded), cut into 8 wedge pieces

1 pound cherry tomatoes

20 pitted kalamata olives

PREP TIME 40 MINUTES

Preheat oven to 350°F.

Mix olive oil, garlic, sea salt, and thyme. Put the fennel, tomatoes, and the olives on a baking sheet. Pour the olive oil mixture over the vegetables. Bake for 20–25 minutes. The fennel should be soft and the tops should be a little bit browned.

Note–All stages of this diet have gradients. If you are easing into Stage 3 this recipe is appropriate. If you are eating a pure Stage 3 diet, omit the kalamata olives unless they are raw.

ROASTED GARLIC

When garlic is roasted, it becomes milder, sweeter, and mellower with a creamy, spreadable consistency. It can be used in a variety of ways—spread on bread, used in recipes such as *Tapenade* (see page 191), and added to mashed potatoes. It can also be substituted in some recipes for raw or sautéed garlic.

Large bulbs of garlic

Olive oil

PREP TIME 25 MINUTES

Preheat oven to 350°F.

Remove the outer skin of large heads of garlic by rubbing with thumb (leave the bulb intact). Cut a ¼ to ½ inch off the top of the bulb to expose the cloves.

Arrange bulbs on a cookie sheet with cut tops facing up. Drizzle a little olive oil (about a tablespoon per bulb) over the cut top. Bake for 15–20 minutes.

Let cool. Ideally, they are still fairly firm and will pop out of the shells when squeezed. If overcooked, garlic becomes too mushy and sticky.

Pack in clean jars and cover with olive oil. Store in the refrigerator

GREENS

Are you one of those people who rejected everything green when you were growing up (except green popsicles)? Maybe they just weren't prepared right. Here is some guidance on how to cook greens.

General recipe for cooking greens—Chop greens, put in a pot, cover with water, and boil until tender. If desired, add onion to the pot while greens are cooking. Soy sauce, persimmons, pesto, red pepper, or other spices or herbs may be added after the greens are cooked and drained.

Refer to the following list for total cooking time if boiling greens and for when to add the onion (optional).

Keep the water used to boil greens and use in soups, as a drink itself, or to cook rice. It has nutrients from the greens. It can be frozen for later use.

Alternate cooking method–Sauté onions in a pan. When onions are cooked, put chopped greens on top. Add water (stand back—it will steam and spit) and cover. Greens will steam-cook. Stir occasionally while steaming until greens are tender.

	Total boiling time:	Add onion after:
collards	30 minutes	15 minutes
kale	20 minutes	10 minutes
turnip greens	15 minutes	10 minutes
mustard greens	15 minutes	10 minutes
chard	15 minutes	10 minutes

KALE CHIPS

One summer we had lots of kale from our garden and didn't know what to do with it. How much steamed kale can you eat? Luckily, our friend from New Jersey was visiting and introduced us to the pleasure of kale chips. The children were licking their plates and asking, "Is there more kale?" Enough said.

1 bunch of kale

Olive oil

Sea salt

PREP TIME 15-25 MINUTES

Preheat oven to 350°F.

Wash kale, spin in salad spinner untilnearly dry.

Lightly rub each leaf of kale with olive oil, front and back. Do not use too much oil or chips will be soggy. Then rip into bite-sized pieces.

Lightly salt. Place on cookie sheet in one layer. Bake until crisp. Baking time will depend on oven and tray but check after 10 minutes. Overcooking makes the chips turn to dust.

BAKED PORTOBELLO MUSHROOMS

If you need a new vegetable idea after having broccoli, cabbage, and carrots all week, baked portobello mushrooms are a good change of pace. Even though they look like small planets or unidentified flying objects in our neighbor's cornfield, they are a well-respected addition to any meal. They have a meaty texture and are called cremini mushrooms before they are large and mature. In this recipe, the balsamic marinade that you brush on before you bake them gives a distinctly festive flavor.

SERVES 4

4 portobello mushrooms

Olive oil

BALSAMIC GLAZE

2 tablespoons olive oil

2 teaspoons balsamic vinegar

2 cloves garlic, peeled and squeezed

1 teaspoon honey

1 teaspoon Dijon mustard

¾ teaspoon salt

¼ teaspoon black pepper

PREP TIME 1 HOUR 15 MINUTES

Preheat oven to 400°F.

Quickly rinse mushrooms and dry off with a paper towel. Coat baking sheet with olive oil. Place mushrooms on baking sheet.

To make glaze, combine all ingredients except olive oil. Drizzle in olive oil, whisking to form an emulsion. Brush on mushrooms.

Bake for 1 hour.

ROASTED SWEET POTATOES OR YAMS

Sweet potatoes and yams are different vegetables. In the Southern part of the U.S., yams are usually called sweet potatoes. These are good for dinner or you can serve them for a hearty brunch. Children often love these. They can also be cooked in a skillet on the stove.

SERVES 3–4

1 tablespoon extra-virgin olive oil

½ teaspoon coarse sea salt

1 pound sweet potatoes or yams, peeled and cut into 1-inch cubes

PREP TIME 1 HOUR 15 MINUTES

Preheat oven to 400°F.

Drizzle olive oil over sweet potatoes and toss to coat. Spread on shallow baking pan. Sprinkle with salt.

Bake for 45–60 minutes or until tender and starting to brown at edges.

Stir occasionally while baking.

Aloo Ki Bhujia

When we were traveling through India we experienced the enormous hospitality of the Indian people. Our hosts served us one incredible meal after another. In India, the way to say "Thank You" is to gratefully accept another plate of food. This potato-tomato dish will make you ask for more. It is best accompanying daal or green lentils and can be served with basmati rice.

Serves 4–6

Prep time 45 minutes

5 medium roma tomatoes, peeled and chopped (see *How To—Peel Tomatoes* in Chapter 6)

1 medium onion

4–5 tablespoons safflower oil

½ teaspoon fenugreek seeds

1 teaspoon black mustard seeds

½ teaspoon onion seeds (if unavailable, can make dish without)

1 teaspoon sea salt

¼ teaspoon turmeric

½ teaspoon cayenne

1 pound potatoes, peeled and cut into small cubes

1 lemon (optional)

Handful of fresh mint, chopped

1 tablespoon black/roasted cumin

Prepare tomatoes and set aside. Cut onion in half lengthwise. With cut side facing down, slice it thinly, starting from side. Set aside.

Coat bottom of a saucepan with oil. Over medium heat, add fenugreek seeds. When seeds begin to brown, add mustard and onion seeds, if using. Fry for about a minute, then add sliced onion. Fry until onion is transparent and starting to brown on edges.

Add salt, turmeric, and cayenne. Onion should be a reddish color when these spices are added. Fry spices with onion for about 2 minutes and add water if mixture is starting to stick.

Add tomatoes and fry with onions and spices until oil and water begin to separate. When oil starts to separate, tomatoes should be dissolving into the sauce and mixture of onions, tomatoes, and spices should be fairly thick.

Add potatoes, coat with sauce, and fry for 3 to 4 minutes. Add enough water to bring level of sauce up to top of, but not covering, potatoes. Bring mixture to a boil.

As potatoes are boiling, cut half a lemon into quarters, if using, and put in with rind for about 2 minutes. When sauce has thickened, turn heat off, stir in mint, and sprinkle roasted cumin on top. Add salt, if desired. Serve hot.

Note–When doubling, tripling, etc., this recipe, be conservative with the amount of spices used or they will dominate the flavor. Add only a third more if doubling or even tripling the ingredients and then adjust the spices later if needed. Turmeric is added mostly for color and usually doesn't have to be increased.

ALOO PALAK

Aloo Palak—potatoes and spinach married with spices. This dish would be sorely missed if it was omitted at any Indian Feast. Serve with *Daal* or *Green Lentil Curry* and rice or quinoa.

SERVES 4

PREP TIME 1 HOUR

1–1¼ pounds fresh spinach, steamed, chopped, with moisture squeezed or pressed out (or 2 packages of frozen chopped)

1 small-medium red onion

3 tablespoons safflower oil

1 teaspoon black mustard seeds

2 cloves garlic, finely chopped

2–3 medium red potatoes, peeled and cut into small cubes

¼ teaspoon cayenne pepper

1 teaspoon sea salt

Prepare spinach and set aside.

Cut onions in half lengthwise, place the cut half flat on the board and then slice onion in thin slices lengthwise. Put enough oil in a skillet to coat the bottom of the pan. Heat oil over medium heat and add mustard seeds. When they begin to pop, add onions and garlic. Fry until the onions begin to turn transparent, approximately 5 minutes.

Add cubed potatoes and cayenne pepper and stir so that potatoes take on a bit of the color of the cayenne. After about 3–4 minutes, push potatoes and onions to the perimeter of the pan leaving a clearing in the center. Put spinach in there with the salt. Add just enough water to cover the bottom of the pan so that potatoes don't burn, bring to a boil, cover, turn the heat down to low and simmer until the potatoes are done, about 30 minutes.

When done, boil any excess water away, and stir to combine spinach and potatoes. This will keep your spinach a little greener than if it is mixed with the potatoes at the beginning.

Note– For Stage 3 use fresh spinach.

When doubling, tripling, etc., this recipe, be conservative with the amount of spices used or they will dominate the flavor. Add only a third more if doubling or even tripling the ingredients and then adjust the spices later if needed. Turmeric is added mostly for color and usually doesn't have to be increased.

ALOO GOBI–POTATOES AND CAULIFLOWER

If you think cauliflower is bland and boring, give it one more try. In this recipe, the cumin, coriander, turmeric, and cloves transform the cauliflower into a flavorful partner for the potatoes. Prepare Aloo Gobi and make your friends and family happy. Serve with *Daal* or *Green Lentil Curry* and brown basmati rice.

SERVES 4

PREP TIME 50 MINUTES

1 small-medium cauliflower (approximately 2–3 cups of florets)

3 medium red potatoes, peeled, cubed, and boiled

3 tablespoons safflower oil

1 teaspoon cumin seeds

1 teaspoon ground cumin

1 teaspoon ground coriander

¼ teaspoon turmeric

¼ teaspoon cayenne pepper

Salt

Black pepper

¼–½ teaspoon ground cloves or ground roasted cumin to taste

Soak the cauliflower florets in a bowl of water for approximately 30 minutes while peeling, cubing, and cooking the potatoes. Drain.

Put oil in a large frying pan or wok over medium heat and add cumin seeds once the oil is hot. When seeds begin to sizzle, put in cauliflower. Fry cauliflower and let it brown in spots. Cover, turn heat down to low, and let it simmer until cauliflower is just done but still crunchy.

Put in potatoes, ground cumin, coriander, turmeric, cayenne pepper, salt, a dash of black pepper, and ground clove or ground roast cumin to taste. Stir in spices so that the dish takes on a gold color and the spices coat the vegetables. Continue to cook and stir gently until potatoes are heated through and flavors combine.

Note–When doubling, tripling, etc., this recipe, be conservative with the amount of spices used or they will dominate the flavor. Add only a third more if doubling or even tripling the ingredients and then adjust the spices later if needed. Turmeric is added mostly for color and usually doesn't have to be increased.

Oven-Roasted Potatoes with Rosemary

Use fingerling or small red potatoes when in season. You do not need to cut these smaller potatoes—just toss them in oil and bake them whole. In the summer, lay whole sprigs of fresh rosemary over the potatoes to intensify the aroma. You can also garnish the serving platter with fresh rosemary springs.

SERVES 6–8 AS A MAIN DISH OR 8–10 AS A SIDE DISH

PREP TIME 1 HOUR 15 MINUTES

10 medium Yukon gold (or fingerling or small red, when in season) potatoes

3–4 tablespoons olive oil

2 teaspoons (or more) dried rosemary

Salt to taste

Preheat oven to 400°F.

Wash and dry potatoes. Cut in half lengthwise. Cut each half into 4 quarters lengthwise.

Toss potatoes in olive oil, put on baking sheet. Sprinkle with rosemary and salt.

Bake in oven for 1 hour, turning every 20 minutes. For crispier potatoes, bake longer.

Marinated Potatoes, Artichoke Hearts, and Asparagus

A friend of ours made this colorful dish for a neighborhood party. People not only emptied the huge bowl but kept asking for more to the point that she had to comfort them by promising them another neighborhood party soon.

Serves 12

Prep time 50 minutes (without chilling time)

1½ pounds small new potatoes

1 small bunch of asparagus, cut diagonally into 1-inch pieces

1 (13 ounce) can artichoke hearts, drained and quartered

1 small green bell pepper, diced

1 small red bell pepper, diced

½ small red onion, diced

3 ounces sliced pitted black olives

1 cup grape tomatoes

¼ cup chopped flat-leaf parsley

Sea salt and pepper to taste

Dressing

¼ cup apple cider vinegar

1 clove garlic, pressed

2 teaspoons Dijon mustard

1 teaspoon sea salt

½ teaspoon black pepper

½ cup olive oil

Put potatoes in large pan and cover with water. Add salt to taste. Cook over medium heat for 15–20 minutes, until tender. Drain.

While potatoes cook, make vinaigrette dressing. Combine vinegar, garlic, mustard, salt, and pepper. Whisk in oil.

Carefully cut hot potatoes into bite-sized pieces and place in a large bowl. Add raw asparagus and gently mix. Let the asparagus get lightly steamed next to the hot potatoes. Pour vinaigrette over potatoes and asparagus.

Add artichoke hearts, peppers, onion, black olives, tomatoes, and parsley to potato mixture. Gently mix well. Add salt and pepper, if needed. Mix again.

Cover and chill for at least 4 hours, stirring occasionally.

Note–For Stage 3, omit artichoke hearts (or use fresh) and black olives.

Potato salad typically makes you think of hard-boiled eggs, sweet pickles, and mayonnaise. This vibrant potato salad, made with parsley, green onions, the slightly sweet touch of tarragon vinegar, and a cherry tomato garnish, is a feast for palate and eyes. It's great for picnics because it doesn't have to be kept refrigerated.

Serves 12

Prep time 45 minutes (without marinating time)

4½ pounds new potatoes

½ cup chopped flat-leaf parsley

½ cup thinly sliced green onion

3 large cloves garlic, minced

1 teaspoon sea salt or more to taste

½ teaspoon dry mustard

2 teaspoons agave syrup or honey

8 ounces olive oil

4 ounces tarragon vinegar

2 ½ cups cherry tomatoes, cut in half

Flat-leaf parsley for garnish

Boil potatoes in salted water. When tender, cut into bite-sized pieces. Sprinkle parsley and green onions over potatoes.

Combine garlic, salt, mustard, agave or honey, olive oil, and vinegar. Pour over potatoes. Stir well. Cover and let rest for at least 4 hours, stirring every hour.

Garnish with cherry tomatoes and fresh parsley, if desired.

Serve at room temperature. Refrigerate leftovers.

Note–All stages of this diet have gradients. If you are easing into Stage 3 this recipe is appropriate for occasional use. If you are eating a pure Stage 3 diet, omit the agave syrup or honey, and substitute apple cider vinegar and fresh tarragon (to taste) for the tarragon vinegar.

STEAMED SPINACH WITH GARLIC

At last, we take a little time to give credit to what we have learned from our mothers. This simple recipe is one of the first things that I (Tika) picked up at my mother's side. It's not like she taught me how to make it, but just by watching her, the recipe got in. She used to make it all the time. The garlic, salt, and pepper give the spinach just the right amount of flavor to allow it to stand on its own.

SERVES 4

4 bunches of fresh spinach

1 tablespoon organic butter

2 medium cloves garlic, minced

Sea salt

Black pepper

PREP TIME 12 MINUTES

Add ¼ inch water to a skillet. Bring to a boil. Add spinach, reduce heat to simmer, and cover. Steam until spinach is tender, adding water if necessary to keep spinach from burning.

While spinach is cooking, melt butter in a pot. Add salt and pepper, stir. Add garlic, sauté for 1 minute. When spinach is drained, add to butter mixture and stir. Serve hot.

INDIAN ZUCCHINI

A few years ago our friend's mother from Pakistan was visiting. When asked if she'd be willing to spend the day in the kitchen teaching us some of her favorite recipes, she happily agreed. Grinding cardamom and cumin, chopping garlic and ginger, laughing in the midst of steaming pots and pans, and having cool lemonade, it was a transmission of Indian/Pakistani cooking that left its mark on our hearts. This recipe is a very easy, delicious, and colorful addition to an Indian dinner (or any kind of dinner). Of all the recipes she taught us that day, this recipe stood out and is now one of our standards. Serve as a side vegetable with daal and basmati rice.

SERVES 4

3 tablespoon safflower oil

1½-inch piece of ginger, peeled and finely minced

1 teaspoon cumin seeds

1/8 teaspoon red pepper flakes

5 small cloves garlic, finely minced

4 medium zucchini, cut lengthwise into quarters and then sliced

2 tablespoons water

½ teaspoon turmeric

2 roma tomatoes, diced in small dices (about ¼-inch cubes)

½ teaspoon sea salt or to taste

PREP TIME 35 MINUTES

Heat oil in a skillet on medium to high heat. Add ginger and sauté for 30 seconds. Add cumin seeds and pepper flakes and sauté on medium heat for 30 seconds. Make sure to not burn the cumin seeds. Add minced garlic. Sauté for another 30 seconds.

Turn up the heat and add zucchini, water, and turmeric. Stir and sauté on medium-high heat for 3 minutes. Then add tomatoes. Sauté for another 2 minutes. Add salt. Vegetables should be slightly firm and already tender but not too soft. Serve hot.

Note–When doubling, tripling, etc., this recipe, be conservative with the amount of spices used or they will dominate the flavor. Add only a third more if doubling or even tripling the ingredients and then adjust the spices later if needed. Turmeric is added mostly for color and usually doesn't have to be increased.

GRAINS

Grains recommended for your Dharma Feast diet include short and long grain brown rice*, brown basmati rice,* millet*, quinoa*, bulgur, buckwheat*, whole barley, oats (whole oat groats, steel-cut, or rolled), teff*, amaranth*, wild rice*, polenta, barley, and sticky sushi rice* (naturally white). These can be bought in bulk. (*Does not contain gluten.)

In Stage 2 use grains not more than once per day and in Stage 3 use grains no more than 3 times per week. If you live in a cold climate, you may need grains more often than this.

Most grains (with the exception of millet) contain phytic acid, which blocks the absorption of minerals, but which can be removed by soaking grain in water. The complex starches in grains create acid. To make grains alkaline, cook them with minerals, such as a little bit of kombu (a sea vegetable) or sea salt.

When grains are sprouted, their natural enzymes and minerals become available, so in a perfect world, it's best to eat sprouted grains. To sprout, a grain requires water, warmth, some acidity, and time. Put grains in enough warm water to keep them covered when they swell. Add a tablespoon of something acidic like vinegar or lemon juice. Cover and soak 36 hours, making sure the grains stay covered with water. Pour out the water and allow the grains to sit covered for about 12 more hours, or until sprouted.

Consider sprouting oatmeal before cooking it. The sprouting process rids it of toxins and puts the nutrients in a form we can absorb. To do this, put oats in warm water with a tablespoon of something acidic, cover it, and leave it on the counter overnight. In the morning, add the oat mixture to boiling water with some salt. This will

cook very quickly, so keep an eye on it or it will burn.

As we noted in Chapter 3, *The Basics*, the healthiest, least-processed rice is brown because only the first hull has been removed, leaving the bran and germ, where all the nutrients are. White rice ("unpolished rice") has had the bran and germ removed. Polished rice is white rice that has been buffed with glucose (sugar) or talc powder to make it bright and shiny. "Enriched rice" is polished rice that has been sprayed with synthetic vitamins and minerals. Converted or parboiled rice is white rice that has been boiled in the husk before milling (removing the outer hull).

Cooking Grains

Soak grains (not millet) overnight or during the day before cooking to remove phytic acid. Soaking shortens cooking time by about 10 minutes. If you soak first, drain the water before cooking the grain and use ½ cup less water than the recipe calls for.

Note: All the following grain recipes use unsoaked grains.

Put the grain in a pot, add water, bring to a boil, then cover and turn heat to low until the water is almost gone. Turn the stove off, keep the cover on, and allow the remaining water to steam away (around 5 minutes). When using a rice cooker, follow the directions.

Roasting gives millet a different flavor. Spread millet in a dry cast iron skillet (do not add oil). Toast over medium-low heat, stirring frequently until it is dark golden yellow or light brown in color. If grain starts to smoke, turn down heat. After toasting, cook millet according to recipe or directions below.

Some rice, especially basmati and sushi rice, needs to be rinsed first or the starch on it can make it stick together. Put the dry rice in a bowl, cover with water, and swirl around. Drain and rinse again until the water is clear.

Yields and approximate cook times (from the time the water begins to boil) are in parenthesis after each grain.

High altitude grain cooking

For brown rice, use 1 cup brown rice and only 1 ¾ cups water; otherwise rice gets mushy.

For basmati rice, millet, and quinoa, use one cup grain and 2 cups water.

1 ½ cups of water per 1 cup grain:	
oats	makes 2½ cups, takes 30 minutes
spelt	makes 2½ cups, takes 30 minutes
2 cups of water per 1 cup grain:	
amaranth	makes 1½ cups, takes 20 minutes
brown rice (short or long)	makes 3 cups, takes 45 minutes
buckwheat (or kasha)	makes 2½ cups, takes 15 minutes
bulgur wheat	makes 2½ cups, takes 15–20 minutes
cracked wheat	makes 2 1/3 cups, takes 25 minutes
quinoa	makes 3 cups, takes 15 minutes
wild rice	makes 3 cups, takes an hour
basmati rice	makes 2 cups, takes 20 minutes
sticky sushi rice	makes 2 cups, takes 20 minutes
any kind of white rice	makes 2 cups, takes 20 minutes
3 cups of water per 1 cup grain:	
barley (whole)	makes 3½ cups, takes 1 hour 15 minutes
millet	makes 3½ cups, takes 30–45 minutes
rye	makes 2½ cups, takes 1 hour
whole wheat berries	makes 2 2/3 cups, takes 2 hours
4 cups of water per one cup grain:	
polenta	makes 3 cups, follow recipe

GARLIC-PARSLEY MILLET

Are you one of those people thinking that millet is boring and dry? Try this recipe. Sauté the millet in olive oil with garlic and chopped parsley. It is delicious and turns a plain "grain" (even though millet is usually referred to as a grain, it's actually a seed) into a favorite dish. It is a nice variation if you have a lot of rice in your diet. It's gluten-free, has lots of vitamins and minerals, and is alkaline unlike most grains.

SERVES 8

PREP TIME 50 MINUTES TO 1 HOUR

2 cups uncooked millet

1/3 Olive oil

2–3 medium onions, chopped

1 bunch parsley, finely minced

2 cloves garlic, finely minced

Combine millet and 4 cups water in pan. Bring to a boil. Once boiling, cover tightly, and reduce heat to lowest temperature. Cook about 40–45 minutes, then turn off heat and let it steam. Fluff with a fork

Heat olive oil in skillet. Sauté onions until translucent. Add parsley and garlic and briefly sauté. Then add cooked millet. Sauté until heated through and thoroughly combined.

SIMPLE STIR-FRIED MILLET

Cooked millet tends to be a bit dry and dense. Sautéed in ghee with onions and garlic, it becomes a fantastic, aromatic, moist main or side dish.

SERVES 4–6

1 cup raw millet

2 cups water

2 tablespoons ghee

½ medium red onion, diced

2 cloves garlic, minced

PREP TIME 1 HOUR 5 MINUTES

Combine millet and water in pan. Bring to a boil. Once boiling, cover tightly, and reduce heat to lowest temperature. Cook about 40–45 minutes, then turn off heat and let it steam. Fluff with a fork.

Heat ghee in a skillet. Add onions and sauté until onions become translucent. Add garlic and continue sautéing for another 2 minutes. Add millet and keep sautéing, stirring frequently, for about 10 minutes.

Serve.

Note–3½ cups leftover millet can be substituted for raw millet and water.

MILLET-QUINOA GRAIN

We still haven't decided whether we want to call this "Minoa" or "Quillet." It has been announced at our dinner table as both. We leave it up to you what you want to call it, but in any case, it's really good. We just know that it is a perfect combination because it gives you the best of both grains—the density of millet and the lightness of quinoa. It's a quick and easy alternative to rice.

SERVES 8

PREP TIME 1 HOUR

1 cup uncooked quinoa

1 cup uncooked millet

4 cups water

Combine quinoa, millet, and water in a saucepan. Bring to a boil. Cover, simmer for 45–50 minutes, turn off heat, and let it steam for 10 minutes. Fluff with a fork.

Quinoa Tabouleh

In Middle Eastern cuisine you find tabouleh served at nearly every meal. Usually it is made with couscous, a refined wheat product, and fresh parsley and mint. Another way to eat tabouleh is to replace couscous with quinoa, which has more protein and is gluten-free. We combine it with fresh vegetables and parsley to give lots of color and flavor. For variety, add a finely chopped tomato and cucumber to this salad, especially in the summer time. Serve it with hummus and freshly cut vegetables and you have a great Middle Eastern meal.

SERVES 10–12

5 cups quinoa

10 cups of water

1 bunch parsley, chopped very fine

1 red onion, chopped very fine

3 red bell peppers, chopped very fine

½ cup lemon juice

½ cup olive oil

½ teaspoon salt

PREP TIME 50 MINUTES (WITHOUT MARINATING TIME)

Cook quinoa. Set aside. It should be fluffy. If it's mushy, use less water next time.

Combine vegetables in a bowl. Mix lemon juice, olive oil, and salt. Pour over vegetable mixture and stir. Let sit 1 hour.

Mix marinated vegetables with cooled quinoa. Add more olive oil and lemon juice to taste.

Aromatic Indian Rice

There is never too much rice. Imagine yourself wearing a saree walking down a street in India, rickshaws honking and moving in every direction, chai stalls on your right, unknown intriguing spices wafting their way into your nose. Try this rice and you will find yourself transported. Serve with *Green Lentil Curry* or other Indian dishes.

SERVES 4

2 tablespoons olive oil

1 teaspoon cumin seeds

½ stick cinnamon

2 cloves

1½ cups brown basmati rice, rinsed

3 cups of water

PREP TIME 50 MINUTES

Coat the bottom of a saucepan with olive oil and set on medium heat. When hot, add cumin seeds, cinnamon stick, and cloves. When cumin seeds begin to sizzle wait for about a minute and then add rice; stir to coat rice with oil, and cook for a couple of minutes.

Add water and bring to boil. Once water is boiling, cover tightly, turn heat down to low, and simmer for about 40 minutes. Leave covered and let sit for 5 minutes. Fluff rice with fork and remove cinnamon and cloves before serving. Rice should have a wonderful aromatic flavor to it.

Note–Keep the spices the same for up to 3 cups of rice. Beyond that, multiply amount of spices by half, so add half more every three cups. So for four cups, add 1½ teaspoons cumin, 1 stick of cinnamon, and 1 or 2 more cloves.

RICE AND PEAS WITH GARAM MASALA

Garam masala is a mixture of Indian spices. Indian families make their own blend that gives their distinct flavor to the family dishes. Usually health food stores or Asian markets offer an already-made garam masala.

SERVES 5–6

1½ cups brown basmati rice

3 tablespoons olive oil

1 small onion, cut into thin half-rings

¾ teaspoon salt

1 teaspoon ground garam masala

4 tablespoons finely chopped fresh dill

16 ounces vegetable stock

4 ounces green peas, cooked in boiling water for 2 minutes or until tender and drained

PREP TIME 45 MINUTES

Wash rice several times and soak for 30 minutes. Drain thoroughly.

Heat oil in a small, heavy sauce pan over medium-high heat. When hot, add onion and stir until brown.

Add rice, salt, garam masala, and dill. Cook, stirring continuously, for a minute.

Add stock and bring to a boil. Cover tightly, turn to very low heat, and cook for 35 minutes.

Add peas. Cover tightly again and cook for 5–7 minutes. Stir gently before serving.

FRIED RICE

Some like fried rice with lots of colorful vegetables while others prefer it plain. This recipe works either way—most of the vegetables are optional. It calls for cooked rice so it's a great way to use the brown rice not eaten at a previous dinner.

SERVES 4–6

PREP TIME 45 MINUTES (WITHOUT OPTIONAL INGREDIENTS)

1 ½ tablespoons sesame oil or more if needed

3 cloves garlic, minced

6 green onions, thinly sliced

1 ½ tablespoons very finely minced fresh ginger

6 cups cold cooked rice

1 cup finely chopped red pepper (optional)

1 cup finely chopped carrot (optional)

1 cup fresh or thawed frozen green peas (optional)

2 teaspoons olive oil

3 eggs, beaten

¼ cup soy sauce or tamari

Heat sesame oil in wok or large cast iron skillet. Add garlic, onions, and ginger; cook for 2–3 minutes. Add rice and pepper, carrot, and peas if using. Cook about 5–7 minutes, until vegetables are a bit tender.

Move the rice back to the edges of the pan to make a 3-inch space in the center. Add oil to center of pan and heat. Add egg and scramble. When just cooked, stir egg into rice. Add soy sauce. Stir to thoroughly combine. Fry a bit more. Adjust seasoning and add more soy sauce if needed.

Soups

Soups are nurturing, grounding, and, because they're mostly liquid, easy to digest. There are two kinds—clear broth and pureed soups, which are creamier. Consider the season, outside temperature, and other dishes in the meal when choosing which kind of soup to make. In colder months, serve a thick, warm soup or for breakfast serve miso soup with vegetables. For a light summer meal, add fresh vegetables from the garden to a vegetable broth base.

Have you had several days of heavy meals? Choose a broth-based soup. Does everyone need a bit of nurturing? A thicker, heartier soup can provide this. In general, serve soups really, really hot, but use common sense—a boiling hot soup during summer is not a good idea.

Pureeing a soup makes it creamy without using dairy products. It's easiest to do this with a stick or immersion blender, although it can be done in a regular blender or VitaMix. Pureed soups often turn brown as the colors blend—sprinkle with freshly chopped herbs to add a bit of color.

Soups are a great dish to make ahead of time and serve over several days. Send some in a thermos for lunch. Or freeze the extra in serving-sized containers for easy re-heating.

Note: If you want to make a creamy soup without dairy: Blend a cup of macadamia nuts in a VitaMix blender with ¾ cup of water and blend until it becomes smooth and creamy. Add more water if you like a thinner consistency, or use less water to begin with if you like it thicker.

CARROT AND POTATO SOUP

It's creamy. It's orange. Your children like it. Your mother likes it. "Mmm, Mmm, Good." Don't forget to serve it with freshly baked whole wheat bread and lots of butter.

SERVES 6-8

4 cups peeled and chopped potatoes

4 cups peeled and chopped carrots

2 tablespoons safflower oil

½ cup rice or oat milk

1 small onion, chopped (optional)

Low sodium soy sauce to taste

Italian parsley, chopped

PREP TIME 1 HOUR

Cut carrots and potatoes into rounds and cubes no thicker than ¼ inch. Cook potatoes in boiling water until soft. Drain.

Heat safflower oil in a pan. Add carrots and onion. Sauté over medium heat for approximately 20 minutes or until soft.

Combine potatoes and carrots. Puree carrot/potato mixture with oat or rice milk in a food processor. If using a blender, puree the carrot/potato mixture with oat or rice milk, batch-by-batch, in small portions.

Season with soy sauce and garnish with chopped Italian parsley.

CARROT-ALMOND SOUP

This recipe makes a big pot of delicious soup so it's perfect for a large gathering or a holiday dinner. The almonds bring substance and a nutty flavor and make it a little creamy. Children like this soup. It might even become one of your family's favorites.

SERVES 10–15

1 large onion, chopped

2 tablespoons olive oil

10–12 large cloves of garlic, pressed or finely minced

10 cups carrots, chopped

2 cups celery, chopped

1–2 bell peppers (any color), chopped

Several bay leaves

Salt and pepper to taste

4 tablespoons fresh sage

1 tablespoon fresh thyme

Bragg Liquid Aminos

2 cups almonds

PREP TIME 1 HOUR 10 MINUTES

Sauté the onion in a large pot in olive oil. Add garlic. Sauté until brown. Add carrots. Once they are well-cooked, add celery, peppers, and enough water so that it covers vegetables plus an inch over them. Add several bay leaves, salt, and pepper in generous amounts, sage, thyme, and a good squeeze (about a tablespoon) of Bragg. Bring to a boil and simmer until carrots are very soft.

In a skillet with NO OIL, roast almonds. Once they are roasted, put a third of them in the blender and add water to cover the almonds. Blend until completely smooth—there should be no almond bits. Add water as necessary during this process. Do three separate batches and then set aside.

When the carrot soup part is well-cooked, remove bay leaves and blend the rest in batches in the blender until smooth. Add water if needed. Add carrot and almond mixes together. It should have a "creamy" look to it.

SPLIT PEA SOUP

This soup is so simple yet delicious. Our recommendation is to use green split peas because they will give your soup the color of summer grass. We use shitake mushrooms. When you store it in the refrigerator the soup gets thicker so add more water when reheating.

SERVES 12–15

5 cups green or yellow split peas

13 cups water

4–5 cups mushrooms, sliced

1 medium onion, chopped

1 tablespoon safflower oil

3 tablespoons shredded ginger

Sea salt to taste

PREP TIME 2 HOURS

Wash and sort peas (see *Cooking Beans* in *Main Dishes*, page 109). Simmer split peas in water until they are very soft, about 2 hours.

After split peas have been cooking for 1½ hours, in a separate pan sauté onion in safflower oil until soft. Add mushrooms. Sauté for another 3–4 minutes, until mushrooms are releasing liquid. Put onion-mushroom mixture in split peas.

Put ginger in a blender with a little water and blend until pasty. Add ginger to soup during last 5 minutes of cooking.

Add additional water to adjust consistency, if needed. Salt to taste.

Vegetable Broth

Vegetables like to be together and cooked in one pot. They give out all their nutrients and make a cleansing broth that is beneficial for the body. Drink it pure as a vegetable tonic or use it as stock for soups.

1 whole onion

1 daikon radish

4 carrots

1 bunch parsley

6 ribs celery

1 bunch hearty greens
(kale, mustard greens,
swiss chard, etc.)

Leeks (optional)

PREP TIME 2 HOURS 20 MINUTES

Fill a stock pot with water. Add whole, unchopped vegetables.

Bring to a boil, then simmer for 1½–2 hours.

Remove vegetables and compost them, as all the nutrients are in your stock.

Variation–See instructions for *Vegetable Broth* included in *White Bean Soup* recipe.

WHITE BEAN SOUP

One of our friends is from Arkansas. She visited one of us and made White Bean Soup. This is her recipe. When she brings this soup to the table people get excited. She says the key is "soft beans" (but not too soft). We take her word on this. For a burst of extra flavor, stir in a tablespoon of pesto (see *Pesto* in *Sauces, Spreads, and Dips*, page 181) just before serving.

SERVES 8

PREP TIME 3 HOURS

3 cups great northern beans

8 cups water

5-inch by 1-inch piece of dried kombu (seaweed)

1 small onion

2 stalks celery

3 carrots

1 clove garlic

¼ bunch flat-leaf parsley

2 bay leaves

1 large onion, chopped

1 clove garlic, minced

1 cup chopped celery

1½ cups diced potatoes

1 cup diced carrots

4 cups vegetable broth (see Note below)

Salt and pepper to taste

Tamari to taste

Soak beans in water overnight, drain, and rinse. Put beans in a large stockpot. Add water, kombu, onion, celery, carrots, garlic, parsley, and 1 bay leaf. Bring water to a boil then reduce heat, cover, and cook slowly for 2–3 hours or until beans are soft. When beans are tender, remove vegetables and compost them because their flavor and nutrients are in the broth.

Add chopped onion, garlic, chopped celery, diced potatoes, diced carrots, vegetable broth, 1 bay leaf, and salt and pepper to taste. Cover and cook over low heat for about 45 minutes or until vegetables are done. Add more liquid during cooking if needed. Adjust seasoning by adding salt, pepper, and tamari to taste. Remove bay leaf before serving.

Note–To make vegetable broth (*ingredients not in ingredient list above*)—While beans are cooking, in a separate pot, combine 1 onion, 3 carrots, 2 stalks celery, 1 clove garlic, ¼ bunch of parsley, 1 bay leaf, and 8 cups water. Bring water to a boil, then lower heat and simmer for an hour. Compost bay leaf and half of vegetables. Puree remaining vegetables in broth either with immersion blender or in blender or food processor. Use 4 cups in above recipe or chill (if it will be used in 2 or 3 days) or freeze until needed.

LENTIL SOUP

An Italian friend of ours gave us this recipe. In Italy, it is common to eat lentils over pasta. Lentils are an inexpensive source of protein and they come in several varieties and colors. When cooked, brown lentils hold their shape better than red lentils, so they're a good choice for soups. Over pasta or as a soup, this recipe works either way.

SERVES 4–5

1 cup brown lentils

8 cups water

2 bay leaves

1 yellow onion, chopped

2 tablespoons olive oil

2 or 3 stalks celery, cut in half lengthwise and chopped

2 carrots, diced (optional)

1 small potato, chopped (optional)

2–3 tablespoons dried oregano (use more if using fresh)

1½ teaspoons ground cumin

3 tablespoons chopped fresh parsley, plus more at the end

Salt and pepper to taste

Tamari (optional)

1–2 (14.5 ounce) cans diced tomatoes (optional)

Tabasco (optional)

PREP TIME 55 MINUTES

Sort and wash lentils (see *Cooking Beans* in *Main Dishes,* page 109). Put in large pot with water and bay leaves. Bring to boil and let simmer for 30–45 minutes, until softened. If more water is needed as lentils cook, add boiling water.

In a large pan, sauté onion in olive oil until almost clear. Add celery and, if using, carrots and potato, and continue sautéing, stirring frequently, until vegetables begin to soften. Add herbs and either ½ cup water or a mixture of water and tamari to equal about ½ cup. Add diced tomatoes, if using, and pour over sauté. Cover and simmer over medium to medium-low heat for about 5 minutes or until vegetable are tender.

When lentils are soft, add the sautéed vegetables, mix well, and adjust seasonings, adding more salt, pepper, tamari, and Tabasco, if using, to taste. Simmer for a few minutes. Add more boiling water if soup is too thick. Remove bay leaves before serving.

Note–All stages of this diet have gradients. If you are still easing into Stage 3 this recipe is appropriate. If you are eating a pure Stage 3 diet, omit the canned tomatoes or substitute diced and peeled fresh tomatoes.

Miso Soup

It takes some practice to make good miso soup, because you need just the right amount of miso for the soup to be tasty, but not too strong. This recipe helps you hit the mark. It's worth the effort when you eat this nurturing, elegant broth which can be served with a little tofu, some seaweed, and a few mushrooms; the broth should not be overcrowded. It needs to be served hot, but should not boil because this kills the enzymes. It's good to heat the serving bowls before filling.

SERVES 4

½ of a 6-inch piece of kombu seaweed

¾ cup dried shiitake mushrooms

6–8 cups water

½ cup red miso

Tamari to taste

2/3 of a block of tofu, small diced

3 chopped scallions for garnish

PREP TIME 25 MINUTES

Soak kombu and dried mushrooms in water in a pot for a few hours. Pull out kombu and mushrooms and slice thinly, then return to water. Bring to boil and simmer for 10 minutes or so.

Put 1–2 cups of this broth in a bowl; dissolve miso in broth. Pour this mixture back into soup pot, heating, but being careful not to let boil. Add tamari to taste.

Put diced tofu in the bottom of heated soup bowls and pour soup over it. Garnish with scallions or serve them on the side.

If serving from pot, add tofu and let it warm. Serve scallions on the side.

HOT AND SOUR SOUP

This Asian standard is a bit spicy. Add udon noodles for a noodle soup. Noodles tend to soak up broth so don't put in too many otherwise you end up with a bunch of noodles and little broth.

SERVES 4

PREP TIME 40 MINUTES

1 ounce dried shitake mushrooms (about 5 mushrooms)

1½ cup water

2 tablespoons olive oil

1 small onion, sliced thinly in rounds and then cut in half for half moons

2 carrots, thinly sliced in rounds

2 tablespoons minced fresh ginger

1–2 cloves garlic, minced

6 cups vegetable (not tomato-based) broth

2 tablespoons soy sauce or tamari

¼ cup rice wine vinegar

1–2 tablespoons sesame oil

2 dashes chile (also called chili) oil

Soak shitake mushrooms in the 1½ cups water.

Heat 2 tablespoons oil in a heavy pot over medium heat. Add onion and carrots; cook, stirring constantly, for 3 minutes. Add garlic and ginger; cook, stirring for 1 minute.

Pull shitake mushrooms out of the water, squeeze (into a bowl), and slice into thin slices. If using fresh mushrooms, no need to soak. Just slice them. Take shitake water (if using dried mushrooms), broth, and soy or tamari sauce, and add to soup. Bring to a boil and cook for 2 minutes. Add mushrooms and boil for 1 minute.

Turn off heat. Cover and let rest for 2 minutes. Stir in rice wine vinegar, sesame oil, and chile oil. Heat through for 1 minute, serve immediately.

SOUTHWESTERN CORN AND POTATO SOUP

You don't have to be from Texas to like this satisfying soup. The cilantro, chiles, and corn lend a robust flavor. Leave your hat on or take it off.

SERVES 4 AS SIDE DISH;
2 AS A MAIN DISH

1 cup onions, finely chopped

2 garlic cloves, minced or pressed

1 small fresh chile, seeded and minced

¼ teaspoon salt

4 cups vegetable broth, more or less as needed

2 teaspoons ground cumin

2 cups sweet potato, diced into small pieces

1 small red bell pepper, finely chopped

3 cups fresh corn kernels (see Note below)

Cilantro, finely chopped (optional)

PREP TIME 1 HOUR

In a covered soup pot, simmer onions, garlic, chile, and salt in 1 cup vegetable stock for about 10 minutes, or until onions are soft.

In a small bowl, make a paste with cumin and 1 tablespoon broth. Stir into mixture in the soup pot and simmer for another 1–2 minutes. Add sweet potatoes and remaining broth and simmer for about 15–20 minutes, until sweet potatoes soften.

Add bell pepper and corn and simmer, covered, for another 10 minutes, or until vegetables are tender.

Puree about half of the soup in a blender or food processor or with an immersion blender and return to pot.

Soup will be creamy and thick. Add another cup vegetable broth if desired. Salt to taste. Gently reheat on low heat.

Top with chopped cilantro.

Note–If corn is out of season, for Stage 2, substitute frozen corn kernels.

VEGETABLE-BARLEY SOUP

Barley feels soft and round in your mouth and thickens the soup a bit. It's a nutritious grain and together with fresh vegetables warms you from the inside out.

SERVES 4–6

4 tomatoes, quartered

3 cloves garlic, minced

1 cup chopped onions

1½ quarts water

2 medium potatoes, cut into
1-inch cubes

1/3 cup barley

2 teaspoons dried basil

1 teaspoon chopped parsley

¼ teaspoon black pepper

½ teaspoon sea salt

2 cups sliced zucchini

3 carrots, sliced

3 stalks celery, diced

½ pound green beans, cut into
1-inch pieces

Sunflower seeds

PREP TIME 1 ½ HOURS

Puree tomatoes and garlic in blender. Pour into large pot, add onions. Cook for 5 minutes on medium heat.

Add water, potatoes, barley, and spices. Cook until barley is almost done. Add all remaining vegetables. Cook on low heat until vegetables are just tender. Add additional salt if needed.

Garnish with sunflower seeds.

Vegetable Garden Chowder

This recipe originated at The Vegetable Garden, a vegetarian restaurant owned by our friends in Little Rock in the '90s. It's called chowder because it's a little creamy from the oat or rice milk and the corn. It has the sweetness that we remember from the creamed corn we grew up with.

SERVES 8

PREP TIME 2 HOURS (WITHOUT SOAKING TIME)

3 cups dried baby lima beans

1 large potato, cut into large pieces

2 cups chopped onion

3–4 cloves garlic, minced

3 stalks celery, minced

1 teaspoon basil

½ teaspoon chopped rosemary

1 tablespoon safflower oil

3 cups corn

1 cup oat or rice milk

1 cup vegetable stock

1 teaspoon salt or to taste

Pepper to taste

Soak lima beans overnight, or cover lima beans with water, bring to a boil, turn off heat and let stand, covered, for 1 hour.

Drain, then re-cover lima beans with cold water and bring to a boil in a 4-quart soup pot. Simmer for 1½–2 hours, or until tender.

Cook potato in boiling water until tender.

While lima beans are cooking, sauté onion, garlic, celery, basil, and rosemary in safflower oil in a skillet.

When lima beans are soft, add onion mixture, potato, corn, oat or rice milk, and vegetable stock. Add pepper and salt to taste.

White Bean Stew with Tomatoes, Garlic, and Sage

"Tuscany, come into my kitchen!"

SERVES 4

PREP TIME 2 HOURS (WITHOUT SOAKING TIME)

1 pound dry white beans

3 tablespoons safflower oil

2 cloves garlic, crushed

5 leaves fresh sage, chopped, or 1 teaspoon ground sage

Coarsely ground black pepper to taste

Sea salt to taste

2 tablespoons cumin (optional)

4 large tomatoes, peeled and chopped, or one (14.5 ounce) can diced tomatoes, drained

Cover beans with water and soak overnight. Drain (discard soaking water) and put in a large pot with fresh water to cover. Simmer beans for 1–2 hours, until tender. Add water as needed. Add salt to taste when beans are just tender. Continue cooking for 15 minutes longer.

During last 15 minutes of cooking, heat safflower oil in a large skillet and add garlic, sage, pepper, salt, and cumin. Sauté until garlic begins to change color.

Add beans and liquid to hot skillet. Stir in tomatoes and simmer for 20 minutes. Add salt if necessary.

Note–For Stage 3, use fresh tomatoes instead of canned tomatoes.

TOMATO-COCONUT SOUP

This is a favorite for many children. It is tomatoey, creamy, sweet, and salty. The honey cuts the acidity of the tomatoes. Blend the diced tomatoes to give this soup its characteristic texture.

SERVES 6–8

PREP TIME 45 MINUTES

4 cups coconut milk

2 teaspoons onion powder

½ teaspoon garlic powder

½ teaspoon salt

¼ teaspoon dried chopped oregano or ¾ teaspoon fresh chopped oregano

½ teaspoon dried basil or 1½ teaspoons chopped fresh basil

1 tablespoon dried parsley or 3 tablespoons chopped fresh parsley

1 tablespoon honey

8 cups diced or crushed tomatoes

Blend coconut milk, seasonings, herbs, and honey until smooth. Pour into large saucepan. Add tomatoes. Simmer for 20–30 minutes for the flavors to blend.

Blend until smooth or to desired consistency with immersion blender or in blender.

PUMPKIN-COCONUT SOUP

This was originally a Thai recipe that we adapted. If you puree the cooked pumpkin in a blender make sure you don't fill the blender too full because the hot pumpkin could explode out of the top. (We learned this the hard way.) You need to blend it batch by batch. Better yet, use a stick blender (immersion blender) right in the pot.

SERVES 4–6

3–4 tablespoons safflower oil

1/3 medium red onion, minced

2 cloves garlic, pressed

2–3 teaspoons dried basil

1 medium-size orange pumpkin, peeled, cut into bite-sized pieces

1 quart vegetable broth, or enough to cover pumpkin pieces

1 can coconut milk

Sea salt to taste

Pepper to taste

2 tablespoons low sodium soy sauce

5–6 fresh basil leaves, sliced (optional)

PREP TIME 1 ½ HOURS

Heat oil in a soup pot. Add onion, garlic, and basil, and cook until onion becomes clear.

Add pumpkin. Add vegetable broth to barely cover pumpkin pieces, cover pot, and bring to a boil. Reduce heat and simmer until pumpkin pieces are very soft, about 10–15 minutes.

Puree in a blender or food processor until creamy. Put back into pot, add coconut milk and water (if needed) to desired consistency. Add salt, pepper and soy sauce. Simmer for 10–15 minutes.

Spoon into bowls, garnish with sliced basil leaves if using, and serve.

German Hokkaido Pumpkin Soup

Some people in Germany make this warming fall soup when pumpkins are in season. Hokkaido pumpkin is also known as kabocha squash. If these aren't available, you can use acorn or delicata squash. Ginger gives the soup a little zing, but if you want it spicier, add crushed red pepper. Garnish with toasted sunflower seeds and, if you want, a dollop of yogurt topped with chopped green onion.

Serves 9

Prep time 1 ¾ hours

¼ cup olive oil

1 small to medium-sized onion, chopped

2 cloves garlic, minced

1 stalk celery, halved and sliced

1-inch long piece of ginger, peeled and minced

1 teaspoon cumin

1 teaspoon garam masala

1 heaping teaspoon curry

Juice of 2 oranges

8½ cups vegetable broth

2 pounds hokkaido pumpkin, peeled, seeded, and cut into pieces

3 cups peeled, diced, russet (mealy) potatoes

2 cups carrots, peeled, cut into pieces

1 pinch cinnamon

1 tablespoon soy sauce

1 teaspoon salt or more according to taste

Toasted sunflower seeds, to garnish (see *Nuts and Seeds*, page 201)

Heat olive oil in a soup pot. Sauté onion, garlic, celery, and ginger until onions are translucent and begin to brown. Add cumin, garam masala, and curry. Sauté briefly. Add orange juice, broth, pumpkin pieces, potatoes, and carrots. Cook everything for 30 minutes until soft.

Puree with immersion blender to desired consistency. Add cinnamon, soy sauce, and salt according to taste.

Garnish with toasted sunflower seeds.

CHICKPEA STEW

The literal translation of "chickpeas" into German is "giggling peas." They are also called garbanzo beans. The onions, olives, tomatoes, and herbs give this stew a Mediterranean flavor. If you brown the onions with the herbs the aroma comes out even more. (Careful, this is easy to burn.) Serve with fresh green salad and hot basmati rice. This stew will probably not make you giggle but it will fill you and satisfy your taste buds.

SERVES 4–6

1 pound dried chickpeas, soaked overnight, then cooked for 2½ hours

3 tablespoons safflower oil

1 large red onion, chopped

1 teaspoon dried basil

1 teaspoon dried chopped oregano

1 pound mushrooms, rinsed and cut into quarters

1 can black olives, drained and sliced

2 cloves garlic, minced

3 tablespoons low sodium soy sauce

2 (15 ounce) cans diced tomatoes or more, not drained

2 bay leaves

Salt

Pepper

PREP TIME 3 HOURS (WITHOUT SOAKING TIME)

Soak chickpeas overnight. (See *Cooking Beans*, page 109) Drain and rinse. Cook for 2½ hours or until tender.

Heat oil in a large pot and sauté onions, basil, and oregano for 3–5 minutes. Add mushrooms and sauté over medium to high heat.

Add olives, garlic, and soy sauce and cook down for another 5 minutes. Add tomatoes, bay leaves, and chickpeas. Let simmer for 15 minutes or more. Add salt and pepper to taste. Remove bay leaves before serving.

YAM AND GARBANZO BEAN SOUP

This soup is wonderfully soft in your mouth. The yams give the soup a creamy texture and the spinach leaves add their softness. A warming winter meal.

SERVES 6–8

PREP TIME 2 ½ HOURS (WITHOUT SOAKING TIME)

2 cups dried garbanzo beans
(or 6 cups cooked)

4 medium yams, peeled and
cut into 1-inch cubes

3 medium tomatoes, diced,
or 1 (15 ounce) can diced
tomatoes

4 big handfuls spinach,
chopped

1 teaspoon dried thyme

2 tablespoons olive oil

1 yellow or white onion, diced

2 cloves garlic, minced

Sea salt to taste

If using dried garbanzo beans, cook them in water until tender, about 1½–2 hours (See *Cooking Beans*, page 109).

Put yams in a large pot and only just cover with water. Boil until tender, about 15 minutes.

Puree 2/3 of garbanzo beans and 1 cup water. Add garbanzo bean puree to yams. Add diced tomatoes and whole garbanzo beans and bring to a boil.

Add spinach, lower heat, and simmer for 5 minutes. Add thyme. Sauté onion and minced garlic in oil in small fry pan until tender. Add to soup. Add salt to taste.

Note–For Stage 3, use fresh tomatoes instead of canned.

ADUKI-SQUASH STEW

Aduki beans, which are also called adzuki or azuki beans, are small reddish-brown beans. They have a strong nutty sweet flavor and are used frequently in a macrobiotic diet. You can buy them at Asian markets or in many health food stores.

SERVES 4

PREP TIME 2 HOURS (WITHOUT SOAKING TIME)

2 cups rice

1½ cups dried aduki beans, washed

5 cups water

3-inch piece of kombu seaweed (look for in same store section as nori, the sushi seaweed)

1 small butternut squash (2 cups)

Shoyu, low sodium soy sauce, or tamari to taste

Begin cooking rice. (See *Grains*, page 136)

Place beans, water, and kombu in a separate 2-quart pot and bring to a boil. Reduce heat, cover, and simmer for 30 minutes.

Chop squash into rounds and cut off peel. Discard seeds. Cut into small chunks and arrange on top of beans, making sure beans are still covered with water. Cover and continue cooking for another 30 minutes. Stir periodically. Add more water if needed so that beans are covered with water.

Mix squash into beans. Remove kombu and discard. Add shoyu, soy sauce, or tamari and cook for 15 more minutes. Add shoyu, soy sauce, or tamari to taste. Ladle bean mixture into bowls over rice.

GARDEN VEGETABLE SOUP

The freshness and bright full flavors of just-picked, sautéed summer vegetables bring a light but deep flavor to this soup. It's best in summer but can be made any time of the year.

SERVES 10–12

2 tablespoons olive oil

2 tablespoons butter

2 large sweet onions, finely chopped

6 stalks celery, finely chopped

2 cloves garlic, minced

1½ pounds carrots, peeled and cut into thin rounds

2 handfuls thin green beans, cut into 1-inch pieces

Additional butter and olive oil

Sea salt and pepper to taste

3 pounds new potatoes, cut into bite-sized pieces, or regular potatoes, peeled and cut into bite-sized pieces

4 large ears organic corn or 1 12-oz. bag frozen organic corn

2 bay leaves

PREP TIME 1 ½ HOURS

Heat olive oil and butter in a stock pot. Add onion and celery and sauté, stirring occasionally. After a while, there should be browning on bottom of pan but vegetables shouldn't turn brown and they should not be scorching or burning.

Add garlic and sauté another minute or two. Add carrots and green beans and continue sautéing. Add small amounts of oil and butter as needed. Add salt and pepper to taste. Add potatoes; continue stirring and sautéing.

In summer, use fresh corn cut off cob. Scrape "milk" from corn cob and add to vegetables along with corn; stir. Continue to cook over low heat. Add bay leaves.

When vegetables are just tender, add water to cover. Stir. Make sure to loosen the browned (not scorched or burned) bits from bottom of pan—this gives flavor to the broth. Simmer for 20–30 minutes. Add more salt and pepper if needed. Remove bay leaves before serving.

MUSHROOM AND BOK CHOY SOUP

This recipe was invented when we cooked for a large group. It was an important time for the people who gathered, and a soup of onions, cabbage, and mushrooms was requested by one of the honored guests. Since we couldn't find a recipe to fit their request, we created this soup. It has a bit of an Asian taste. Baby portobello mushrooms and shitake mushrooms blend with bok choy to make the soup grounding and nourishing.

SERVES 12

PREP TIME 1 ¾ HOURS

VEGETABLE BROTH

3 carrots, cut in chunks

4 stalks celery, cut in chunks

1 onion, quartered

1 clove garlic

1 handful fresh flat-leaf parsley

2 bay leaves

Salt and pepper to taste

4 quarts water

MUSHROOM/BOK CHOY COMBINATION:

2 tablespoons butter

2 tablespoons extra virgin olive oil

2 medium onions, chopped

3 stalks celery, chopped

1½ pounds baby portobello mushrooms, cut in half and sliced

½ pound shitake mushrooms, sliced

1 tablespoon butter

1 tablespoon extra virgin olive oil

¼ head white cabbage, sliced and cut into 1-inch pieces

1 medium head bok choy, sliced

3 tablespoons soy sauce or tamari

Vegetable Broth–Put all ingredients in large stock pot. Bring to a boil; lower heat. Simmer one hour.

Remove and discard bay leaves. Remove half of vegetables and compost. Puree remaining vegetables and broth with immersion blender.

Mushroom and Bok Choy combination–Melt 2 tablespoons butter in a large skillet. Add 2 tablespoons oil. Sauté onion and celery until tender. Add mushrooms. Sauté until tender and liquid from mushrooms evaporates. Add to broth in stockpot.

In remaining butter and oil, sauté cabbage and bok choy for about 5 minutes, or until barely tender. Add to broth. Add soy sauce. Stir. Season with salt and pepper. Simmer for 20–30 minutes.

BREADS

All breads at Stages 1, 2, and 3 should be whole-grain, not made from white flour, as it is highly processed. In Stage 2 of the diet we begin to limit the use of bread and by Stage 3 it is for special occasions only. We've included a few recipes for breakfast breads and cornbread that are great for those times. Also, sometimes on a cold winter's night a steaming bowl of White Bean Soup and a chunk of hot cornbread makes the perfect hearty meal.

Because grains contain phytic acid which blocks the absorption of minerals, their flours do as well. The complex starches and sugars in grain flours remain intact and are difficult to digest. Also, the cellulose in grains is a great source of minerals but we can't absorb it.

There are two methods for overcoming these problems—fermenting and sprouting. Fermented breads are also called sourdough. The process of soaking flour for at least 12 hours (24 is better) in either (1) a cultured dairy product (buttermilk or yogurt, for example—also called soured dairy), or (2) water with a small amount of cultured dairy or vinegar or lemon juice, breaks down phytic acid. The lactobacilli in soured dairy breaks down the starches and sugars. The process of fermentation breaks down the cellulose, making its nutrients available to us in a form we can absorb. Sprouting a grain before grinding it into flour also eliminates these problems.

Modern sourdough- and bread-making techniques have done away with the fermentation process, replacing it with the faster and more reliable yeast-culture process. This process, however, produces an alcoholic fermentation, which destroys some of the nutrients and is not acidic enough to remove phytic acid or break down starches, sugars, and cellulose in the same way.

This is why we recommend traditionally-made sourdough breads and breads made from sprouted grains, like Ezekiel bread. Many health-food stores are beginning to sell traditionally-fermented sourdough. Make sure the breads you buy are whole-grain, not made from overly-processed white flour. If you would like to make your own traditional sourdough bread, there is a recipe for the starter and the bread in *Nourishing Traditions* by Sally Fallon (Newtrends Publishing, Inc., 2nd Edition: Warsaw, Indiana, 1999).

There are many gluten-free breads made from grains such as millet and brown rice available in stores but use these sparingly. They are heavily processed.

To make your own gluten-free breads it's best to have a gluten-free baking book, but a good all-purpose gluten-free flour mixture is 1 cup rice flour, ¾ cup potato starch, and ¼ cup tapioca starch/flour (from http://www.csaceliacs.org/recipes/FlourFormulas.php). This is a one-for-one replacement for gluten flours, which means if the recipe calls for one cup of wheat flour, substitute one cup of this flour. The mix you use will depend on what type of cooking you are doing. See http://www.csaceliacs.org/recipes/FlourFormulas.php for more mixtures.

A note on baking powder—several of these recipes call for this ingredient. Make sure to use an aluminum-free baking powder like Rumford, which is also gluten-free and uses non-GMO cornstarch.

CORNBREAD (GLUTEN-FREE)

To make your bean soup perfect, serve cornbread. No one will know this one is gluten-free. It's the old-fashioned kind—with a course texture and baked in a cast iron skillet. It's hard to find something better than a hot wedge dripping with melted butter. If you like your cornbread spicy, chop up a few jalapenos and add them to the batter. Sliced jalapenos served on the side could also be a welcome addition.

SERVES 8

PREP TIME 1 HOUR

2 cups stone-ground cornmeal

1 teaspoon baking soda

2 teaspoons baking powder

1 teaspoon sea salt

1¾ cup milk

1 egg

1½ teaspoons apple cider vinegar

2 tablespoons honey or agave syrup (optional)

¼ cup melted butter

1 cup fresh or thawed, frozen corn, chopped

Preheat oven to 400°F. Heat cast iron skillet in oven for 10 minutes.

Combine dry ingredients in a mixing bowl.

Combine milk, egg, vinegar, and honey or agave, if using, in a medium bowl. Pour into dry ingredients and stir to combine. Fold corn into batter.

Carefully remove hot skillet from oven. Coat bottom and sides of skillet with butter. Pour excess butter into batter; stir just to combine. Pour batter into skillet. Bake for 25-35 minutes or until golden brown.

Turn skillet upside down onto wooden cutting board. Cornbread should release from pan. Cut into wedges. Serve hot with butter.

CORN MUFFINS

These corn muffins have a more delicate texture than cornbread. If you use grapeseed oil, which has a bit of a buttery taste, instead of butter, they are vegan. Savoring one while still hot, with melted butter, will make you feel that you are in the right place at the right time.

MAKES 12 MUFFINS

1 cup cornmeal

1 cup whole-wheat pastry flour

1 teaspoon baking soda

1 teaspoon sea salt

1 cup applesauce

1 cup almond milk

½ cup honey

½ cup melted butter or grapeseed oil

PREP TIME 45 MINUTES

Preheat oven to 350°F. Butter or oil a 12 unit, regular size muffin pan. Combine cornmeal, flour, baking soda, and salt in a large bowl. Add applesauce, almond milk, and honey. Stir. Add butter or oil; stir to combine. Fill each unit ¾ full with the batter.

Bake until a toothpick inserted in center of muffin comes out clean, about 12–15 minutes.

MAPLE-PECAN SCONES

Scones originated in Scotland. They make a delicious addition to a special breakfast anywhere in the world. We love the combination of maple syrup and pecans in this recipe. The maple syrup also gives just the right amount of sweetness. We have doubled and tripled this recipe with great success. Substitute a gluten-free flour blend for the whole-wheat flour if needed.

MAKES 8–16 SCONES
DEPENDING ON SIZE

3½ cups sifted whole wheat pastry flour or gluten-free all-purpose flour

1 cup finely chopped pecans

4 teaspoons baking powder

1 teaspoon salt

2/3 cup softened butter

1 cup (more with whole wheat flour) rice or almond milk

1/3 cup + 3 tablespoons Grade B maple syrup

PREP TIME 1 HOUR

Preheat oven to 425°F.

In a large bowl, combine flour, chopped pecans, baking powder, and salt. With pastry blender or 2 knives, cut in butter until mixture resembles coarse crumbs.

Put 2/3 cup milk in a bowl. Add 1/3 cup maple syrup to milk and add to dry ingredients. Mix lightly with a fork until the mixture clings together and forms a soft dough. Drizzle and work in more milk if necessary to make dough workable and the right consistency.

Turn dough out onto lightly floured surface or pastry cloth and knead gently 5 or 6 times. Divide in half. With lightly floured rolling pin, roll one half of dough into a 7-inch round. Cut into pie wedges. Repeat with remaining half of dough.

Place scones 1 inch apart on baking sheet. Pierce tops with a fork and brush with remaining maple syrup.

Bake 15–18 minutes or until golden brown. Brush with remaining maple syrup. Serve warm.

WHOLE WHEAT BANANA BREAD

What is a cookbook without a good Banana Bread recipe? This is a healthier version than those you'll find in most cookbooks. It uses whole-wheat pastry flour instead of white flour and is sweetened with honey. It's a great way to use up bananas that are turning brown.

MAKES 1 LOAF

3 large ripe bananas, mashed

1¾ cups whole wheat pastry flour

2 teaspoons baking powder

¼ teaspoon baking soda

½ teaspoon salt

1 teaspoon cinnamon

1/3 cup butter, room temperature

2/3 cup honey

1 egg

PREP TIME 1 HOUR TO 1 HOUR 15 MINUTES

Preheat oven to 350°F.

Mix all ingredients well, so there are no lumps. Put in greased loaf pan. Bake for 45–60 minutes or until knife inserted in center comes out clean. Remove from oven and place on a wire rack to cool. When pan is no longer too hot to touch, remove banana bread from pan. Cool. Slice and serve.

BANANA BREAD MUFFINS (GLUTEN-FREE)

We love having delicious recipes that just happen to be gluten-free. This one is good enough to serve to family and friends. We make this banana bread in muffin pans which works well with the gluten-free flours and makes serving easy. This is a versatile recipe—you can make it by hand or in a food processor.

This recipe calls for xanthan gum, which is derived from corn sugar. This white powder looks a lot like baking powder and is used in similar amounts. Invaluable in gluten-free baking, it provides elasticity and helps to prevent dryness and crumbling. It can be found in natural food stores.

Almond and coconut flours are also often used in gluten-free baking and are available at health food stores. It is good to keep these ingredients at hand, since many gluten-free baking recipes call for them.

MAKES ABOUT 2 DOZEN MUFFINS

2 cups almond flour

½ cup coconut flour, sifted

1 teaspoon xanthan gum

4 teaspoons baking powder

½ teaspoon baking soda

½ teaspoon sea salt

1 teaspoon cinnamon

3 large ripe bananas, mashed

½ cup butter, room temperature

2/3 cup agave syrup

4 eggs

1 cup chopped pecans (optional)

Pecan halves (optional)

PREP TIME 50 MINUTES

Preheat oven to 350°F. Butter muffin pans.

Combine almond flour, sifted coconut flour, xanthan gum, baking powder, baking soda, salt, and cinnamon in medium bowl. In a separate bowl, combine bananas, butter, agave syrup, and eggs. Add to dry ingredients. Mix well so there are no lumps. Fold in chopped pecans if using.

Fill muffin pans ¾ full. Top with pecan half if desired. Bake for 20–25 minutes, until golden brown and toothpick inserted in center comes out clean.

Note—You can prepare using a food processor if desired. Puree the bananas; add butter and process until combined. Add agave syrup and process. Add eggs and process. Add dry ingredients and pulse a few times until combined. Stir in the nuts by hand and it's ready to bake in a matter of minutes.

BASIC MUFFINS

Use this recipe to make basic muffins, served hot from the oven with butter, or spice up a special breakfast with the variations for Lemon or Ginger Muffins.

MAKES ABOUT 15 MUFFINS

3 cups whole wheat flour

2 cups buttermilk or yogurt

2 eggs lightly beaten

1 teaspoon sea salt

¼ cup Grade B maple syrup

2 teaspoons baking soda

1 teaspoon vanilla extract

3 tablespoons melted butter

PREP TIME 45 MINUTES (WITHOUT SOAKING TIME)

Preheat oven to 325°F.

Soak flour in buttermilk or yogurt in a warm place for 12–24 hours (see introduction to *Breads*). Muffins will rise better if flour is soaked for 24 hours. Blend in remaining ingredients. Pour into well-buttered muffin tins, filling about ¾ full. Bake for about 25–30 minutes or until a toothpick comes out clean.

Variations–Lemon Muffins–Add grated rind of 2 lemons and ½ cup chopped pecans.

Ginger Muffins–Add 1 tablespoon freshly grated ginger and 1 teaspoon ground ginger. Omit vanilla.

APPLE, DATE, AND OATMEAL MUFFINS

Another healthy muffin recipe. If you are trying to limit your and your family's intake of processed sugars, these muffins are perfect because this recipe doesn't use any sugar. The sweetness comes from the dates.

MAKES 12 MUFFINS

1½ cups whole wheat
pastry flour

½ teaspoon cinnamon

Pinch of ground cloves

3 teaspoons baking powder

½ cup rolled oats

1 cup chopped pitted dates

1/3 cup oil

2 eggs

1/3 cup water or rice or
almond milk

¾ cup grated apple
(1 medium apple)

PREP TIME 50 MINUTES

Preheat oven to 375°F.

Sift together flour, spices, and baking powder. Add rolled oats and dates and mix well.

In separate bowl, beat together oil and eggs. Beat in milk then add the apple. Mix well.

Stir the flour mixture into the wet mixture just enough to mix; don't overbeat.

Spoon batter into well-oiled muffin tins. Bake for 20 minutes or until golden brown.

CRANBERRY MUFFINS

These muffins are a little tart because of the cranberries but this is nicely balanced by the sweetness of the maple syrup. Fresh cranberries are available in autumn.

MAKES 12 SMALL MUFFINS

1½ cups whole wheat pastry flour

1 tablespoon baking powder

¾ cup Grade B maple syrup

3 tablespoons oil

2 eggs

¼ cup milk or rice milk

1 teaspoon vanilla

1 cup whole cranberries

½ cup chopped pecans (optional)

PREP TIME 45 MINUTES

Preheat oven to 350°F.

Sift together flour and baking powder.

In separate bowl, beat together maple syrup, oil, eggs, milk, and vanilla.

Stir dry ingredients into liquid ingredients. Beat enough to blend well, but don't overbeat. Fold in cranberries and pecans, if using. Spoon mixture into well-oiled muffin tins until they are ¾ full.

Bake for 15 minutes or until toothpick inserted into the center of a muffin comes out clean.

SAUCES, SPREADS, AND DIPS

Sauces, spreads, and dips enhance a meal partly by giving it more flavor. They also tie dishes together. For example, when we think of a vegetable and a grain, we think of them as separate. But Tahini Sauce brings steamed broccoli and rice together deliciously.

Sauces, spreads, and dips are also a great way to bring more raw foods into our diet—a few cut-up raw vegetables and a dip can be added to any meal. Be careful because we don't want to bury a fresh vegetable under a lot of sauce.

It's easy to experiment and create your own recipes. Grind different nuts into flour in a blender and add water, vinegar or lemon juice, oil, different spices, and fresh herbs to make an original sauce.

Except for *Guacamole*, it's best to make the raw dips and spreads with a food processor or a heavy-duty blender such as a VitaMix. Some regular blenders will work but for the most part they are not designed for these recipes.

WHITE MISO SAUCE

This sauce came into our repertoire sixteen years ago when I, Tika, was cooking for the first time for a large group of people. Working non-stop to prepare meals at a retreat center and running on an average of three hours of sleep every night, I remember the moment I finally tasted the white miso sauce over steamed broccoli—somehow the simplicity of this dish made all the effort worth it.

MAKES 2½ TO 3 CUPS

PREP TIME 10 MINUTES

4 cloves garlic, peeled and squeezed

¾ cup white miso

1 cup olive oil

½ cup apple cider vinegar

½ cup apple juice

Put all the ingredients in a blender and blend. If you like it thinner, add more water.

Note–For Stage 3, use fresh apple juice.

NUT PÂTÉ

Several years ago we experimented a lot with raw food dishes. Tika invented a bunch of hearty nut pâtés because we needed something more filling to serve that was raw. Nut pâtés go well with salad, and in this recipe you can substitute other nuts such as cashews or pine nuts. You can also experiment with spices and flavors; for example, dulse, fresh herbs, or dried dates. These additions may require a little water to achieve the desired consistency.

SERVES 4

PREP TIME 15 MINUTES

1 cup almonds, soaked (or 1 cup walnuts, soaked)

3 green onions, cut into small pieces

½ red bell pepper, minced

Lemon juice to taste

Salt to taste

Cayenne pepper to taste

Put everything in a food processor and blend into a paste

TAHINI SAUCE

③

Tahini is a paste of ground sesame seeds used for cooking in North Africa and the Middle East. We love this Tahini Sauce because it completes grains and vegetables to make a satisfying meal. Sometimes tahini, especially if it is raw, can taste just a little bitter. Experiment with different kinds. Our favorite is roasted tahini because it's nuttier tasting and less bitter, but it's not raw. The best recipe for tahini sauce is John's Tahini Dressing in *May All Be Fed: Diet for a New World* (Harper Perennial: New York, New York, 1993). Ours is a close second.

MAKES ABOUT 2 CUPS, DEPENDING ON AMOUNT OF WATER USED

1 cup tahini (see Note below)

1/3 cup warm water or more, depending on thickness desired

Juice of ½ lemon or 1–2 tablespoons apple cider vinegar

2 cloves garlic, crushed and minced

Salt and Pepper

PREP TIME 15 MINUTES

Add some warm water to tahini and stir until creamy. Right after it gets creamy it gets firm again. Add as much water as needed for it to be creamy but not too watery.

Add all other ingredients and stir until everything is well blended.

Pour over baked potatoes or steamed broccoli or other steamed vegetables. It is also good as a dip for raw veggie sticks.

Note–For Stage 3, use homemade *Tahini* (see recipe in *Nuts and Seeds*, page 202) or a good quality tahini from a natural food store.

TURKISH YOGURT MINT SAUCE

I (Tika) spent a week at the Turkish Coast and had the pleasure of every meal being served with a variety of Turkish appetizers—tomato cucumber salad, lentil salad, different types of olives, baked and marinated vegetables, and the always-at-hand and most delicious Yogurt Mint Sauce. I had it for break-fast, lunch, and dinner and never got tired of it!

SERVES 4

2 cups yogurt

3 tablespoons finely chopped fresh mint

¾ teaspoons salt

¼ teaspoon pepper

PREP TIME 15 MINUTES

Whisk the yogurt until smooth. Add mint, salt, and pepper. Mix well.

Serve with eggplant slices, with baked or raw vegetables, or as a side dish with a Mediterranean dinner.

RAITA

Raita is an Indian yogurt dish that is served with basmati rice, daal and vegetables. The freshness of the yogurt balances the spiciness of typical Indian food. There are many different kinds of raita, each one using different spice combinations. This is a basic recipe.

MAKES ABOUT 2 CUPS

1 cup plain yogurt, stirred

Juice of one lemon

½ cup very finely chopped red onion

½ cup very finely chopped cucumber

Sea salt and pepper to taste

Pinch of cayenne (optional)

Finely chopped cilantro or mint (optional)

PREP TIME 15 MINUTES

Add ingredients together, mix, and serve. You can make the raita thicker by adding more yogurt or thinner by adding water.

TZAZIKI SAUCE

In the 1980s in Germany, *Tzaziki Sauce* was the party food that people often brought to a potluck dinner. The only disadvantage is the amount of garlic. Needless to say, the consumption of this much garlic sometimes interfered with the desired amount of kissing.

SERVES 8

2 English cucumbers

1 container (about 32 ounces) plain Greek yogurt

3–4 cloves garlic, minced

1 tablespoon dried dill

1 tablespoon olive oil

½ teaspoon salt

PREP TIME 15 MINUTES

Peel and shred cucumber. Squeeze the liquid out with your hands or wrap it in a clean dish towel and twist to remove liquid.

Mix all ingredients. Refrigerate for at least 2–3 hours before serving.

PESTO

"Pesto per pasta o pizza! Pronto! Gracie! Mille gracie!" ("Pesto for pasta or pizza! Quick! Thank you. Thank you so much.") After this enthusiastic Italian repartee, you now know how some people speak about this pesto.

SERVES 8–10

1½ cups fresh basil leaves

2 cloves garlic, finely minced

¼ cup pine nuts

¾ cup olive oil

¾ teaspoon salt

PREP TIME 15 MINUTES

Put all ingredients in a blender or food processor. Blend until smooth, scraping sides with a rubber spatula to keep it mixing well.

Variations–Add lemon or lime juice. Or use walnuts, cashews, or sunflower seeds instead of pine nuts, or cilantro instead of basil.

RED HOT SAUCE

You can wear your little black dress for this *Red Hot Sauce*. Serve with barbeque tofu kabobs or as a spicy sauce on the side as part of a Mediterranean dinner, or with baked vegetables such as baked eggplant slices.

MAKES 1 CUP OR 6 SERVINGS

PREP TIME 25 MINUTES

2 tablespoons safflower oil

¾ teaspoon crushed red pepper flakes

3 cloves garlic, pressed or finely minced

1 can (14.5 ounces) diced tomatoes

1 tablespoon rice vinegar

½ tablespoon Grade B maple syrup

¾ teaspoon sea salt

Heat safflower oil in a medium-size skillet. Sauté red crushed peppers for 30 seconds. Add garlic and sauté for 1 minute. Add diced tomatoes and sauté over medium-high heat for 10 minutes. Once tomato juice has cooked off, add rice vinegar, maple syrup, and salt. Stir. Put everything in a small mixing bowl and puree with an immersion blender.

Note–For Stage 3, replace canned tomatoes with fresh tomatoes and omit maple syrup.

YEAST GRAVY

For anyone who can't live without gravy, this is for you. We substituted the yeast for the cream, butter, and bacon grease. Try it. It is surprisingly good and goes well over your chicken-fried steak. (Excuse us, we meant to say your brown rice.)

1½ cups unbleached wheat flour

3 cups nutritional yeast

1½ cups safflower oil

8 cups vegetable stock

Low sodium soy sauce to taste

PREP TIME 25 MINUTES

Put all ingredients in a large heavy-bottomed pan. Cook over medium heat until golden brown.

TOMATO CHUTNEY

One of our friends calls this "The Indian Ketchup" with a big grin on her face. We think she's exaggerating a bit. Still, the maple syrup, the chiles, and the cinnamon make this dish irresistible. People tend to eat a lot so make more rather than less. It goes well with basmati rice, *Kitchari*, and other Indian dishes.

SERVES 2–3

PREP TIME 55 MINUTES

2 tablespoons butter, oil, or ghee

1 teaspoon cumin seeds

1–2 whole dried red chiles

1-inch piece of cinnamon stick

1 2/3 cups chopped tomatoes or diced canned tomatoes

3 tablespoons honey or Grade B maple syrup

½ teaspoon salt

Heat butter, oil, or ghee over moderate heat in a large frying pan. Add cumin, chiles, and cinnamon stick; fry until cumin turns brown. Add tomatoes, then honey or maple syrup, and salt. Continue cooking and stirring until it has cooked down (about 45 minutes). Serve at room temperature in bowls.

HOOCHIE-KOOCHIE SAUCE

The name of the sauce gives it all away—you taste it and it's so delicious you dance the Hootchie-Kootchie. It's great to serve with all sorts of dishes including *Polenta, Baked Vegetables*, and baked potatoes, and as a dipping sauce for warm whole-grain bread or artichokes. Both children and adults love it.

MAKES ABOUT ½ CUP

PREP TIME 15 MINUTES

¼ cup olive oil

1–2 cloves garlic, minced

Fresh ground sea salt to taste

½–¾ cup Italian flat-leaf parsley, finely chopped

In a small bowl, add garlic and sea salt to olive oil. Add enough parsley to oil to reach almost the consistency of a paste.

Burrito Spread

Most of us don't go to Taco Bell any more for the Mexican food that we love so much. This mix can be spread on lettuce leaves for a raw meal. Or it's a healthy version of what could go into your burrito. Add *guacamole* and you will have a delicious and satisfying quick lunch.

MAKES ABOUT 2 CUPS

1 cup walnuts

Juice of ½ lemon

2 teaspoons chile (also spelled chili) powder

2 tablespoons chopped onion

1 large red bell pepper, diced

½ cup sun-dried tomatoes, soaked for a few hours and diced

PREP TIME 20 MINUTES

Liquefy walnuts and lemon juice in blender or food processor. Add a small amount of water if needed. Then add other ingredients slowly. Stop blending when the dip is still slightly chunky.

Serve wrapped in lettuce leaves. (from *Raw Soups, Salads, and Smoothies* by Frederic Patenaude)

Coconut-Pine Nut-Apricot Pâté

This pâté is a great combination of flavors, and a good raw snack that can also be eaten as a side dish with salad. It's rich and a little sweet. You can also substitute 1 cup finely chopped macadamia nuts for half of the pine nuts.

SERVES 4

12 sun-dried apricots

1 cup pine nuts

1 cup shredded unsweetened coconut

PREP TIME 10 MINUTES (WITHOUT SOAKING TIME)

Soak apricots until soft, then rinse with water until water is not brown. Combine everything in a food processor and blend until it becomes a paste.

ORGANIC GHEE (CLARIFIED BUTTER)

Ghee is often used in Indian cooking but often it can be used instead of butter. It doesn't need to be refrigerated and will last for months if kept tightly sealed away from light and high temperatures. Test by tasting it—if it tastes bitter, throw it out. Ghee has a high heat tolerance so it is good to use when sautéing. This is the same ghee used in ghee lamps.

MAKES ABOUT 1½ CUPS

PREP TIME 25 MINUTES

Heat 1 pound organic, unsalted butter over medium-low heat. Don't stir. Once it's melted completely, turn heat down to low.

Some milk solids will form a foam on top—skim this off. Milk solids will then sink to the bottom and form a layer. This layer will brown, adding a nutty flavor to the ghee, while the butter gently boils away any water. Keep turning the heat down so the bottom layer doesn't burn and ruin the flavor of the ghee.

Once boiling stops and layer is brown, ghee is finished. Pour through a fine mesh strainer or several layers of cheesecloth to keep the layer at the bottom from getting into the ghee. Seal in a glass canning jar.

GUACAMOLE

Who doesn't know guacamole in the United States? It seems like guacamole is a lot of people's best green friend. Here's a good basic recipe. Tip: If you have leftover guacamole, cover the surface with plastic wrap (we don't recommend plastic wrap; this is a rare exception so food is not wasted) leaving no air between the wrap and the guacamole. This way it will stay green.

SERVES 3

PREP TIME 15 MINUTES

2 ripe avocadoes

1 tablespoon minced red onion

1 tablespoon lemon or lime juice

1 clove garlic, pressed or minced

Sea salt to taste

Mash avocadoes. Add onion, lemon juice, garlic, and salt. Combine. Serve soon after preparation, otherwise it will turn brown.

Avocado-Pepper Dip

This is an uplifting avocado dip that is a little bit fruity because of the orange and lemon juices. Serve it as a dip with fresh vegetables or as a spread.

MAKES 2 CUPS

2 avocados
1 large red bell pepper
Juice of ½ orange
Juice of 1 lemon
1 teaspoon sea salt

PREP TIME 15 MINUTES

Blend in food processor until smooth.

(from *Raw Soups, Salads, and Smoothies* by Frederic Patenaude)

Avocado Mayonnaise

A good, healthy mayonnaise substitute.

MAKES ABOUT ¾ CUP

1 avocado
Juice of 1 lemon
2 tablespoons olive oil
2 tablespoons dulse flakes (see Note below)
1 teaspoon Grade B maple syrup

PREP TIME 15 MINUTES

Blend avocado and lemon juice in a food processor. Add the oil a bit at a time and then add the other ingredients.

Notes–This recipe doesn't work in a blender. You can replace dulse flakes with sea salt. Add to taste.

PICO DE GALLO

Pico de Gallo (Salsa Fresca) is a Mexican uncooked condiment made from tomatoes, onions, bell peppers, and jalapeño peppers. It's bright, colorful, and bursting with flavor. Though it's best with garden tomatoes in the summer, at other times roma or vine-ripened tomatoes can be used. How much heat it has is up to you—if you like it hot, use the seeds and white membrane of the jalapeño; if not, discard them or omit the jalapeños altogether. Eat it with burritos and *guacamole.* Garnish with a dollop of yogurt.

MAKES ABOUT 3 CUPS

PREP TIME 45 MINUTES

5–6 fresh, ripe tomatoes, seeded and diced (about 2 cups)

½ cup finely chopped white, yellow, or red onion

2 tablespoons very finely chopped green bell pepper or more to taste

2 tablespoons very finely chopped red or yellow bell pepper or more to taste

1–2 finely minced fresh green jalapeño peppers (about 2 tablespoons) (optional)

2 tablespoons chopped cilantro, plus extra for garnish

1 clove garlic, pressed or finely minced (optional)

Juice of 2 limes

Salt and pepper to taste

Combine all ingredients and add a bit more of those ingredients with the flavors you are missing. Keep experimenting until this salsa tastes the way you like it.

FRESH TOMATO SALSA

This recipe makes a world-rocking tomato salsa. You'll never find this kind of flavor in a store-bought salsa. One of the secrets is fire-roasting the tomatoes and chile peppers. It's best made in the summer because tomatoes are fresher and more delicious, but this can be made any time of the year. Serve with organic corn chips, *Mexican Tortilla Buffet*, *Breakfast Burritos*, or your favorite Mexican food.

MAKES ABOUT 5 CUPS

7 medium vine-ripened tomatoes

2 Anaheim green chile peppers

3 cloves roasted garlic, minced (see *Roast Garlic*)

¼ cup fresh cilantro, chopped

3 green onions, cut into 1-inch pieces

¼ cup chopped red onion

2–3 whole jalapeños, deveined, seeded, and diced, or to taste

2 teaspoons olive oil

1 tablespoon lime juice

1 teaspoon sea salt

1 (8 ounce) can tomato sauce or 1 cup pureed fresh tomatoes

Sea salt and pepper to taste

1 teaspoon cayenne pepper (optional)

PREP TIME 1 HOUR

Char (lightly burn the skin off) tomatoes and Anaheim chiles over a gas grill, under the flame of a hot broiler, or over the flame of a gas stove (holding the vegetable over the flame with long tongs), frequently turning until the peel blisters on all sides.

Remove and discard tomato peel; the flesh will still be firm. Remove core and cut tomatoes in half vertically. Use a teaspoon to scoop out the seeds. Cut into chunks and set aside.

Remove and discard skin from charred Anaheim peppers. Cut in half lengthwise. Remove seeds and discard. Cut into chunks and set aside with tomatoes.

With the food processor running, drop in garlic, cilantro, green onions, red onion, and jalapeños. Process for just a few seconds. Scrape down sides of the bowl using a rubber spatula. Use processor on Pulse if still needed to chop vegetables.

Add tomatoes, roasted Anaheim chiles, olive oil, lime juice, and sea salt. Process with brief pulses. Don't blend so much that it becomes a paste—you want to see bits of all the vegetables in the salsa. Put in a bowl. Stir in tomato sauce to reach desired consistency. Season with salt, pepper, and cayenne, if using, to taste.

Note–For Stage 3, use fresh pureed tomatoes rather than tomato sauce.

FLUFFY HUMMUS

Hummus is another staple food of Middle Eastern cuisine. A friend of ours spent several months in Israel many years ago. He told us that every restaurant and corner booth offered hummus, and he ate it every day. Hummus is inexpensive, easy to make, lasts a while (good to make a big batch), nutritious, and filling. Most types of hummus contain tahini; this one doesn't. Fresh cilantro and parsley add to the freshness and fluffiness of this recipe.

9 cups cooked garbanzo beans

½ cup water

½ cup olive oil

2 cloves garlic

3–4 tablespoons lemon juice

4 teaspoons cumin powder

2 teaspoons coriander powder

1 bunch fresh cilantro

1 bunch fresh parsley

Sea salt to taste

PREP TIME 15 MINUTES

Put everything in a food processor and blend until fluffy.

Note–It doesn't work in a blender, but it will work in the blender attachment that looks like a small food processor.

HUMMUS

This is a more traditional hummus recipe than *Fluffy Hummus*. If you can't eat or don't like tahini (sesame), substitute raw cashew butter.

MAKES ABOUT 4 CUPS

3½ cups cooked garbanzo beans

2 tablespoons *Tahini* (see Note below)

3 tablespoons olive oil

3 tablespoons water

¼ teaspoon cayenne pepper or more to taste

2 teaspoons ground cumin

2 teaspoons ground coriander

2 cloves garlic, pressed or very finely minced

1 teaspoon sea salt

Juice of ½ lemon or more to taste

PREP TIME 15 MINUTES

Combine all ingredients in a food processor or VitaMix and blend until smooth.

Serve with raw vegetables.

Note–For Stage 3, use homemade *Tahini* (see recipe in *Nuts and Seeds,* page 202) or good-quality tahini from a natural food store.

TAPENADE

Here are two versions of easy-to-make tapenade. Serve it on the side or as an elegant appetizer with rice crackers and *Rosemary Cashews* (page 203).

Equal amounts green olives, kalamata olives, and artichoke hearts

Olive oil

ALTERNATE RECIPE

1 bulb roasted garlic (see recipe in *Vegetables*)

1 jar green olives with pimento

1 jar black olives or Greek kalamata

1 jar capers

1 lemon, grated zest and juice

1 medium onion, cut into ½ inch rings and caramelized

About ½ bunch fresh flat-leaf parsley, chopped

Olive oil

PREP TIME 15 MINUTES

Put olives and artichoke hearts into food processor or blender (food processor works better) with a little olive oil or water and blend until finely chopped—not chunky but not absolutely smooth.

Alternative Recipe—Squeeze roasted garlic from bulb into food processor or blender. Add remaining ingredients and enough olive oil to keep them moving. Blend until not chunky, but not completely smooth.

Fermented Foods

Fermented foods are important in The Traditional Diet and the Macrobiotic Diet. The salt in the pickling process gives these foods expansive energy, which we could all probably use a bit of. Eating them refreshes us by slowly moving our energy from inside to the surface.

Lacto-fermentation is a process of breaking down the sugars in vegetables and fruits by using beneficial bacteria (lactobacilli, also called probiotics). The word "lacto" used here has nothing to do with dairy. The process produces lactic acid, which naturally preserves foods and gives them their distinctive taste.

Probiotic bacteria aid the growth of helpful bacteria in our digestive tract, which supports digestive health and strengthens the immune system. They also help stop harmful bacteria and assist in the absorption of minerals.

Fermented dairy products are also referred to as "cultured." Fermentation breaks down caesin, or milk protein, which is one of the most difficult proteins to digest. It also restores many of the enzymes destroyed during pasteurization including lactase, which helps digest lactose (milk sugar).

Traditional lacto-fermented foods are raw. They are easier to digest than in their unfermented raw forms and make foods eaten with them easier to digest as well. In Europe the principal lacto-fermented food is sauerkraut. Cucumbers, beets, and turnips are also traditionally lacto-fermented. Asian cuisines use pickled cabbage, turnip, eggplant, cucumber, onion, squash, and carrot. Korean Kimchi is lacto-fermented cabbage, along with other vegetables and seasonings.

Mass-produced pickled products do not have the same benefits. The substitution of vinegar instead of brine makes them too acidic and pasteurization kills all the lactobacilli so we lose the beneficial effect on digestion. They are still okay for us to eat, but as usual, it's best to make your own if you can. This is also a wonderful weekend project to do with children.

When fermenting foods it is important to use the best-quality ingredients available. For dairy use either cow or goat milk, preferably goat, as it is not homogenized. If you can get it, use raw milk. For lacto-fermentation of vegetables and fruits use organic produce, sea salt, and filtered or pure water.

Fermented foods are meant to be eaten as condiments, not as main or side dishes.

For those of us who really want to "get out of the box," fermenting vegetables provides a sensual metaphor of the alchemical process of transformation. In this case, the kimchi or sauerkraut is pressed with your hands until it loses its sharp resistance and becomes softer. The different characteristics of the vegetables, salt, and spices lose some of their distinct personalities as they meld together into an entirely different substance. This can be an unpleasant, smelly, painstakingly long process. But in the end, the fermenting that is forced to occur in that tight jar allows for the creation of something incredibly healing, powerful, and delicious.

YOGURT

This produces a low lactose, naturally low-fat yogurt. It may not be as thick as commercial yogurt but virtually all the lactose has been digested by the bacterial culture, meaning no further digestion of lactose is required by us and there's little chance of any intolerance or ill effects.

1 quart (1 liter) skim milk

1 tablespoon Ultra Dopholus or 1 tablespoon Ultra Bifidus or 2 teaspoons of each

PREP TIME **30** MINUTES (WITHOUT FERMENTATION TIME)

Bring milk to a simmer and remove from heat. Stir often to prevent scorching.

Cover and cool until it has reached room temperature. Can be put in the refrigerator to cool down. It's important that the temperature drops below 120°F (48°C) or the heat will kill the bacterial culture you are about to introduce.

Remove ½ cup of cooled milk and make a paste with the Ultra Dopholus or Ultra Bifidus or both. Mix the paste with the remainder of the cooled milk and stir thoroughly. Pour the milk into a container, cover, and let stand, following heating instructions in next paragraph, for at least 24 hours. The fermentation should not be less than 24 hours.

The source of heat during this 24-hour fermentation is critical. It is important to get the temperature between 100–110 °F (38–43°C) before you proceed with the fermentation. Too high a temperature will kill the bacterial culture and will prevent the proper conversion of lactose. Too low will prevent the activation of bacterial enzymes and will result in incomplete digestion of lactose.

An electric yogurt maker controls the temperature perfectly but the amount you can make at one time is limited. A temperature-regulating electric warming tray is ideal. Use a mouth thermometer to set it properly. An electric crock pot (set low) or a heating pad may be used also. If you have a gas oven, the pilot light usually keeps the temperature within the correct range. Turning the oven light on (replace regular stove light with a 60 watt bulb) also creates enough warmth.

Allow the yogurt to remain in the heat for at least 24 hours to insure that all lactose is completely digested. Remove from heat and refrigerate.

(from *Infant Nutrition,* Health Coach Systems Int'l, Inc. Canada, 3rd Ed., 1995)

KOMBUCHA

This fermented tea has been around for centuries all over the world in various forms. It's a probiotic drink that aids in digestion and was described to us as "effervescent wonderfulness." It's filled with antioxidants which remove free radicals and has been shown to boost the immune system. We feel that kombucha is such a good thing that we're willing to use it even though it has sugar. (Though during the process of fermentation, the sugar is broken down by yeast and converted into carbon dioxide, acids, and other substances.)

To make kombucha a "mushroom" or starter culture is required. (It isn't really a mushroom—it's a symbiotic combination of good bacteria and healthy yeast.) Traditionally people have gotten one from a friend. If you don't know anyone who makes kombucha, check at a health food store to see if anyone makes kombucha. People are often happy to help others get started. Or you can order one online (see Note below).

MAKES ABOUT 1 GALLON

PREP TIME 55 MINUTES (WITHOUT FERMENTATION TIME)

1 gallon filtered water

2 cups white sugar (do not substitute honey)

3 tablespoons loose organic black tea (preferably Assam)

3 tablespoons loose organic green tea (preferably Sencha)

1 kombucha mushroom starter (see Note below)

About a cup of kombucha from a previous batch

Bring filtered water to a boil. Add sugar, stirring, and simmer until dissolved. Remove from heat. Add teas. Steep until water completely cools. (This usually takes all day or overnight.)

Strain to remove tea leaves. Put cooled tea into a 4-quart clear glass container (do not use metal, plastic, colored glass, crystal, ceramic, or porcelain). We find that a gallon glass jar with a wide mouth works best. Others prefer a large glass bowl such as a punch bowl because it has a very large surface area and a shallower depth.

Add 1 cup kombucha from a previous batch to the tea. (If this is your first batch, add the liquid that comes with your starter mushroom.) Put kombucha mushroom on top of tea. Cover jar with a lint-free cotton dishtowel or 4 layers of cheesecloth and secure with a rubber band around top of jar. If using a bowl, put several perpendicular strips of masking tape across top and then cover with a clean, lint-free dishcloth; secure cloth to bowl. The container must be covered to keep out dust and insects such as fruit flies.

Set container in a warm (80–85°F), dark place away from contaminants for 7–10 days. If the room is cooler, it may take up to 14–21 days or longer, and you don't end up with optimal metabolites. Avoid putting jar where temperature will be below 73°F. Do not move container.

If mushroom sinks to bottom of jar, leave it there. A new one will form on the surface of the tea.

Check after 7 days. You are looking for the liquid to be fizzy and mellow rather than sour and for there to be no taste of tea left. It should be acidic and not sweet. How long it takes depends on the temperature and your personal taste of how sour you prefer the kombucha to be. One suggestion is "It's ready when it stops smelling as strong as it smells in the first few days."

When it is ready, remove the kombucha mushroom(s) or culture, which grows and covers the surface of the tea. As it grows, it thickens considerably and is composed of layers, one on top of the other, that can easily be peeled off. Each can be used to produce kombucha.

Rinse mushroom(s) under cold running water. Do not allow them to touch metal—sink, tap, wedding rings, etc. Gently wipe off brown tendrils so you have a clean, fresh mushroom. Lay right side up on a glass plate or in a glass container.

The original mushroom can be reused dozens of times unless it turns black or kombucha doesn't sour as it should. In that case mushrooms from that batch should be thrown away and a new one used for the next batch.

Using a glass measuring cup as a ladle, pour mature kombucha through cheesecloth or a German cotton tea filter into glass bottles or jars. Even after filtering it may have some sediment, which is yeast. Drink it or discard it, whichever you prefer. Cover and refrigerate.

Store the new mushroom refrigerated in a covered glass container with a small amount of kombucha around it. If you give one away, put it in a jar with kombucha liquid for their first batch. It can be kept in the refrigerator for several weeks.

Adults drink 1 or 2 ounces, once or twice a day; up to 4 ounces total. Increase your water intake. Children can drink 1 ounce once or twice a day, up to 2 ounces total, but only if they want to drink it.

Note–A "mushroom" is necessary for making kombucha. If you can't find one locally, you have several online options: (1) go to the Worldwide "Kombucha Exchange" at www.kombu.de (choose English, German, French, or Spanish language). Mushrooms are often available for the cost of shipping or free for pick up; (2) order a starter kit including mushroom from Laurel Farms at www.laurelfarms.com. Can be shipped to U.S. or Europe; (3) order mushrooms, supplies, and kits from www.kombu.de (choose from many languages). These can be shipped in the U.S. or to Europe; (4) look for one on craigslist.com. You can also get more information on making kombucha online.

Tip–Make sure all utensils, containers, and your hands are clean so that you don't pick up a contaminant.

SAUERKRAUT

This is probably the most recognized German dish, especially if you picture it with lots of sausages, a big Humpen of beer, sweaty Lederhosen, and thousands of people crowding you at the Octoberfest. If you want to eat a more modest version here is the recipe. Tika's grandmother bought fresh, raw sauerkraut in "Reform Houses," the precursor to health food stores in Germany. She would literally walk miles to buy it. In Germany, it is traditionally prepared with caraway seeds and cloves.

MAKES 1–2 PINTS

1-2 heads savoy cabbage

Fresh garlic (optional)

Caraway seeds (optional)

Filtered water

1–2 tablespoons sea salt

PREP TIME 45 MINUTES (WITHOUT FERMENTATION TIME)

Chop or grate the cabbage as thickly or finely as you wish. Include a few cloves of chopped garlic and a few teaspoons caraway seeds if desired. Place cabbage and any additional ingredients in a bowl and sprinkle with salt (1 tablespoon per head of cabbage). Stir well and then mash cabbage down with clean hands or a pestle-like instrument like a wooden citrus reamer. A potato masher also works well. Try to create as much juice as possible so that the cabbage, once in a jar, will be covered with its juice. This takes 5–10 minutes.

Transfer cabbage to a sterile wide-mouth quart jar and mash it down as much as possible. Place a smaller jar, filled with water, into this jar to keep the cabbage submerged beneath the juice. Use a jar that is as close as possible to the size of the larger jar's opening. If you have more juice than you need, remove some so it won't overflow. Leave the jars on the counter covered with a towel to keep out insects and dust for at least four days. Occasionally press the second jar down to keep packing down the cabbage. Or remove upper jar and pack the cabbage daily. The more packed the cabbage is, the quicker the fermentation.

Start tasting it after four days. If any mold has formed spoon it off. It won't affect the submerged cabbage. When it tastes strong enough, take out the weighted jar and transfer the sauerkraut to a smaller covered jar. Refrigerate. Use part of the juice from this sauerkraut to start your next batch. If making a larger quantity, a good ratio is 5 pounds of cabbage to 3 tablespoons of sea salt. Use a gallon-sized food-grade plastic bucket or a ceramic crock for the cabbage and then fit a plate or a 1-gallon jug filled with water inside to weigh down the cabbage.

If cabbage is not fresh the fermentation will take longer. Also, the larger the quantity, the longer the fermentation takes.

KIMCHI

Kimchi is Korean sauerkraut. Koreans eat kimchi every day, adding it to breakfast and even using it as a cure for hangovers. They say it keeps the doctor away. Its spice can enliven all kinds of rice dishes and soups, even matzoh ball soup.

We love how colorful it is and how much room there is for creativity in the particular mix of vegetables you choose. Try different vegetables depending on the season—for instance, use green onions and napa cabbage as a base in the spring and add cucumbers in the summer. You can also add all kinds of root vegetables, Jerusalem Artichokes, snow peas, seaweed, and spicy peppers to taste. It is common to add fish sauce to the recipe as well. This recipe has no chile in it but is plenty spicy, in a more kid-friendly way, due to the garlic. But add the chiles if you wish.

Fermented foods like kimchi take patience and experimentation. The time it takes to wait for them to ferment only adds to the joy you feel when you finally get to taste them. A small bit of kimchi goes a long way towards waking us up and slowing us down. Sounds better than meditation.

MAKES ABOUT 14 OUNCES

PREP TIME 35 MINUTES (WITHOUT FERMENTATION TIME)

2 cups filtered water

2 tablespoons sea salt

1 head napa or savoy cabbage, chopped or grated (you can also use bok choy)

½ daikon radish or a few red radishes

2 carrots, sliced

4–6 cloves garlic, chopped

1–2 green onions and/or shallots or leeks

3 tablespoons grated ginger

1–4 red chiles, either whole, dried, or in a sauce (optional)

Mix together water and sea salt in a large jar or in a bowl; mix or shake well to dissolve salt.

Place cabbage, radishes, and carrots in half of the brine and mash them down with hands or with any pestle-like tool until they are submerged by the liquid. Add more brine if necessary. Place a plate over the mixture to keep vegetables submerged and cover with a clean cloth.

A few hours later or even the next day, once the vegetables are soft, prepare the spices. Blend garlic, onions, ginger, and chiles (seeded), if using, into a paste. If using fish sauce, add it to paste. (Make sure that the sauce has no chemical preservatives in it or fermentation will be prevented.)

Drain brine off vegetables into a bowl and set aside. Taste vegetables for saltiness. If they're too salty, rinse them. If they aren't salty enough, add a few more teaspoons of salt but be careful not to add too much.

Mix together vegetables and paste and press this mixture into a quart-sized jar or a bowl. Press it down until juices are higher than vegetables. You can add some brine back in if necessary. Weigh down vegetables with another smaller jar or with a plate. At least once a day, or several times, pack kimchi down further with your hands and re-cover. Always cover the set-up with a clean cloth.

After about a week, start tasting. When it tastes sharp, move it to the refrigerator.

BEET KVAAS

Many Americans have never heard of it, but in the Ukraine beet kvaas is found in most kitchens. It adds a sour saltiness to their soups and is also used as a health tonic.

While for most people it wouldn't win awards for taste, some people crave it because of how good it makes them feel. Like other lacto-fermented drinks, it provides a hydrating balance in the body similar to electrolyte drinks, but in a much more natural way. Folk medicine teaches us that beets contain high levels of anti-carcinogens; they can be especially strong in preventing colon and stomach cancers. They also support liver health, increase the oxygen-carrying ability of the blood, and are an easily assimilated, high-quality source of iron.

Anybody that hangs in there long enough through experimenting to create the appropriately mellowed taste of beet kvaas ends up hooked on it and keeps a batch continuously going, adding new beets and using ¼ cup of this liquid instead of whey for the next batch.

MAKES ABOUT 14 OUNCES

¼ cup whey (see Note below)

3-5 medium beets, peeled and roughly chopped (Don't cut them too thinly or you will create alcohol rather than lactic acid.)

1 tablespoon sea salt

Filtered water

PREP TIME WHEY: 10 MINUTES (WITHOUT SEPARATION TIME); BEETS: 10 MINUTES (WITHOUT FERMENTATION TIME)

Combine whey, beets, and salt in a 2-quart container. Add filtered water to fill. Stir well and cover. Let this sit on the counter for 2 days and then transfer to the fridge. If any mold forms, just scoop it off the surface. This will probably only occur if it is very warm or it is left longer than 2 days.

One-fourth cup of this liquid can be used to start another batch, removing the need for whey.

Many people find beet kvaas tastes better if left for a week or more in the refrigerator. This further fermentation mellows the saltiness.

Note–Make **whey** from good-quality raw milk or from whole-milk plain yogurt. If using raw milk, place it on the counter in a glass jar and allow it to separate. This should take anywhere from 1–4 days. Place a dish towel over a strainer. Place this lined strainer over a bowl. Pour the separated milk or yogurt, if you're using yogurt, into the lined strainer and then tie up the towel into a package, being careful not to squeeze the milk solids inside. Place a wooden spoon through the knot and then rest it on top of the container. This will allow more of the whey to drip out. When the whey stops dripping, put whey and resulting cream cheese (what's in the towel) into separate covered glass jars. Refrigerate. 3 cups yogurt makes about 1¼ cups whey. Use ¾ cup yogurt if you only need the ¼ cup whey for this recipe.

Nuts and Seeds

Roasted nuts and seeds are a wonderful way to add protein and good fats to breakfast, lunch, or dinner. They bring flavor and variety to any meal. Sprinkle them over salads and vegetables, mix them in with cooked grains, or eat them on their own as part of a lunch or dinner, or as a snack.

Homemade nut butters contain more nutrients than store-bought ones because they are fresh, but make sure to refrigerate them so the naturally-occurring oils don't go rancid. They can be used in dressings, desserts, smoothies, or even eaten straight. They can also be used as a base for sweet or savory sauces.

Don't eat too many nuts at once. They contain enzyme inhibitors, which makes them very difficult to digest. To rid them of enzyme inhibitors and activate the enzymes needed for digestion, soak them overnight in water or in water with a little pineapple juice, or toast them. See *Soak and Toast Nuts and Seeds* in *How To*, Chapter 6. Even when soaked or toasted, it's best to eat only a handful or so at a time.

GOMASIO (SALT SUBSTITUTE)

Gomasio is traditionally from Japan and is a principal table condiment in macrobiotic cooking. It's made out of ground, toasted sesame seeds (with or without salt) and sprinkled over food. It can be used as a topping for any dish. The smell of toasted, ground sesame seeds can be counted among the best smells in any kitchen.

MAKES 2 CUPS

PREP TIME 15 MINUTES

2 cups raw sesame seeds

Put seeds into a cast iron frying pan. Roast over medium heat, stirring constantly, until brown but not dark. If seeds start to smoke, turn down heat.

Let seeds cool and put into food processor, coffee grinder used just for spices, or Vita-Mix, and grind until desired consistency is reached. Don't grind too long or it will turn into tahini.

TAHINI

MAKES 2 ¼ CUPS

PREP TIME 25 MINUTES

2 cups raw sesame seeds, toasted

¼ cup olive oil (or more, to desired thickness)

Toast sesame seeds in a heated dry skillet over medium heat, stirring constantly, until barely light brown. Pour onto baking sheet and let cool.

Once cool, put sesame seeds in food processor. Blend until finely ground. Add oil and blend until smooth.

ROSEMARY CASHEWS

Coating roasted cashews with butter and fresh rosemary makes them quite rich and gives them a wonderful flavor. Serve them as a small side dish or use them to top a salad. Whether it's for a special occasion or with a simple meal, they make the simplest of salads seem festive, while adding protein to a meal.

SERVES 3

PREP TIME 25 MINUTES

1 cup cashews

1 tablespoon butter

1 teaspoon fresh rosemary leaves, finely chopped

Pinch of sea salt

Preheat oven to 350°F.

Spread cashews on baking sheet; roast in oven for 10–15 minutes, depending on your oven. Watch closely so they don't burn.

Melt butter. Add rosemary and a pinch of salt; mix. Remove cashews from oven. Put in bowl. Pour rosemary butter over nuts; mix to coat nuts.

ROASTED SUNFLOWER SEEDS

Roasted Sunflower seeds are a great addition to any salad or sprinkled over brown rice. They bring protein to a meal and most children love them.

SERVES 4

PREP TIME 25 MINUTES

1 cup raw sunflower seeds

1 tablespoon Bragg Liquid Aminos, low sodium soy sauce, or tamari

Heat a dry iron skillet. Add sunflower seeds. Roast at medium-low heat, stirring occasionally, for 5–7 minutes until brown. If seeds begin to smoke, turn heat down immediately.

Pour Bragg, soy sauce, or tamari over them and stir rapidly for 30 seconds.

Spread on a cookie sheet. Put cookie sheet in oven at 350°F for 15 minutes or until seeds are dry.

Let cool or serve immediately.

ROASTED ALMONDS

We serve roasted almonds as a side dish with any simple meal. They are also a good traveling snack or addition to children's lunches.

SERVES 4

PREP TIME 30 MINUTES

1½ cups raw almonds

2 tablespoons Bragg Liquid aminos, low sodium soy sauce, or tamari

Heat a dry iron skillet. Add almonds. Roast at medium-low heat, stirring occasionally, for 5–7 minutes until brown. If nuts begin to smoke, turn heat down immediately.

Pour Bragg, soy sauce, or tamari over them and stir rapidly for 30 seconds.

Spread on a cookie sheet. Put cookie sheet in oven at 350°F for 15 minutes or until nuts are dry.

Let cool or serve immediately.

ROASTED ALMOND BUTTER

Nut butters are quite expensive if you buy them at the health food store. The alternative is to buy a big bag of almonds, roast them, and make almond butter yourself. We can hardly keep up with making new batches because some people in our family eat it by the tablespoon during the day. Serve it with bread or vegetable sticks. It also makes for great sauces and dressings.

QUANTITY: 32 OZ. ALMOND BUTTER

PREP TIME 25 MINUTES

3-pound bag raw almonds

Olive oil

Pinch of salt

Spread almonds in one layer on cookie sheet. Bake at 350°F for 15–20 minutes until toasted. Keep an eye on them so they don't burn.

Cool almonds, then put in a bowl. Add 1 tablespoon olive oil and toss nuts until coated.

Put into food processor and start processing. Gradually add one tablespoon of olive oil at a time if needed, but not too much or the consistency will become too thin. Continue processing until it is as chunky or smooth as desired. Refrigerate.

RAW NUT BUTTER

Use raw nuts instead of roasted if you want a completely raw nut butter. The time to process depends on the type of nut that is used.

QUANTITY: 5 ½ OZ.

PREP TIME 25 MINUTES

2 cups almonds, Brazil nuts, pecans, hazelnuts, or macadamia nuts

1 tablespoon raw honey (optional)

½ teaspoon sea salt (optional)

Place nuts in food processor. Process for 8–12 minutes, scraping down the sides as needed, especially in the beginning. Continue processing until the nut butter is creamy and all the oils come out. If using honey and salt, stir in by hand after the butter is made. Put in a covered glass jar. Refrigerate.

GRAIN AND NUT MILKS

Grain and nut milks are a good alternative to cow milk and soy milk, which are not recommended on this diet for health reasons. Making them is easy and much cheaper than buying them in the store. They also taste better homemade and don't contain artificial vitamins and preservatives. Because they don't contain preservatives, they only last for a few days.

These milks can be used as a dairy substitute in tea and other beverages and can be drunk as a beverage on their own. Consider using them to add creaminess to soups and smoothies.

RICE MILK

This recipe is so easy and it's so inexpensive to make. One cup of brown rice makes 4 quarts of creamy rice milk. Try this in our *Chai* recipe or in one of the soups.

MAKES 4 QUARTS

1 cup uncooked organic long grain brown rice

8 cups water for cooking

More water for diluting

1 teaspoon finely ground sea salt

PREP TIME 3 HOURS 45 MINUTES (WITHOUT SOAKING TIME)

Thoroughly wash rice. Soak overnight.

Put 8 cups water in a big pot and bring to a boil over high heat. Pour in rice. Cover and lower the heat. Simmer for 3 hours. It will look like soupy rice pudding. Add salt.

In batches, fill your blender one-third full with rice mixture and then add an equal amount of water. Blend until very smooth. Strain twice through a fine mesh strainer into a mason jar. Repeat with the remainder of the rice. Cover jars and refrigerate. Shake before using.

It will be thicker than commercially-produced rice milk. It can be diluted with additional water at the time of serving, if desired.

Raw Hazelnut or Almond Milk

Homemade is the way to go with nut milks. You can buy a special bag for straining the nut pulp from the milk but we use a fine mesh strainer—it does the job, it's easy to clean, and we didn't have to spend money on another kitchen tool. Make only what you will use in about 3 days.

Makes 6 cups

Prep time 20 minutes using VitaMix or blender (without soaking time)

1 cup raw hazelnuts or almonds

2 cups filtered water, for soaking

6 cups filtered water

¼ cup raw honey or several Medjool dates (optional for sweetening)

Using Vita-Mix

Soak nuts in 2 cups of water overnight or up to 24 hours, then drain and rinse.

Put 6 cups of fresh water, nuts, and honey or dates, if using, in Vita-Mix. Turn on to low speed, increase variable speed to 10, and then switch to high. Blend on high for 2 ½ minutes, until milk is smooth. It will be quite foamy on top.

Let milk sit until foam settles down, about 5 minutes. Pour through a fine mesh strainer into a glass storage container or jar, using a rubber spatula to press the liquid from the almond pulp.

Refrigerate. Shake before serving.

Using Blender

Soak nuts in 2 cups of water overnight or up to 24 hours, then drain and rinse.

Place half the nuts and 3 cups fresh water into blender. Blend on high speed until smooth. Pour through fine mesh filter into a storage container or jar. Repeat with second half of nuts and 3 cups water.

If sweetening, pour 2 cups of the milk into the blender container and add honey or dates. Blend well and add to the rest of the milk. Mix well. Refrigerate. Shake before serving.

Notes–Nut milks keep for about 3 days in refrigerator. For Stage 3, do not sweeten milk with honey.

DESSERTS

Dessert can be the perfect last touch to a meal shared with good company. We think that dessert made with processed sugar and flour does not fit well with a beautiful meal of whole, delicious foods. This does not mean it's never appropriate to have desserts made with these ingredients, but the mood created during a meal can be destroyed if dessert turns into nothing more than a way to satisfy our "sweet tooth" or an indulgence in large portions.

Most sweeteners are simple sugars which convert instantly to energy and wreak havoc with blood sugar levels, causing mood swings, fatigue, and even immune system malfunction. Many studies show that two of the most highly-processed sweeteners, high fructose corn syrup and refined white sugar, are at the root of a variety of the health issues in the U.S., yet they are found in most of the processed foods sold in grocery stores and served in restaurants, and are in virtually every commercially-produced and homemade dessert.

The dessert recipes we offer here are made with natural ingredients and sweeteners. They tend to be light and don't have the same impact on the body that more processed desserts do. However, we only eat these on special occasions. In Germany and France, desserts are served in small portions and in general are not nearly as sweet as desserts in the United States. In Europe, they are a food served as part of a meal, rather than a neurotic indulgence. Part of the Japanese macrobiotic diet is to eat a small sweet with most meals, as a part of this diet's emphasis is on having all four tastes at most meals.

Many of these recipes use blanched almond flour. Two sources in the U.S. that we are familiar with are Benefit Your Life (www.benefityourlifestore.com or 1-877 295-2407) and Honeyville (www.store.honeyvillegrain.com or 1-888 810-3212). Or make your own in a food processor. Use blanched (the brown skin has been removed) slivered almonds. Use a fine strainer to get the bigger nut pieces out. For a finer flour, you can use a coffee grinder dedicated just to grinding spices.

Dark chocolate is a simple dessert that doesn't need to be prepared. We consider it to be a food, not a candy, because it's made from cacao beans which contain all the nutrients of beans. This is not true of milk chocolate. Because of its added milk and sugar, milk chocolate is really nothing more than candy.

The higher the percentage of cacao "solids" a dark chocolate bar has, the better. Cacao contains minerals such as copper, magnesium, potassium, calcium, and iron. It has been proven to contribute to heart and cardiovascular system health. It contains concentrated amounts of anti-oxidants, which rid the body of free radicals, which can cause chronic disease.

This is not an invitation to over-indulge in chocolate. We bring attention to our relationship to sweets and are careful not to eat them mindlessly, which is often the case if because we are addicted to them.

DATE-NUT BALLS

A mother we know invented these so her children could have a healthy "sweet." We love these *Date-Nut Balls* and if you use raw nuts and sun-dried dates, they make a wonderful raw dessert. They can also be served with *Chai* or mint tea. We think the Medjool dates provide just the right amount of sweetness. If you want them to be less sweet, substitute walnuts for the pecans.

MAKES ABOUT 4 DOZEN
SMALL BALLS

PREP TIME 30 MINUTES

1 cup pecans

1 cup almonds

2 cups pitted Medjool dates

Shredded, unsweetened coconut (optional)

Toss everything, except the coconut, into a food processor and process until it starts to "ball up." (This will be obvious.) It should still be a bit chunky, not totally smooth. Form the mixture into small (about 2 teaspoon-sized) balls and roll in coconut, if desired.

STUFFED DATES

For several years, whenever our friend from Mexico came to visit us, we put her to work making stuffed dates for festive occasions. Now we call her the "Stuffed Date Specialist." These dates along with hot mint tea, when enjoyed in good company, catalyze a mood of friendship and appreciation for each other.

MAKES ABOUT 60 DATES

PREP TIME 45 MINUTES (WITHOUT CHILLING TIME)

1 cup raw almonds

½ cup crystallized ginger, sliced

½–¾ stick of butter

1 teaspoon vanilla

60 pitted Medjool dates

Put all ingredients, except dates, into a food processor and chop until roughly blended to your satisfaction. Slit dates on one side lengthwise. Fill amply but don't overstuff.

Put into freezer for 10 minutes to chill. Serve.

(from *Hohm Cookin': Music for the Tastebuds*)

Apple Pudding

Originally a dessert, we also recommend it as a breakfast. It is warm and nurturing in the morning, especially in the winter.

SERVES 4

PREP TIME 40 MINUTES

¼ cup rolled oats

2 apples, peeled, cored, and sliced

½ cup apple juice

1/3 cup water

½ cup cooked brown rice

¼ teaspoon cinnamon

1 tablespoon honey or Grade B maple syrup

Dash of allspice

Lightly roast oats by stirring in a dry saucepan over medium heat until they smell toasty. Add apples and other ingredients. Bring to a boil, cover, and simmer on lower heat for 20 minutes. Blend until completely smooth in a blender. Serve topped with chopped roasted almonds or sunflower seeds.

Note–For Stage 3, omit honey or maple syrup. Use fresh apple juice.

Tart Shell (Gluten-Free)

Dates add sweetness and an interesting texture to this tart shell. Fill it with the non-dairy *Chocolate Filling* or with *Macadamia Cream* topped with fresh fruit (both recipes follow). Bake it the same day you will serve it and wait until shortly before serving to fill it.

SERVES 8

PREP TIME 35 MINUTES

3 cups blanched almond flour

1/8 teaspoon sea salt

½ teaspoon xanthan gum

8 Medjool dates, pitted

¼ cup toasted sliced almonds

2 tablespoons agave syrup

½ cup cold butter, cut into chunks

Preheat oven to 350°F. Put almond flour, salt, xanthan gum, dates, and almonds in food processor. Pulse until dates are chopped into small pieces and ingredients are evenly combined. Add agave syrup and butter and pulse until evenly mixed. Press into bottom and sides of an 11–inch tart shell. Bake at 350°F for 10–15 minutes, until lightly browned. Cool before filling.

Note: See description of xanthan gum in recipe for *Banana Bread Muffins (Gluten Free)*, page 172.

CHOCOLATE FILLING FOR TART

This non-dairy chocolate filling is sure to please every chocolate lover. Dark chocolate makes it satisfying and not too sweet. Most people don't even taste the coconut milk. It's thickened with agar-agar, a vegetarian gelatin substitute made from seaweed, and sweetened with a small amount of agave syrup, but honey can also be used. For variety, top with chopped toasted pecans instead of toasted sliced almonds. Or, if you're a coconut lover, as a final touch, sprinkle with lightly toasted unsweetened coconut.

MAKES ENOUGH FILLING FOR ONE
TART SHELL

1 (13.5 ounce can) regular coconut milk

Pinch of sea salt

5 teaspoons agar agar

2 tablespoons agave syrup

6 ounces dark (70%) chocolate

PREP TIME 15 MINUTES (WITHOUT CHILLING TIME)

Pour coconut milk into small saucepan. Whisk to combine liquid and solid parts. Whisk in salt and agar-agar. Stir continuously over low heat until agar-agar dissolves. It may take 5 minutes or longer. Mixture should thicken. Add agave and chocolate and stir until melted. Refrigerate for about an hour. Before putting in tart shell, whisk or beat with mixer until it is smooth.

To assemble, spoon filling into *Tart Shell* (page 213). Spread evenly and smooth the surface. Sprinkle toasted almonds over filling. Serve immediately.

MACADAMIA CREAM

A light, orangey cream that miraculously has no dairy in it. Serve it instead of whipped cream. Or spread it evenly in a tart shell and top with nicely arranged fresh fruit, such as raspberries and blueberries, or thinly sliced peaches and raspberries or blueberries.

MAKES 2 CUPS

1 cup macadamia nuts

Juice of 2 oranges

2 teaspoons natural vanilla extract

Squeeze of lemon or lime juice

PREP TIME 15 MINUTES

Blend macadamia nuts into a powder in a blender. Add the other ingredients and blend into a cream.

LEMON SORBET

Here is a sorbet is not made with processed sugar. The lemon zest intensifies the lemon flavor. Use it as a refreshing dessert after a special summer meal or a palate cleanser between courses. If you wish, serve a cookie on the side for a more substantial dessert. For a different twist, add finely minced fresh mint leaves just before freezing in ice cream machine. Garnish with mint leaves.

SERVES 4

PREP TIME 20 MINUTES (WITHOUT CHILL/FREEZE TIME)

1 cup water

¾ cup agave syrup or raw honey

1 cup fresh lemon juice

1 tablespoon finely grated lemon zest, chopped

Put water and agave syrup or honey in a small saucepan, heat and stir until combined. Pour into a glass bowl and cool. Once cool, add lemon juice and zest. Put in freezer for about a half hour to chill. Pour into the bowl of an ice cream machine. Freeze according to the manufacturer's instructions. After the sorbet is made, transfer to an airtight container. Freeze for an hour before serving.

Note–If you use dark agave syrup, the sorbet will have a brownish color. It tastes great but it may not appear as appetizing.

ORANGE SORBET

We wanted a sorbet that could be used on our Stage 3 diet so we came up with this. It's a nice alternative to the more traditional lemon sorbet. Be sure that the oranges are naturally sweet and juicy. It's not as sweet tasting as most sorbets but we've found that when we rarely eat sweets, naturally sweet fruits have just the right amount of sweetness.

SERVES 4

PREP TIME 20 MINUTES (WITHOUT CHILL/FREEZE TIME)

3 cups fresh-squeezed orange juice

1 tablespoon finely grated orange zest, chopped

Combine juice and zest in bowl or container. Chill in the refrigerator for several hours.

Strain juice into bowl of ice cream maker. Freeze according to manufacturer's directions.

Once frozen, transfer to air-tight covered container. Freeze for an hour before serving. Garnish with mint or basil leaves.

MANGO SORBET

We love to serve sorbet but the sorbets that are available commercially (and the recipes to make them) are sweetened with lots of processed sugar. This recipe, which is sweetened with agave syrup or honey, is perfect to serve on a special occasion, especially after a Japanese or Indian meal. Make sure the mangoes are ripe and juicy.

MAKES ABOUT 3 CUPS

PREP TIME 20 MINUTES (WITHOUT CHILL/FREEZE TIME)

1½ cups fresh-squeezed orange juice (about 8 small juice oranges)

1½–2 cups very ripe mango (2 mangos, peeled and flesh sliced off the pit)

¼ cup agave syrup or honey

Put orange juice, mango, and agave syrup into blender. Blend until smooth. If there are any fibers in the puree, strain it before proceeding.

Freeze in a small ice cream freezer (like a Cuisinart) according to manufacturer's instructions.

Remove from ice cream freezer bowl and put into a glass container. Freeze for several hours before serving.

CHOCOLATE-COCONUT ICE CREAM (NON-DAIRY)

More and more people these days can't eat dairy or processed sugar. They try many of the commercially available non-dairy "ice creams" but sometimes these don't hit the mark. If you want something that tastes more like homemade ice cream, try this recipe that uses coconut milk and agave syrup or honey. Top it with toasted sliced almonds or chopped pecans. It's a cool summer treat.

SERVES 4

PREP TIME 45 MINUTES (WITHOUT CHILL/FREEZE TIME)

5.3 ounces dark (73%) chocolate bar

1 cup almond milk (see *Grain and Nut Milks*)

1 (13.66 ounce) can regular coconut milk (tested with Thai Kitchen), not "lite"

½ cup agave syrup or honey

1 teaspoon vanilla extract

Gently melt chocolate over double boiler. Add almond milk; whisk and heat until blended. Cool until warm.

Pour mixture into blender. Add coconut milk, agave syrup or honey, and vanilla. Blend. Chill for at least an hour, or until mixture is cold.

Freeze in ice cream freezer according to manufacturer's instructions.

Spoon into another container, cover, and freeze for at least an hour before serving.

Dark Chocolate Chip Cookies (Gluten-Free)

Most everyone loves chocolate chip cookies! We were celebrating with some of our closest family and friends and we wanted to serve one cookie that would meet everyone's special needs. It couldn't contain wheat flour, processed sugar, or eggs so we came up with this recipe and it was a hit. It can also be dairy-free by substituting grapeseed oil for butter. They are best baked the day they are served.

MAKES APPROXIMATELY 20 COOKIES

2¼ cups blanched almond flour (see Note below)

½ cup brown rice flour

¼ teaspoon sea salt

½ teaspoon baking soda

½ cup melted butter

1 tablespoon vanilla extract

½ cup raw honey or agave syrup

4 ounces (2/3 cup) high-quality vegan/gluten-free dark chocolate chips

PREP TIME 35 MINUTES (WITHOUT BAKING TIME)

Combine dry ingredients in a large bowl.

Stir together wet ingredients in a smaller bowl.

Mix wet ingredients into dry ingredients.

Form into 1-inch balls and press onto a parchment-lined baking sheet. Press tops of balls to flatten.

Bake at 350°F for 8–12 minutes, until golden brown.

Cool before removing from pan.

Note–You can purchase blanched almond flour online if it is not available where you live.

CHERRY-PECAN-OATMEAL COOKIES

This is a versatile cookie recipe. Use dried cherries, raisins, or another chopped dried fruit. Substitute walnuts for the pecans or omit them. Or add dark chocolate chips. They can be made gluten-free by using brown rice flour and gluten-free oats (make sure your other ingredients are gluten-free). They are delicious as a dessert or with a cup of tea.

MAKES 24

PREP TIME 45 MINUTES (WITHOUT BAKING TIME)

2 cups rolled oats (use gluten-free oats, if needed)

½ cup unbleached almond flour

½ cup brown rice flour or whole wheat pastry flour

¾ cup shredded unsweetened coconut

1 tablespoon cinnamon

¼ teaspoon sea salt

¾ cup Grade B maple syrup

½ cup grapeseed oil

1 teaspoon vanilla

1 cup chopped pecans

1 cup dried tart cherries

Combine oats, almond flour, rice flour, coconut, cinnamon, and salt in a bowl.

In another bowl, combine maple syrup, grapeseed oil, and vanilla.

Add wet ingredients to dry ingredients and stir to combine. Fold in pecans and cherries.

Line baking sheet with parchment paper. Form into 1-inch balls and press onto a baking sheet. Press tops of balls to flatten.

Bake at 350°F for 20 minutes or until lightly browned on top.

Variations

Reduce dried tart cherries to ½ cup and add ½ cup vegan chocolate chips,

or omit dried cherries and add 1 cup raisins,

or omit dried cherries and add 1 cup vegan chocolate chips.

PECAN COOKIES (GLUTEN-FREE)

This cookie resembles a shortbread cookie but it's gluten-free. We love blanched almond flour because it is made from almonds—and only almonds. It's high in protein and low in carbohydrates. It may be hard to find in your area, but you can order it online and keep it in the freezer so that you'll have it on hand. This cookie can be sweetened with honey, agave syrup, or, for a slightly different twist, maple syrup. It's worth the extra effort to toast the pecans.

MAKES ABOUT 2 DOZEN COOKIES

2½ cups blanched almond flour

½ teaspoon sea salt

¼ teaspoon baking soda

1 cup chopped pecans, toasted

1/3 cup agave syrup, honey, or Grade B maple syrup

½ cup unsalted butter, melted

1 tablespoon vanilla extract

PREP TIME 45 MINUTES (WITHOUT BAKING TIME)

Preheat oven to 350°F.

In a medium bowl, combine almond flour, salt, and baking soda.

In a small bowl, combine agave, butter, and vanilla. Add to flour mixture; mix well. Add pecans; mix. Let dough rest for a few minutes.

Using a small scoop (about 1½ tablespoons), place mounds of dough on baking sheets lined with parchment paper about 2 inches apart. Lightly flatten tops of dough.

Bake for 10–12 minutes, or until golden brown. Cool before removing from baking sheet.

Best served the day they are baked.

OATMEAL-DATE COOKIES (GLUTEN-FREE)

This is a great cookie. It's gluten-free but delicious enough to serve to cookie lovers everywhere. The dates are a wonderful addition; they add texture and sweetness. If you don't need gluten-free cookies, use regular old-fashioned rolled oats; they're cheaper.

This recipe calls for xanthan gum, which is derived from corn sugar. This white powder looks a lot like baking powder and is used in similar amounts. Invaluable in gluten-free baking, it provides elasticity and helps to prevent dryness and crumbling. It can be found in natural food stores.

Almond flour is also often used in gluten-free baking and is available at health food stores. It is good to keep these ingredients at hand, since many gluten-free baking recipes call for them.

MAKES ABOUT 40 COOKIES

PREP TIME 55 MINUTES (WITHOUT BAKING TIME)

2 cups blanched almond flour

½ teaspoon xanthan gum

¾ teaspoon sea salt

1 teaspoon baking soda

3 cups gluten-free old-fashioned rolled oats

1 cup unsalted butter, room temperature

1 cup agave syrup

2 large eggs

1½ teaspoons vanilla extract

8 large Medjool dates, chopped

1 cup toasted pecans, chopped (optional)

Preheat oven to 350°F.

Combine almond flour, xanthan gum, sea salt, baking soda, and oats in a medium bowl. Set aside.

Beat together butter and agave syrup until combined and creamy. Add eggs, one at time, beating to combine after each addition. Add vanilla.

Add oat mixture; stir to combine. Add dates and pecans, if using; stir to combine.

Line baking sheets with parchment paper. Using a medium-size cookie scoop or 2 tablespoons, drop mounds of dough onto sheet pans. Flatten slightly with damp fingers. Bake for 11–14 minutes, until lightly browned. Cool for 5 minutes or until cookies hold shape when removing with a spatula. Cool completely. Store in an airtight container.

CARDAMOM SHORTBREAD COOKIES (GLUTEN-FREE)

One of our favorite cookies to serve after an Indian meal is Cardamom Shortbread. The traditional recipe contains wheat flour and processed sugar so we started looking for a "healthier" alternative. This version is gluten-free so it works for almost everyone. It's also wonderful served with chai or tea. If you can't find the little round black cardamom seeds to grind, buy the pods, open them up, scrape out the seeds, and grind them.

MAKES 3½ DOZEN SMALL COOKIES

PREP TIME 45 MINUTES (WITHOUT BAKING TIME)

2½ cups blanched almond flour

½ teaspoon sea salt

¼ teaspoon baking soda

1½ teaspoons crushed or ground cardamom seeds

1/3 cup agave syrup, honey, or Grade B maple syrup

½ cup unsalted butter, melted

2 teaspoons vanilla extract

Preheat oven to 350°F.

In a medium bowl combine almond flour, salt, baking soda, and cardamom.

In a small bowl combine agave, butter, and vanilla. Add to flour mixture; mix well. Let dough rest for a few minutes.

Using a small scoop (about 2 teaspoons), place small mounds of dough on baking sheets lined with parchment paper about 2 inches apart. Gently flatten tops of dough.

Bake for about 10 minutes or until golden brown. Cool before removing from baking sheet.

Best served the day they are baked.

CHAI

If you have ever traveled in India you will never forget the smell of chai. Cardamom, hot milk, black tea... At many street corners in every Indian city you can find chai stalls, where you can buy a cup of steaming hot chai for a few rupees. Friends of ours from India gave us this traditional recipe. We adapted it by substituting decaffeinated Earl Grey tea for black tea, and rice and almond milk for cow's milk, and honey for sugar.

MAKES 14 MUGS / SERVES 14 PEOPLE

2½-inch piece of fresh ginger
3 tablespoons water

2 quarts unsweetened rice milk (see recipe in *Grain and Nut Milks*)

½ quart unsweetened almond milk (see recipe in *Grain and Nut Milks*)

1 quart water

2 heaping tablespoons ground cardamom

¼ cup loose decaffeinated Earl Grey tea

1 cup honey

PREP TIME 45 MINUTES

Peel ginger, cut into pieces. Blend in Vitamix or regular blender with 3 tablespoons water into a ginger puree.

Combine rice milk, almond milk, and water. Add cardamom and ginger puree. Bring to a boil, stirring occasionally from the bottom so the milk/water combination doesn't burn.

Once it is boiling turn burner off. Add tea, cover pot, and let sit for 2 minutes.

After 2 minutes stir and strain into another pot. Add honey and bring to a boil again, whisking lightly to combine all the flavors.

Serve hot.

JUICE

Fresh fruit and vegetable juices give us vitamins, minerals, electrolytes, amino acids, antioxidants, and enzymes in forms that are easy to digest and absorb. They strengthen the immune system and help remove free radicals, which have been found to cause many chronic diseases. When we are sick, fresh juices rebalance the body and help it heal by providing needed electrolytes, fluids, and glucose. Their minerals and amino acids help restore a depleted body.

Fruit juices feed the brain and the nervous and glandular systems and also help cleanse toxins from the body. Drink them during the day, as the sugars can make it hard to fall asleep at night. Vegetable juices tone and rebuild the body, especially bones, muscles, and connective tissues, because they are more protein-rich. The juice of water-based vegetables like cucumbers and celery can be relaxing in the evening.

It's best to drink juice immediately after making it so the nutrients aren't lost. But we are all busy, and this isn't always possible. Consider making enough for one day and storing it in the refrigerator. As with water, stop drinking at least a half-hour before a meal and don't drink anything until an hour after a meal, as, contrary to popular practice, fluids interfere with digestion.

Add a little lemon, garlic, or ginger juice to any juice for added cleansing benefits. These ingredients have been used medicinally for thousands of years. Consider adding the juice from greens (spinach, kale, chard, parsley, etc.) to your mix as well. Green juice supports the health of virtually every system and organ in the body. It provides minerals and chlorophyll in liquid form, which is more easily absorbed. Chlorophyll helps in the growth and repair of tissues and helps eliminate toxins. It also aids in the absorption of magnesium, calcium, and other minerals.

If drinking straight fruit and vegetable juices is too strong, dilute with at least 25 percent water. Dilute 50 percent for children.

Start by choosing fresh, organic fruits and vegetables. If you're using root vegetables like carrots, cut off the tops. Scrub clean with a stiff brush and soak in GSE water (see *How To—Soak with Grapefruit Seed Extract [GSE] Water* in Chapter 6) unless the peel is going to be removed, such as with lemons and oranges. When peeling citrus, leave as much of the white "pith" as possible as it contains many nutrients.

Recipes with greens require a twin-gear juicer. (See *Choose a Juicer* in *How To*, Chapter 6.) Bunch greens into a small ball and process with a harder ingredient such as carrot or apple.

The following fruits and vegetables are good bases. Use them to create your own mixtures and keep track of the recipes.

Apple Provides calcium. It helps cleanse the liver and kidneys and feeds the nervous and glandular systems. It also contains enzymes which help digestion and amino acids which rid the body of free radicals.

Cabbage Used to successfully treat many gastrointestinal illnesses, such as bleeding peptic ulcers, colitis, and indigestion, for over fifty years. The American Cancer Society recommends we eat more cruciferous vegetables like cabbage and broccoli because they help protect against cancer; they also support a healthy spleen.

Carrot Tastes great, which is why it is the base for so many juices. Cut the top off and scrub with a tough brush before juicing. If you peel the outer layer, important nutrients are lost. Carrots are high in vitamin A and support the health of the eyes, liver, and lungs.

Cucumber In this case, peel before juicing as skins typically are covered with wax to make them last longer at the store. Cucumbers support heart and pancreas health and can help with edema, which is swelling that results from the retention of water.

Grape Use seeds and stems, too—they contain nutrients that strengthen the heart and vascular system, support the lymph system, and eliminate free radicals. Provides calcium. Also cleanses the liver and kidneys and feeds the nervous and glandular systems. Supports colon health.

Whether it is vegetable juice, fruit juice, or a combination of both, juices are the elixir of life. They may seem elaborate to make, but once you get used to making them, it's actually quite easy.

Tip: Clean your juicer right away after juicing so the pulp does not stick to it. It is harder to clean it later once it is dry.

APPLE JUICE

SERVES 1

PREP TIME 10 MINUTES

3 apples

Cut to fit opening of juicer and process.

APPLE-STRAWBERRY JUICE

SERVES 2

PREP TIME 15 MINUTES

2 cups strawberries

4 apples

Remove tops of strawberries.

Cut apples to fit opening of juicer and process.

CARROT JUICE

SERVES 2

PREP TIME 10 MINUTES

12 carrots

Remove tops of carrots.

Cut to fit opening of juicer and process.

CARROT-CELERY JUICE

SERVES 2

PREP TIME 10 MINUTES

12 carrots
4 stalks celery

Remove tops of carrots and celery. Cut to fit opening of juicer and process.

ORANGE JUICE

SERVES 2

PREP TIME 15 MINUTES

6 Valencia oranges

Peel oranges, leaving as much of the white pithy skin as possible. Cut to fit opening of juicer and process.

PINEAPPLE JUICE

SERVES 1

PREP TIME 15 MINUTES

3 1-inch-thick rings pineapple

Cut to fit opening of juicer and process.

V-6 Juice

SERVES 2

PREP TIME 20 MINUTES

4 tomatoes

2 stalks celery

1 sweet green pepper

2 carrots

1 small onion

1 clove garlic

Remove tops of carrots and celery. Peel onion and garlic. Cut to fit opening of juicer and process.

Watermelon Juice

SERVES 2

PREP TIME 10 MINUTES

1 medium watermelon

Remove rind but not seeds. Cut to fit opening of juicer and process.

Carrot-Apple Juice

SERVES 2

PREP TIME 10 MINUTES

8 carrots

2 apples

Remove carrot tops. Cut to fit opening of juicer and process.

CARROT-CELERY-APPLE-PARSLEY JUICE

SERVES 2

PREP TIME 15 MINUTES

10 carrots

1 stalk celery

1 apple

½ cup parsley, chopped

Remove tops of carrots and celery. Cut to fit opening of juicer and process.

CARROT-KALE PLUS JUICE

SERVES 2

PREP TIME 20 MINUTES

10 carrots

1 apple

1 1/8-inch-thick slice ginger root

1 stalk celery

1 cup kale, chopped

Remove tops of carrots and celery. Peel ginger.

Cut to fit opening of juicer and process.

When juicing kale, bunch leaves into a small ball, then push through along with either carrot or apple.

CARROT-SPINACH-APPLE JUICE

SERVES 2

PREP TIME 15 MINUTES

5 carrots

1 apple

1 cup spinach leaves

Cut top off carrots. Cut to fit opening of juicer and process. When juicing spinach, bunch leaves into a small ball, then push through along with either carrot or apple.

Tomato-Carrot-Celery Juice

Serves 2

Prep time 10 minutes

2 tomatoes

6 carrots

1 stalk celery

Cut tops off carrots and celery. Cut to fit opening of juicer and process.

Carrot-Cucumber-Apple-Chard Juice

Serves 2

Prep time 15 minutes

4 carrots

½ cucumber

2 apples

1 cup Swiss chard leaves, chopped

Cut tops off carrots. Cut to fit opening of juicer and process. When juicing Swiss chard, bunch leaves into a small ball, then push through along with either carrot or apple.

You and I possess within ourselves, at every moment of our lives,

under all circumstances, the power to transform the quality of our lives.

– WERNER ERHARD

How To

Soak With Grapefruit Seed Extract (GSE) Water

Soak non-organic and organic lettuce, vegetables, and fruit in GSE water. This helps remove pesticides and any residue from people handling the food before we bought it.

Use 7–10 drops per liter of water. Rinse fruits and vegetables before and after soaking. Soak most fruits and vegetables for about 20 minutes.

Most fruits with peels do not need to be soaked unless the peel is used for zest or it remains on the fruit (such as a slice of lemon in tea). Soak fruits separate from vegetables, and soak tomatoes and grapes separate from anything else.

Soak lettuce and any fruit or vegetable that gets waterlogged for less time. Some people never soak mushrooms and strawberries while others soak them for a minute or two.

Ripen Fruit

Put unripe fruit in a brown paper bag with an apple slice. The apple releases ethylene gas, which helps fruit ripen.

Mince, Dice, Cube, Chop, Slice

Mince–Cut into very small pieces. **Dice**–Cut pieces about 3/8 inch wide. **Cube**–Cut pieces in a cube shape. **Chop**–Cut pieces as close to the same size as possible. **Coarsely chopped**–The pieces don't have to be the same size. **Slice**–Cut right through it.

Cut Onions

Store onions in the refrigerator and cut them under cold running water to avoid tears. This is easy if slicing, but difficult if dicing.

Peel Tomatoes

Boil enough water so that, when dropped in, the tomatoes are covered. Drop tomato in for 10–15 seconds. Remove. Run under cold water to cool. The skin peels right off.

Peel, Crush, Press, Mince Garlic

To **peel** a garlic clove, put it on a cutting board under the side of a large knife and press down on the knife until the clove is **crushed**. The peel is easily removed and discarded. The crushed clove can be used as is or, if a finer texture is needed, it can be minced or finely minced. To **mince**, use the knife to cut the crushed clove into tiny pieces. Or put the crushed clove through a **garlic press,** which is sometimes called "pressed" or "squeezed."

Peel Broccoli Stalks

The inner part of the thick, main stalk can be eaten. It is sweet and tender if peeled first. Peel the outer layer by cutting up into it from the bottom. Hold the cut part against the knife with the thumb and peel up toward the head. This leaves the lighter middle intact.

Work With Beets

Beets stain. Cover work surfaces and clothing when working with them. Bake them with a piece of foil on the pan, as they leak. Golden beets are sweeter and won't stain.

Revive Leafy Greens

If leafy greens have wilted, cut or tear them up and put them in a bowl of cold water. They will be crisp again in 10–15 minutes.

Use Spice Alternatives

Instead of spices, use different foods to bring out flavors. Instead of adding sugar, add onions or carrots. For a salty flavor, add tomatoes or celery. Mushrooms, zucchini, and squashes act like sponges—put them in first so they can absorb all the other flavors in the dish.

Sauté

Put a little bit of organic butter or oil in a pan (enough to make a 1/16-inch covering on the bottom) and then cook the ingredient for a short time until it is brown or caramelized (onions) or cooked (mushrooms, carrots, etc.). Sautéing is good for foods that don't need to be cooked a long time or foods that have already been cooked and are being warmed up.

If you want to use less oil to sauté, heat a small amount of oil and add a bit of water. Add water before oil is hot or it will spit everywhere. When water is almost boiling, add food and sauté to desired texture.

Soak And Toast Nuts And Seeds

Soaking starts the germination process, which releases the enzymes in the nuts and seeds that are needed for digestion. To soak, cover nuts or seeds in water overnight or for 6–7 hours. Make sure there is extra water covering them because as they soak they will swell. If you wish, add some pineapple juice to the water.

To toast them, spread soaked nuts or seeds on a baking sheet. Put them in the oven at no more than 150 °F (slightly higher than having the pilot light on) for 12 hours or overnight, until they are completely dry and crisp. Turn occasionally. Store in an airtight container. By toasting them slowly and at such a low temperature, enzymes are not destroyed.

For pecans, almonds, and macadamia nuts, toast 12–24 hours. Store walnuts in an airtight container in the refrigerator because they contain oils that will go rancid. For cashews, whose enzymes have already been destroyed by processing by the time they arrive in the store, toast in a 200–250 °F oven for 12–24 hours.

Steam Vegetables

Fill a stock pot with two inches of water. Bring water to a boil. Put vegetables in colander and put colander in pot. Reduce heat to low and cover pot. Test vegetables every few minutes with a fork—they should be tender but still firm to retain the most nutrients. Keep an eye on the water level so you don't boil it dry.

Cook Hard Squash

Hard squashes includes acorn, butternut, and spaghetti. Cut a triangular hole in the squash (the sides of the triangle should be no longer than the edge of your paring knife's blade) that goes all the way in to the middle of the squash. Remove the triangle. Place it whole on a rack in the oven with the triangle on top. Put a pan underneath it to catch any juices that leak out.

Bake at 350°F for 45–50 minutes or until flesh is tender. Large squash may take 60–70 minutes.

Squash can also be cut in half before baking. Cut triangular hole in top of each half and place cut-side-down on a baking sheet filled with 1/4 inch water. Cook until flesh is tender. Scrape meat out when it has cooled enough to do so.

Reheat Food

Microwaves are not recommended (see *Microwaves* in *Resources and Recommendations*, Chapter 8). A good bamboo steamer is inexpensive and easily heats up solid foods (don't clean it with soap as the soap is absorbed by the natural bamboo and steamed into the food). The steamer insert in a big cook pot works well also—boil an inch of water in the bottom.

Another good method is to fill a pot, pan, or skillet with about 1/8 inch of water. Heat the water to boiling and put the food into the pot, but don't stir it. Just put on a lid. The steam both heats it and keeps it moist. Keep an eye on it so it doesn't burn.

Clean a Burned Pan

First, try a nylon scrubber (like steel wool, but orange and yellow). If that doesn't work, fill the pot with hot water and some dish liquid and soak overnight. If that still doesn't work, fill the pot with a solution of 1 teaspoon baking soda or cream of tartar per quart of water and bring to a boil. Boil for 5 minutes or so.

Make Natural Household Cleaner

For 16-oz spray bottle, combine 4 ounces vodka, 3 ounces witch hazel, and 1 ounce white vinegar. Pour into spray bottle and fill the rest up with water, leaving room for the following essential oils: 20 drops Tea Tree oil, 20 drops lemon oil, and 15 drops rosemary oil. Optional essential oils are orange, grapefruit, etc.

Convert Fahrenheit to Centigrade

Subtract 32, multiply by 5, divide by 9.

Example:
$$350\,°F - 32 = 318$$
$$318 \times 5 = 1590$$
$$1590 \div 9 = 177\,°C$$

Convert U.S. Measurements to Metric

—www.worldwidemetric.com/metcal.htm

1 gallon	= 4 qt	= 16 cups	= 8 pt	= 3.76 l	
1/4 gallon	= 1 qt	= 4 cups	= 2 pt	= .94 l	
1/8 gallon	= 1/2 qt	= 2 cups	= 1 pt	= 16 fl oz	= .47 l
1 cup	= 8 fl oz	= 16 Tbs.	= 48 tsp.	= 237 ml	
3/4 cup	= 6 fl oz	= 12 Tbs.	= 36 tsp.	= 177 ml	
2/3 cup	= 5 1/3 fl oz	= 10 2/3 Tbs.	= 32 tsp.	= 158 ml	
1/2 cup	= 4 fl oz	= 8 Tbs.	= 24 tsp.	= 118 ml	
1/3 cup	= 2 2/3 fl oz	= 5 1/3 Tbs.	= 16 tsp.	= 79 ml	
1/4 cup	= 2 fl oz	= 4 Tbs.	= 12 tsp.	= 59 ml	
1/8 cup	= 1 fl oz	= 2 Tbs.	= 6 tsp.	= 30 ml	
1 Tbs.	= 3 tsp.	= 15 ml			
1 tsp.	= 5 ml				

Key

fl oz = fluid ounces
gal = gallon
pt = pints
qt = quart
tsp. = teaspoons
Tbs. = tablespoons
ml = milliliters
l = liters

If something calls for ¼ cup, don't divide the liter equivalent—multiply the tablespoon equivalent. Example: ¼ cup = 4 tablespoons. 1 tablespoon = 15 ml, so ¼ cup = 4 tablespoons x 15 ml each = 60 ml

Choose A Juicer

There is no "best" juicer. Just like we would dress differently for different occasions, each juicer type matches a different need. All that really matters is that you get one that fits your needs. If all you want is fresh orange or grapefruit juice in the morning, then all you need is a manual press juicer.

The Norwalk brand is well-reviewed. Or consider an old-fashioned glass juicer, the kind where youpress half an orange down on it and voila—juice.

If you decide you'd like to add more and different fresh juices to your diet, there are three types of juicers—centrifugal, masticating, and twin-gear.

In a centrifugal juicer, fruit pieces are pushed against a spinning mesh basket, which shreds them into a pulp. The spinning motion also separates the juice. The pulp either stays in the basket or is expelled depending on the model. If it isn't expelled it has to be removed from time to time during juicing.

These juicers make juice quickly because of their large intake tubes—foods do not need to be cut up as much, and more can be added at once. They work well with most fruits and vegetables and are cheaper than the other two types. They are easy to clean but the mesh basket must be cleaned

immediately or it can become very difficult to get the dried pulp out.

However, they don't do so well with leafy greens and smaller pieces of produce, which just fall into the mesh basket, leading to wasted food. The fast spinning of the basket also adds heat and air, which oxidizes the juice, resulting in faster nutritional loss than juice produced by the other two kinds. Some work at lower speeds but this means less juice is produced. Centrifugal juicers are the loudest of the three because of the motor power required to spin the basket.

The Omega Big-Mouth Juicer and the Breville Juice Fountain Elite 800 JEXL both get consistently good reviews.

Masticating, or single-gear, juicers grind food into a pulp and squeeze it against a mesh strainer. This results in more juice from the same amount of produce than a centrifugal juicer. The pulp is continuously ejected so it is not necessary to stop juice production to remove it. They run at a much lower speed than a centrifugal so there is less oxidation. Most brands do well with a wide variety of fruits and vegetables and some can even make nut butters and baby foods, but they don't work as well with leafy greens. They have big feed tubes but, unlike with centrifugal juicers, smaller pieces of food are fully processed.

The best-reviewed ones are from the Omega brand, with the J8006 slightly beating out the J804 and J8005 models. The Champion brand is also well-reviewed and is easy to clean.

Twin-gear (sometimes called triturating) juicers have two interlocking gears that grind food to a pulp to extract the juice. They get the most juice from foods and run at the lowest speeds—juice can be stored for up to two days without significant nutrient loss. They are also the only juicers that work with leafy greens.

Because of their low speeds, though, they do take longer. They also have more parts to clean. They can be less efficient with soft fruits like oranges, although some now have soft-fruit attachments.

The best twin-gears are the Green Star Elite and the Green Power, by Tribest.

Have the following considerations in mind when shopping for a juicer:

Power—The more power, the faster the juicer works. But the faster the juicer, the more oxidation occurs.

Produce used—If you want to juice only fruits and vegetables, either a centrifugal or masticating is fine. But if you also want to juice greens then you need a twin-gear.

Feeder tube size—The smaller the tube the more

produce must be chopped and the longer it takes to make juice.

Simplicity—The less parts, the easier it is to clean.

Noise—Centrifugals are the loudest but that doesn't mean the others are quiet. Still, this is one place where the adage "you get what you pay for" applies—the more expensive juicers are quieter.

Warranty and parts—All juicers break eventually. A good warranty can mean your juicer gets fixed for free. If you don't want a warranty, make sure parts are easily available. Buying a bargain discontinued model or an older used model may not be worth it if the manufacturer no longer makes parts for it.

We are the arbiters of our destiny.

— Irina Tweedie

Farmers Markets

The *supermarché*, or supermarket, is a relatively new phenomenon in France. Just like Walmart and other large chain stores have put small retail stores out of business, the *supermarché* has to a large degree done the same to traditional open-air markets. These traditional markets are places where people get vegetables and cheese from *producteurs* (farmers), choose cuts of meat, and buy fresh what they will cook for dinner. The *boulangerie* and *charcuterie*, or bread and meat shops, are also dwindling in numbers. Much to their credit, some French people refuse to shop at the supermarket because they view them as the death of their food culture.

In the U.S. we no longer have a culture of food that is connected to the earth. We have lost relationship with the people who grow our food. What we have lost is the relationships that stretch from the soil of the farm to the plate on our table, and this is partly responsible for our lack of appreciation and connection to what we eat.

Farmers markets are making a comeback in America—they are the fastest-growing segment of agricultural business. It may not be possible to buy everything we need at a farmers market, but by buying as much there as possible we are rebuilding food culture by meeting the person growing our food and having them be a part of the experience.

We have found that if we go to a market in France and buy wine from the person who makes it, there is something subtly different in the experience of drinking that wine. For those of us who work at offices, retail businesses, and all those places where we are far from the natural world, going to a market on a Saturday or Sunday takes us out of the technological influences that we exist in all week long. We can meet a whole variety of people, handle real food, and have an expanded experience of community.

When we buy food directly from the person who grew it we are holding them accountable. They aren't going to be able to sell us the kind of bruised or unripe tomatoes we may see in a grocery store if the table down the row is selling juicy red tomatoes plucked from the vine that morning. We can take a stand for healthy food in many ways, even engaging in political action. And, we can start in our own hometowns by supporting people of like mind.

It can be difficult to step away from the convenience and comfort of the supermarket, but there is power in the money we work for and spend on food. We are giving our support, consciously or unconsciously, for the way the food we buy is grown. Once we've tasted a "real"—local, organically grown—tomato, we are spoiled, in a way, and less inclined to buy chemicalized varieties.

To find a farmers market in the United States go to ams.usda.gov/farmersmarkets and type in a state. This will provide a list of all the farmers markets registered with the USDA. Local Harvest, localharvest.org, also lists local farmers markets. There are lots of farmers markets that are not registered—check local papers. To find a farmers market internationally, check in travel guide books or search for "farmers markets" for the city or region you are in on the internet. You can also check city websites—they often provide a list.

When we do shop in a grocery store or supermarket, often we can still buy food that is grown locally and in season. Food grown far away from us was picked before it was ripe and this forces it to ripen without the life-support system of the plant and the earth. Also, the longer it takes to get food from its source to our table, the more nutrients are lost. People who work in the produce section of your supermarket can be good resources, as they often know what's in season and where the food comes from if we're not sure.

Gardens

Gardening gives us a connection to our food and where it comes from that nothing else can. My husband and I (Theresa) live near San Francisco. We have a tiny back yard, but we dug up a strip next to the fence and planted zucchini, onions, cucumbers, basil, Swiss chard, and red bell peppers. As our little garden began to produce we were shocked at how good our produce tasted. It was like the difference between hearing a symphony through laptop speakers and hearing it live. Greens as soft as butter melted on our tongues. Onions were sweet and alive in our mouths.

Our next garden was a salad garden. We picked lettuce, arugula, chard and basil and made a salad that went from the garden to being eaten in thirty minutes. Our young son routinely asked if we could have a salad for dinner, he loved the flavor of living greens so much. I reduced my salad dressing to just a bit of olive oil.

You can have a garden planted in pots even if you don't have some land. Since greens are important, try to grow at least a salad garden. *Salad Gardens: Gourmet Greens and Beyond* by the Brooklyn Botanic Garden has a section on container gardens for salad greens as well as other vegetables.

In creating your garden, rotate crops year to year so the soil isn't exhausted, and use good fertilizer, like Fertrell (www.fertrell.com). This brand is made with seaweed, which puts the trace minerals we need in the food. *Four-Season Harvest: Organic Vegetables from Your Garden All Year Long* by Eliot Coleman and Barbara Damrosch and *The New Organic Grower: A Master's Manual of Tools and Techniques for the Home and Market Gardner* by Eliot Coleman are two good resources.

I also get a "farm box," which is delivered every two weeks and which I share with another family. Our box brings us a variety of picked-that-morning, seasonal produce from a CSA farm (Community Supported Agriculture—a farm that brings its produce directly to a home or drop-off point). It's a wonderful thing to go to that box, pick out two or three fresh vegetables, and build a meal around them. Go to csacenter.org and click on "Locate a CSA Farm near you" or go to localharvest.org. For international CSAs, again, search the web for your country or region.

If this aspect of food and diet intrigues you, please read *In Defense of Food* by Michael Pollan and *Animal, Vegetable, Miracle* by Barbara Kingsolver. Mr. Pollan uses humor and hard facts to discuss the state of our food culture and explains how we went from eating good, nutritious food to, in his words, "edible foodlike substances." Ms. Kingsolver and her family lived only on what they could produce on their land or buy in local farmers markets for a year. They ate with the seasons. Then they wrote about it.

Kitchen Tools

The culture of food extends to our kitchen. A well-equipped kitchen helps support an intentional diet. That doesn't mean that we need every gadget and tool that's available in all the fancy catalogues that sell expensive stainless steel and wooden utensils. In general, simply get what you need and have it be functional.

Several things to keep in mind:

- Purchase well-made products—two sources are restaurant supply stores and Lehmans (www.lehmans.com), which is an Amish company in the United States that sells everything from kerosene lanterns to cheese makers to canning supplies to wooden spoons. If you're a catalogue junkie this will take you to new heights of your addiction. In Europe you can try www.riess.at or www.purenature.de.

- Purchase items made from natural materials such as stainless steel, wood, bamboo, or glass. Avoid those made from aluminum, Teflon, and plastic.

- Buy versatile items rather than single-use items. Single-use items are highly advertised gadgets that you spend your hard-earned money on because you think you need them, rather than using your physical body to do the work. You can buy an apple corer, an apple peeler, a strawberry huller, a strawberry slicer, a banana slicer, a corn zipper (for removing the corn from the cob), and an egg slicer. Or you can buy a good paring knife and use it to peel, slice, and core apples; remove the tops from and slice strawberries; slice bananas; remove corn from the cob; and slice eggs, among other things.

Several small appliances that are useful:

- A good juicer—The type that is best for you will depend on what you will be juicing. Get a good-quality machine that will last a lifetime. See *Choose a Juicer* in *How To*, Chapter 6.

- A powerful blender such as a VitaMix—It can be used for pureeing or juicing whole vegetables and fruits, making smoothies, grinding grains, and making nut butter. A VitaMix is expensive so if you can't afford one, you can get a good-quality blender for much less. Or you can buy a VitaMix for less on any used-goods lists like craigslist.org and ebay.com.

- An immersion or stick blender—This is used for blending or pureeing soups in the pot to thicken them. Immersion blenders are easier and safer to use than a regular blender. Hot foods have to be blended with care in small batches in a regular blender so that steam does not force the lid off and explode the hot liquid upward. Stick blenders also save time because we don't have to transfer the food from pot to blender.

- A small electric coffee grinder for grinding spices and grains. You won't want to use the same grinder for coffee, if you drink it, and spices unless you clean it thoroughly.

- A Cuisinart or other brand food processor.

- A handheld mixer, if you will have need for one.

- Some of the tasks done by these appliances can be done by hand as well. Spices can be ground in a mortar and pestle, batter and dough can be mixed with a spoon, and nuts and other foods that need to be ground can be processed with a hand-grinder.

Let me emphasize something; life is entirely positive. It is the manner in which life is expressed that takes on the form of creation or destruction.

— Arnaud Desjardins

For Making Informed Decisions

We are, as they say, what we eat.

We know what's in *our* homemade soup, salad dressing and dip, but processed foods contain sometimes dozens of ingredients we can't even pronounce. Even the healthiest canned, frozen, and packaged choices usually contain extra ingredients, including additives, preservatives, and chemicals. The purest ones still lose nutritional value over time as they sit on the shelves.

To make life positive changes in our diet we can educate ourselves as much as possible regarding how to do that in a very practical way. In this section we offer you background and some of the latest research on these topics so you can make the best choices possible.

Water

No healthy lifestyle can succeed without the bedrock of hydration. Every biological system uses water to function. Water is the "river" of the body—it carries hormones, amino acids, oxygen, and neurotransmitters where they need to go. Water is what fills every cell, regulates its pressure from the inside, and allows the system of the cell to function. It carries the enzymatic messages in the brain from neuron to neuron. It keeps the blood flowing and maintains the correct pressure within the veins. And much more. Sources differ as to what percentage of a human body is water, but there is agreement that it is more than 50 percent.

When we are not getting enough water the body prioritizes how the water we do have is used. Life-sustaining organs, such as the brain and the heart, receive water first, while many other organs, systems, and functions receive less or none. As we become more and more dehydrated, we develop acute and chronic disease.

The following bullet points are synthesized from the book *Your Body's Many Cries For Water*, by F. Batmanghelidj, M.D., and are a short list of water's health attributes, as well as symptoms that may result from dehydration. There are other causes of illness but Dr. Batmanghelidj makes such a strong case for adequate hydration being able to heal disease that it makes sense to us to follow his recommendations and pass them along to you. We recommend reading this engaging book.

- Water fills the discs in our spines. If we are dehydrated, the water in our discs is low priority, and we may have back and neck pain.

- Water is essential in the digestive process. If there isn't enough water the acid in the stomach become too concentrated, leading to pain in the digestive tract as this acid irritates the delicate lining.

- Heartburn can be another result of the body's attempt to protect the intestine from insufficiently-diluted stomach acid. Stomach acid is pushed back up into the stomach to protect the intestines, but it is also pushed through the stomach into the esophagus, resulting in heartburn.

- The mucus layer formed during digestion to protect the lining of the stomach is 98 percent water. If there isn't enough water to form that layer, the stomach lining is compromised, which can lead to ulcers.

- A lack of water leads to constipation because water is essential to moving fecal waste through the intestines. With the additional strain of elimination without hydration the intestinal lining is pushed out, resulting in hemorrhoids.

- Dehydration can also cause or exacerbate allergies. Histamine, the hormone responsible for fighting bacteria, viruses, and foreign bodies, also regulates water distribution. If there is a shortage of water, the body produces an over-abundance of histamine to help regulate what little water there is. It then becomes much more responsive to the foreign bodies that cause allergies.

- Skin problems are another symptom of dehydration. Tremendous amounts of water are lost through the skin as it, like the lungs, has a huge surface area. Because of this, when water is scarce, getting it to the skin is a low priority. Pimples and eczema can form when there is not enough water to wash away impurities. Wrinkles can form when there is not enough water to hydrate the skin (that will get some of us drinking). Waking up with puffy eyes may be caused by the lymph, the fluid in the lymphatic system, not being sufficiently liquid, making it stagnate in the face as we sleep.

- Because we lose a lot of water during the night through breathing, it's an excellent idea to drink a glass of water when we wake up.

- Lack of hydration affects more than the physical body. If it is not getting enough water, the body sends a message to the brain that our life is in danger and we can live in a state of alarm without knowing why. This can have a profound effect on our mind and emotions. Receiving this message and not understanding where it is coming from, we project inappropriate reactivity on our partners, our children, our friends, or the jar of olives we can't open.

Our recommendation, based on our experience and what we have read and researched, is to drink three to four liters of water a day. This may sound like a lot but when we consider everything in us that relies on water, it makes sense. It only takes about two weeks to form a habit and to make drinking this much water a part of our routine. It takes about six months of this practice to completely hydrate oneself.

It's not effective to drink large quantities of water at one time, however, because it is too much to absorb at once. Eight to twelve ounces every hour or so is appropriate. Each of us can regulate the timing of our water intake differently based upon our daily activities. For example, if we are riding in the car for eight hours we may not want to drink a lot of water unless we don't mind stopping a lot. The point is to give the body an ongoing supply of water to meet its needs.

It's best not to drink liquids a half-hour or less before eating and for at least forty-five minutes after eating. A few sips during a meal are fine, but drinking liquid before, during, or after a meal disrupts digestion by diluting saliva and gastric juices. If we follow this schedule for a while we will no longer feel thirsty or have the need to drink during meals, but it will continue to astonish our waiter or waitress when we say we don't want anything to drink with our meal.

Water is the only liquid that does not require digestion. Tea, soda, juice, electrolyte drinks, coffee, or anything else must go through the process of digestion like any other food, so we don't include other beverages as a part of our three-or-four liters a day.

When we really start drinking water, for the first week or two we might find ourselves feeling a little bit sick, or at least sick and tired of going to the bathroom as our body adjusts. What happens when we begin drinking water consistently is that our cells and intestines begin to dump toxins they had not been able to flush for a long time. After this stage we might have the experience of being thirsty all the time. Keep drinking; this will pass.

One way to gauge whether or not we are beginning to drink enough water is the color of our urine. It should consistently be either colorless or very, very light yellow—anything darker means we need to drink more.

As we hydrate more and more, we need to consider what we're drinking out of. All plastic water bottles and cups, including Nalgene or other brands that use thick and hard plastic, leak chemicals and plastic into the water. This may not seem like such a big deal, but if we're drinking a lot of water every day those minute particles add up, and they have been linked to degenerative disease. Stainless steel or glass water bottles and glasses have been tested and proven to leach nothing.

Water is expensive to buy, and most of it comes in plastic bottles. We recommend having a good water filter in your home. The most basic kind is an activated carbon filter, which removes bad tastes and odors as well as reducing (but not eliminating) heavy metals, parasites, and chemicals. The most popular of this variety is the countertop pitcher, like the Brita. There are also cation-exchange systems. A "cation" is a positively-charged ion, which exchanges calcium and magnesium ions, responsible for "hard water," with sodium ions. This softens hard water and removes some minerals and ions. Ultraviolet disinfectors remove bacteria and parasites. The two best filters are distillers, which work by boiling and condensing the water;

and reverse osmosis, which remove the widest range of contaminants including bacteria and viruses, chlorine, and heavy metals. The more a filter removes, the more expensive it is. Consider what you need and the quality of water where you live when deciding on the filter that will work best for you.

Supplementation

The body is designed to absorb and assimilate vitamins and minerals from whole foods. The large-scale industries that grow food in the United States and countries around the world use petroleum-based fertilizers that strip soil of these nutrients, so foods grown in this soil lack them. It is wise to replace these missing nutrients through food supplements.

One way of looking at supplementation is by thinking of it as horses pulling a wagon up a hill. In order to do the job, a specific number of horses are needed. Supplementation is like making sure we have enough horses.

Whole food supplements (i.e., herbs, green powders, liquid minerals) and "food-*grown*" supplements, which are grown on plants or derived from dehydrated fruit, vegetable, and grass juices, as well as homeopathics, are easily absorbed and assimilated. "Food-*based*" supplements are the next best choice. These use synthetic nutrients but with food-based binders— such as green powders or herbs, which prime vitamins and minerals for absorption. These are less expensive than "food-grown" supplements.

Most commercial vitamins and minerals that are sold in pharmacies, supermarkets, and health food stores in the United States and Europe are made from isolated, synthetic nutrients. For example, a vitamin B-complex is made by producing all the different B vitamins (i.e., B-1, B-6, B-12, etc.) from synthetic sources and then combining these in one capsule, tablet, or liquid and selling it as a B-complex supplement. In the United States these supplements are often labeled as "natural." The problem is our bodies absorb only a tiny percentage of a synthetic nutrient.

The best course of action is to have a natural health practitioner design a supplement program specifically for you. Another way is to visit a reputable natural foods store and talk to the person in charge of the supplement department.

In general herbs should be taken without food, and vitamins and minerals should be taken with food, but read the labels.

The following is a partial list of absorbable supplements. We have researched each one and feel confident in our recommendation.

Liquid Minerals

Minerals build bones and soft tissue and help regulate the heartbeat. They are essential in blood clotting, nerve response, and the transportation of oxygen, among other things. The body needs them to properly use amino and fatty acids and vitamins. Our glandular system feeds on minerals. We recommend:

Youngevity Majestic Earth Plant-Derived Minerals (liquid minerals)—In the U.S. order from their website: www.majesticearth-minerals.com. Click on "liquid supplement" to find product. Outside the U.S., call 00-1-801-756-4949 (corporate office).

Växa Daily Essentials—Order from their website: www.vaxa.com. For international orders you will receive an email with the total cost of the order including shipping. Respond to email to confirm order.

Electrolytes

Electrolytes are necessary for nerve reactions and the electric charge that fires muscles, including the heart. Research indicates that if we don't have enough of them we become confused or fatigued. We may also develop nervous system or bone disorders. Other symptoms of lowered electrolytes include depression, headaches, mouth ulcers, muscle spasms, overall muscle weakness, twitching, convulsions, irregular heartbeat, blood pressure changes, and numbness.

We suggest: *Ultima Replenisher*, which uses maltodextrin derived from organic corn as the chelating agent. In the U.S. order from their website: www.ultimareplenisher.com. Can be ordered *internationally* at www.iherb.com.

Green Powder

We believe that green powders are the best way to give ourselves a nutritional support base because they are 99 percent absorbable. They contain highly absorbable protein and valuable phytonutrients such as enzymes, chlorophyll, and carotenes from herbs, algae, grasses, sprouts, vegetables, and fruits. Our recommendations:

The company *Synergy* arguably makes the best green powder in the world. In the U.S. order from their website: www.synergy-co.com. For international orders, please go to www.synergy-co.com/international.html and follow the directions for your country.

Two other excellent green powders that are less expensive than Synergy are *Dr. Schulze's SuperFood* and *Vibrant Health's Green Vibrance*. Order *Dr. Schulze's SuperFood* from their website: www.herbdoc.com

Order *Vibrant Health's Green Vibrance* in the **U.S.** from their website: www.vibranthealth.us. Can also be found in most health food stores. Order internationally through www.iherb.com.

Flaxseed Oil and/or Cod Liver Oil

These oils contain fatty acids essential to the health of the nervous and cardiovascular systems and the eyes. Fish oil is also a good source of vitamin B-12, which we need to prevent neurological damage from pernicious anemia (a blood disorder caused by inadequate vitamin B12 in the blood). Studies indicate that these oils protect cells from degenerative disease and help with depression and inflammations such as arthritis. While we don't recommend eating fish because of the contaminants, fish oil is heavily filtered and tested.

We also recognize that recommending cod liver oil is not consistent with a plant-based diet or with the scientific arguments of *The China Study.* Some people, however, don't absorb the fatty acids in the form they are found in flax seed oil and everyone needs vitamin B-12. It's so important to get these that we are recommending cod liver oil just to be sure you get them.

We appreciate these:

OmegaBrite—Their process pulls out heavy metals and other toxins found in fish. In the U.S. order from their website: www.omegabrite.com. Place international orders on their website and make sure to select USPS Global Priority Mail International for shipping preference.

Wholemega is made by New Chapter. Their fish oil is pressed out much like extra-virgin olive oil. It is not chemically treated and so retains the natural beneficial compounds processing can destroy. This product is also contaminant-free. In the U.S. go to www.newchapter.com/fish-oil and click on "Store Locator" in the panel on the right.

Udo's Oil contains flaxseed and other beneficial oils. We recommend taking this product along with fish oil because it is a high-quality blend of a number of oils. In the U.S. go to their website to find a store: www.udoerasmus.com. To order internationally, go to www.udoerasmus.com/contact/contact_distributors_en.htm and click on your country.

Digestive Enzymes

Plant-based food enzymes are needed to replace the natural enzymes destroyed through cooking, freezing, or canning.

Ron Schneider's Plant Enzymes, sold under the name *Enriching Gifts Plant Enzymes,* are, in our view, the best in the world. In the U.S. order from their website: www.enzymesfordigestion.com or www.enrichinggifts.com. For international orders, download an order form from www.enrichinggifts.com: click on "how to order," then click "click here for a printable order form." Fax order to the number on the form.

Food-Grown Supplements

New Chapter—We find New Chapter to be the best source for food-grown supplements. They also have other excellent products. In the U.S. order from their website: www.newchapter.com. They can also be found in health food stores. For international orders, please contact them through their website (www.newchapter.com/contact) to find a local dealer.

Garden of Life—In the U.S. order from their website: www.gardenoflife.com. They can also be found in health food stores. Order internationally through www.iherb.com.

Food-Based Supplements

Rainbow Light—In the U.S. order from their website: www.rainbowlight.com. Can also be found in health food stores. Can be ordered internationally at www.iherb.com.

SuperNutrition—In the U.S. order from their website: www.supernutritionusa.com or look for them in health food stores. Order internationally through www.iherb.com.

Organics

When something is organic it means it was grown without using petroleum-based fertilizers, pesticides, or herbicides. It also means it isn't genetically modified (GMO—see *Genetically Modified Organisms* in this chapter).

Organic farmers use natural fertilizers such as cow manure and seaweed. These add trace minerals and vitamins to the dirt, which are then pulled into the foods as they grow. Most organic farmers also rotate their crops so the soil doesn't get depleted. Industrial farms put genetically modified seeds in petroleum-fertilized soil which has been stripped of nutrients. The vegetables and fruits grown in such soil are, therefore, also mineral- and vitamin-deficient. They also absorb whatever chemical fertilizers and pesticides were used on them, transferring them directly to whomever eats them. The soil on commercial farms is often so depleted that it literally will not grow a plant without the petroleum fertilizers. Critics of such farming say that on commercial farms the only purpose of the soil is to hold the plants upright.

We recommend buying organic food as much as possible, and non-GMO food all the time. We do not recommend making "organic" a "religion" by obsessing to make sure every last bit of food we buy is organic. However, fruits and vegetables, which are mostly water, take in a greater quantity of pesticides and chemicals than other foods. At least try to buy organic strawberries, squashes, potatoes, and thin-skinned fruits like grapes, because chemicals soak right into them. If your children drink milk or eat yogurt and cheese, buy organic because conventional dairy products are filled with hormones and antibiotics. (See *Dairy Products* in this chapter)

While labeling is not uniform throughout the world, we can ask the knowledgeable owner or buyer at a health food store what definitions mean in the country we are shopping in.

The following are three categories of organic labeling and what they mean in the United States:

"100% organic" Has not been produced using sewage sludge, ionizing radiation, artificial growth hormones, genetically modified crops, and most synthetic fertilizers and pesticides. If it's a processed food, it must contain 100-percent organically-produced ingredients.

"Organic" The product consists of at least 95 percent organically-produced ingredients. Any remaining ingredients must consist of nonagricultural substances approved on the national list of products that are not commercially available in organic form.

"Made with organic ingredients" The product contains at least 70 percent organic ingredients. These ingredients can either be listed individually or as a group as in "soup made with organic peas, potatoes, and carrots" or "soup made with organic ingredients."

Processed products that contain less than 70 percent organic ingredients can't use the term "organic" anywhere on the label. They can only identify the specific organic ingredients in the ingredients list.

Genetically Modified Organisms

A genetically modified organism (GMO) is one in which one or more genes from an outside source (either from the same or a different species) have been added to a food through genetic engineering. These genes make a plant or animal resistant to insects or bacteria or make them grow faster, among other uses.

Because of the way GMOs are spoken about and marketed in the U.S. many people tend to have a feeling of "no big deal" about them. Yet **the advice of the American Academy of Environmental Medicine is to avoid GMOs.** The Center for Food Safety (www.centerforfoodsafety.org) states, "A number of studies have revealed that genetically engineered foods can pose serious risks to humans, domesticated animals, wildlife and the environment. Human health effects can include higher risks of toxicity, allergenicity, antibiotic resistance, immune-suppression and cancer. As for environmental impacts, the use of genetic engineering in agriculture could lead to uncontrolled biological pollution, threatening numerous microbial, plant and animal species with extinction, and the potential contamination of non-genetically engineered life forms with novel and possibly hazardous genetic material."

Barbara Kingsolver, respected author and biologist, says in her essay, *A Fist in the Eye of God:*

> 'Single transplanted genes often behave in startling ways in an engineered organism, often proving lethal to themselves, or sometimes to neighboring organisms. In light of newer findings, geneticists increasingly concede that gene-tinkering is to some extent shooting in the dark. Barry Commoner, senior scientist at the Center for the Biology of Natural Systems at Queens College, laments that while the public's concerns are often derided by industry scientists as irrational and uneducated, the biotechnology industry is—ironically—conveniently ignoring the latest results in the field "which show that there are strong reasons to fear the potential consequences of transferring a DNA gene between species."

According to a U.S. Department of Agriculture statistic released in 2010, 70 percent of corn, 78 percent of cotton (cottonseed oil), and 93 percent of soy are genetically modified. These crops show up in almost every processed food on the market unless it is certified organic. GMO soy is even found in mainstream baby formulas. By-products of these crops include hydrolyzed vegetable protein, high fructose corn syrup, natural flavorings, soy lecithin, and vegetable oil (which is soy oil). The Food and Drug Administration (FDA) representatives have admitted that everything that contains corn or soy in any form—soy lecithin, hydrolyzed soy protein, etc.—and does not explicitly say "non-GMO," is GMO.

There is massive resistance in the European Union population to GMO crops, so virtually no GMO are grown. Of 331 billion acres of farmland in the 27 E.U.-membership countries, only 247,000 acres total are permitted to grow GMO crops. The resistance is so strong that the National Institute for Agrarian Reform (INRA), which functions in many countries in the E.U. and employs over 1,800 scientists, has stopped researching GMO crops. But Monsanto, a major GMO seed producer, has submitted an application for authorization every year since 2009.

The United States is the only first-world country that does not label GMO foods. But, since most of the GMO crops of the world are made into animal feed, products from animals that eat these feeds contain GMO residues. There are no laws stating these products must be labeled as GMO.

Other labeling gaps exist. For example, foods imported from other countries—especially the U.S.—often contain ingredients made from GMO crops but are not labeled as such. Another gap is ingredients that have been produced with GMO bacteria or yeast, such as flavor enhancers and vitamins; or with GMO soy, such as soybean oil and soy lecithin, which are in almost every processed food.

There are hundreds of genes being spliced into agricultural products across the board both in the United States and Europe and most of them are genes that we would not normally eat in any food, such as Bacillus thuringiensis (Bt). Bt is a soil bacterium that produces toxins which kill certain insects. The specific genes responsible for this are pulled out of the bacteria and put into corn. The corn then produces an insecticidal toxin that kills those same insects. When we eat Bt corn, we are also eating this toxin, which in the normal course of our lives, we would never ingest. In an article entitled "Maternal and fetal exposure to pesticides associated to genetically modified foods in Eastern Townships of Quebec, Canada," published in *Reproductive Toxicology* in May 2011 (Vol. 31, Issue 4), scientists found evidence of the Bt toxin in the blood of pregnant women and their fetuses, as well as in non-pregnant women, despite Monsanto's assurance that Bt would not survive the digestive process in humans.

According to an article written by Jeffrey M. Smith, Executive Director of the Institute for Responsible Technology[1] and published on foodconsumer.com in May 2011:

> There's already plenty of evidence that the Bt-toxin produced in GM corn and cotton plants is toxic to humans and mammals *and* triggers immune system responses.... In government-sponsored research in Italy, mice fed Monsanto's Bt corn showed a wide range of immune responses. Their elevated IgE and IgG antibodies, for example, are typically associated with allergies and infections. The mice had an increase in cytokines, which are associated with "allergic and inflammatory responses." The specific cytokines (interleukins) that were elevated are also higher in humans who suffer from a wide range of disorders, from arthritis and inflammatory bowel disease, to MS and cancer. The young mice in the study also had elevated T cells (gamma delta), which are increased in people with asthma, and in children with food allergies, juvenile arthritis, and connective tissue diseases. The Bt corn that

was fed to these mice, MON 810, produced the same Bt-toxin that was found in the blood of women and fetuses.[2]

We in America are a living, breathing science experiment, and no one is telling us we are participating in it.

Soy

Soybean products have been controversial for decades. One source will say they are excellent for our health and another will say they cause disease. Since soy is in almost everything (i.e., baby formulas, prepared soups, baked goods, some yogurt and ice cream products, sauces, frozen foods, bread, salad dressings) it's worth it to investigate what's going on.

Studies done over the last seventy years on humans and animals have shown that soybeans affect the thyroid. The goitrogens in soy act like a hormone and disrupt (or even suppress) the thyroid's (and the endocrine system's) delicate balance. If we are using thyroid replacement drugs and also eating a lot of soy, we are putting an enormous amount of pressure on our thyroids. In fact, environmental toxicologist Michael Fitzpatrick says the combination of thyroid drugs and high soy intake is how scientists induce thyroid cancer in lab animals.

Soy also contains enzyme inhibitors that stop trypsin and similar enzymes (needed for the digestion of protein) from working. The phytic acid in soy products can block absorption of calcium, magnesium, copper, iron and especially zinc. (All legumes have phytic acid, but soy has an unusually high amount.)

---

[1]He is also the author of the #1 international bestselling book on GMOs, titled *Seeds of Deception*, and of *Genetic Roulette: The Documented Health Risks of Genetically Engineered Foods*.

[2]www.foodconsumer.org/newsite/Safety/gmo/dangerous_toxins_from_genetically_modified_plants_0527110452.html

Soy contains haemagglutinin, which causes red blood cells to clump together. This is why soy is on the list of foods people on blood thinning medication can't eat. Soy also coats the insides of the intestines, which can result in cramping and gas. This coating can also produce long-term problems in the ability to absorb amino acids. Other side effects are constipation, fatigue, and lethargy.

Much of the confusion around whether soy is good or not is the result of the advertising campaigns of Protein Technologies International, the American Soybean Association, and Archer Daniels Midland, who have spent hundreds of millions of advertising dollars promoting this message in order to ensure a market for the over seventy million acres of genetically modified soybeans planted each year by commercial farmers. This confusion is worsened by not knowing the difference between "whole soy foods" and "processed soy products."

Whole soy foods are made from the whole bean and are fermented, which neutralizes the soybean's known toxic effects. For centuries Asian cultures have eaten whole soy foods including tempeh, natto, miso, and soy sauce. Whole soy foods are a good source of protein and vitamins, and fermented food has many health benefits, introducing beneficial bacteria to the digestive tract and enhancing amino acid content.

Processed soy products, on the other hand, retain much of the inherent toxicity of soy. They are made from soy protein isolates (SPI) and textured soy protein (TSP). SPI is the concentrated protein pulled from soybeans. It is made by taking defatted soybean meal (soy meal soaked for twelve hours in hexane, petroleum ether, and/or a chloroform/methanol solution) and washing it in an acid solution to pull the protein from it. This protein is put into another solution and then dried at extremely high temperatures, which strip it of any usable proteins. This process has been proven to produce carcinogens. As early as 1979 the Federation of American Societies for Experimental Biology (FASEB) reported that the only safe use of such a product was as a glue for cardboard boxes.

SPI is added to products to increase their protein content, even though it is indigestible, and to give them a smoother feel in the mouth. It is also used to keep foods from separating or crumbling and to help them hold their water and fat content.

Hundreds of studies over the last seventy years have linked SPI and TSP to malnutrition, digestive problems, immune-system breakdown, thyroid dysfunction, reproductive disorders, infertility, cancer, heart disease, and a decline in mental abilities. Processed soy products, including tofu and soy milk, coat the insides of the intestines, which can result in cramping, constipation, and gas. If we eat them long enough, this coating interferes with the body's ability to absorb nutrition. (Fortunately, you can replace soy milk with rice, almond, or oat milk.)

It has been pointed out for decades that Asians who eat soy don't have the Western diseases linked to the intake of soy. But the soy industry's own studies reveal that Asians eat whole soy foods, not processed soy products, in quantities ranging from 9 to 36 grams per day. Whereas one cup of processed soy milk contains 240 grams!

Never in history have so many people eaten so much soy. Over 60 percent of the food products on the market in the U.S. contain SPI or TSP in one of its various names—textured vegetable protein, soy protein isolate, hydrolyzed plant protein, hydrolyzed soy protein, hydrolyzed vegetable protein, or soy lecithin, to name a few. New soy-based products with new names are continually being developed.

Vegetarians have relied heavily on SPI and TSP products as a source of protein. Daniel M. Sheehan, formerly senior toxicologist with the FDA'S National Center for Toxicological Research, said that those who choose to eat SPI and TSP products are engaging in "a large, uncontrolled and basically unmonitored human experiment."

Dairy Products

While we don't recommend drinking milk or eating milk products on the Dharma Feast diet with the exception of organic butter or ghee, we recognize that some people will choose to do so. We want to make sure you have enough information to make healthy choices.

The U.S. National Dairy Council has spent decades making sure we believe we can't have healthy bones and teeth unless we drink milk and eat dairy products. If we're following the standard American diet, we're eating and/or drinking a cow milk product at every meal.

Our recommendation is to avoid cow milk and it's based on the health effects of these products. For example, according to a 2001 Harvard review of current research, there is a direct correlation between high dairy intake and prostate cancer. This is just one example of the negative results of eating dairy products.

Many of the problems associated with dairy intake are due to modern processing methods. Mechanical homogenization forcibly breaks up the fat globules in milk, which frees the enzyme *xanthine oxidase.* This enzyme can then enter the bloodstream. Studies published by the U.S. Department of Agriculture (USDA) have proven that this enzyme is capable of creating scar damage in the heart and arteries. The body releases cholesterol to form a protective fatty layer over the scarred areas. Over time this leads to arteriosclerosis, also called "hardening of the arteries," a known cause of strokes and heart attacks.

The high heat of pasteurization destroys enzymes, including lactase and galactase. Lactase is necessary for digesting lactose. Undigested lactose is responsible for most allergic reactions and intolerance to cow milk products. Galactase is needed to assimilate calcium and its loss is one reason we can't absorb most of the calcium in cow milk.

Cow milk is acidic after digestion and creates an acidic environment in the body. Calcium is used to neutralize acid. Since the calcium in cow milk isn't absorbed, it can't neutralize this acid, so calcium is pulled from our bones instead. Many studies have found a link between milk consumption and osteoporosis, which is a weakening of bones due to calcium loss, in older women and men. Europe, Australia, and New Zealand have higher rates of osteoporosis than the U.S. and these are also the only places where the population eats more milk products than we do in the U.S.

Another problem with dairy consumption is that we don't know the long-term effects of drinking or eating milk and meat from animals treated with artificial growth hormones, as they have only been in use for a short time. However, studies have shown that drinking milk from cows treated with rBGH/rBST increases Insulin-like Growth Factor 1 (IGF-1) levels in blood. This hormone occurs naturally to regulate cell growth and remove old cells, but at increased levels it leads to uncontrolled cell growth and slows down the removal of old cells. Both of these situations may set the stage for cancer. Once cancer has set in, higher IGF-1 levels make cancer cells grow faster, especially in breast cancer. Despite this and many other human health concerns, no labeling of dairy products containing rBHG/rBST is required.

Studies at Cornell University proved that antibiotics given to cows end up in their milk.

Frequent exposure to antibiotic residues through milk or dairy products is a health concern for people over the long term. In the normal body, there are bacteria that live in the gut and mouth and help in the digestion of food in the gut. These "friendly" bacteria do not normally cause disease since the immune system keeps them in check. ... Bacteria in the normal body that come across small amounts of antibiotics frequently can develop ways to survive the antibiotics and become "antibiotic resistant." In cases of infection and illness, it then becomes more difficult to control such resistant bacteria with the available antibiotics.[3]

We recommend butter from raw, organic cow milk, or organic ghee (clarified butter) on this diet. Raw cow milk still has the enzymes necessary for digestion because it has not been pasteurized or homogenized. If raw butter is not available in your area, then organic butter is recommended. However, we recommend eating any non-organic butter sparingly because of the health risks and possible chemical and antibacterial content discussed above.

For those who would like to keep milk in their diets but who now wish not to drink cow milk, goat milk is a healthier alternative. It is naturally homogenized, so the enzyme xanthine oxidase is not freed and absorbed into the bloodstream. Goat milk is also higher in many vitamins and minerals than cow milk, and its higher amount of medium chain fatty acids (MCT) means it forms smaller and softer curds, which are easier to digest, making it easier for us to absorb the calcium, vitamins, and minerals.

The protein lactalbumin, responsible for most cow milk allergies, is genetically different in goat milk. Many people who are lactose-intolerant can eat goat milk products. There is debate over whether goat milk ends up slightly acid or slightly alkaline after digestion, but even if it ends up slightly acidic, it is less so than cow milk, resulting in less calcium loss over time.

[3]www.envirocancer.cornell.edu/Factsheet/Diet/fs37.hormones.cfm

Raw goat milk is best, as the enzymes required for easy digestion are not destroyed, but pasteurized goat milk and its products are still better choices than cow milk.

Fish

While this book recommends a vegetarian diet, some of us may eat fish and meat, if not on a regular basis, then for special occasions. We offer the following in this spirit.

We do not recommend eating most fish because wild-caught fish has extremely high levels of heavy metals and other toxic substances. Farmed fish contain pesticides, antibiotics, and parasites and have significantly less nutritional value than wild-caught fish. Taras Grescoe's article, "The Trouble with Salmon," in the May 2009 issue of *Best Life* magazine, is a must read—www.bestlifeonline.com/cms/publish/health/The-Trouble-with-Salmon.php. (If the link no longer works the article has been incorporated into the chapter "An Economy of Scales" in *Bottomfeeder: How to Eat Ethically in a World of Vanishing Seafood*.) The following is synthesized from his recommendations:

- Instead of eating carnivorous fish like swordfish and salmon, eat those lower on the food chain (sushi names italicized)—anchoveta, arctic char (*iwana*), barramundi, capelin, Pacific halibut, herring (also called kippers, rollmops, solomon gundy), jellyfish, Spanish (not Gulf of Mexico) mackerel (*sawara*), mullet, oysters, mussels, pollock (the U.S. fishery is Marine Stewardship Council certified), sablefish (also called black cod), sand lance, sardines (also called sprats, brisling, pilchard) (*iwashi*), squid (also called *calamari*), trout (*nijimasu*), and blue whiting are the best choices.

- Don't eat long-lived predator fish like tuna, swordfish, shark, and Chilean sea bass. They have the highest levels of mercury.

- Avoid farmed shrimp, tuna, salmon, and other species that are fed animal protein. Dioxins and other toxins concentrate in their flesh.

In this article Mr. Grescoe thoroughly investigates the farmed salmon industry. Canadian salmon farmers have added the marine toxin Slice, or emamectin benzoate, to the food given to the fish in order to kill a particular parasite. This is more or less true for any farmed fish in the world. Emamectin benzoate, when given to rats and dogs, "causes tremors, spinal deterioration, and muscle atrophy." It is a known neurotoxin listed by the United States Environmental Protection Agency as "highly toxic."

Mr. Grescoe goes on to say that:

> Wild and farmed salmon have similar levels of beneficial omega-3 fatty acids, but feed makers are increasingly bulking up the pellets fed to the fish with soy, which increases the ratio of omega-6 fatty acids. A disproportion of omega-6 fatty acids promotes chronic inflammation, which has been associated with everything from heart disease and cancer to Alzheimer's and depression.

> Analyzing two tons of salmon bought in stores from Edinburgh, Scotland, to Seattle, Washington, a team led by Ronald Hites, PhD., of Indiana University, found that farmed product contained up to ten times more persistent organic pollutants (POPs) than the wild variety. The chemicals in question are among the most toxic known to man such as the dioxins from herbicides (the most infamous being Agent Orange) and the polychlorinated biphenyls used in paints and pesticides, among other things. All are suspected carcinogens; most cause behavioral, growth, and learning disorders.

It's better to eat wild-caught than farmed fish, but even labels in supermarkets can be misleading. In an undercover operation across America, *Consumer Reports* found that 56 percent of salmon labeled "wild" was actually farmed.

For constantly updated information on healthy fish choices, go to Seafood Watch, which is part of the Monterey Bay Aquarium's website (www. seafoodwatch.org). The Aquarium is one of the most respected aquatic research facilities in the world. They offer a printable wallet-sized list for easy reference while shopping and a safe-choice card for sushi as well. Their website offers information on dozens of fish with extensive notes on why each variety is listed as Best Choice, Good Alternatives, or Avoid. They do recommend farmed fish, but these would be from closed-containment farming systems, which Mr. Grescoe recommends as well.

The section titled Seafood Watch on the Monterey Bay Aquarium site presents a separate category labeled *The Super Green List*, which "highlights products that are currently on the Seafood Watch 'Best Choices' (green) list. These are low in environmental contaminants and are good sources of long-chain omega-3 fatty acids. This effort draws from experts in human health, notably scientists from the Harvard School of Public Health (HSPH) and Environmental Defense Fund (EDF)." Also, look for the seal of approval of the Marine Stewardship Council (www.msc. org) on packaging, menus, and advertising for products. They are the most reliable sustainable-fisheries certifier in the world.

Meat

As we noted above in the section on Fish, while we don't include meat recipes in the *Dharma Feast Cookbook*, we believe you should know as much as possible about anything you intend to eat.

To get the healthiest meat we need to know what the animals have been eating. Cows, sheep, goats, pigs, and chickens naturally eat grass, not grain. Chickens should get as much as 30 percent of their nutrition from greens. In the United States these animals are fed "junk corn" that is not fit for humans and often genetically-modified. These animals then require growth hormones because they do not reach maturity on this diet. They are also given antibiotics on a regular basis because a grain diet makes them vulnerable to disease. Their meat, eggs, and milk are contaminated with hormones and antibiotics.

A grass-fed cow or chicken grows naturally. They are raised outside in the sun, which provides vitamin D in the meat in a form we can absorb. The green grass they eat puts nutrients and vitamins, as well as omega-3 fatty acids into their meat. In the U.S. buy grass-fed meat.

The following information will give you a sense of what is happening in the commercial beef industry, at least in the United States. There are equally disturbing stories from other countries.

On the website of the U.S. Centers for Disease Control and Prevention, an article entitled "Preliminary FoodNet Data on the Incidence of Infection with Pathogens Transmitted Commonly Through Food" states "foodborne diseases remain an important public health problem in the United States." Every year we hear about outbreaks of illness and the recall of plant and meat food products due to contamination of food sources. The outbreaks can be caused by a number of different organisms.

A virulent strain of bacteria commonly called E. coli, found in feces, makes tens of thousands of people sick each year. Most of the infected people will recover, but some will die and others will have life-changing injuries. The most common food source of this bacteria is hamburger. But, even though the cuts of meat used in hamburger are from areas of the cow that are most likely to be contaminated by feces, there are no federal requirements to test for E. coli.

Ground beef is not produced by grinding one piece of meat; at least not in the United States.

Instead, a single portion of hamburger meat often consists of various grades of meat from different parts of different cows, possibly from different slaughterhouses that may not even be located in the same state or country. Since this meat is not tested there is no traceable chain of accountability.

In addition, in the article "E. Coli Path Shows Flaws in Beef Inspection" by Michael Moss, in the October 7, 2009 issue of *The New York Times*, says that fatty trimmings, which are 50 to 70 percent fat, are turned into "fine lean textured beef" through a process that warms the trimmings, removes the fat in a centrifuge, and treats the remaining product with ammonia to kill E. coli. U.S. Agriculture Department regulations allow this fine lean textured beef to be added to ground chuck and ground sirloin as long as it comes from the same place in the cow as these cuts. It is also used in hamburger meat sold by grocers and fast-food restaurants and served to children in the U.S. through the National School Lunch Program.

If you intend to serve hamburgers at a barbeque or other special occasion, we recommend, if possible, buying ground beef from a local butcher you may trust; or buying grass-fed beef and having the butcher grind it, or grinding it yourself.

Gluten

Gluten is the sticky protein in wheat, barley, spelt, rye, and oats that are not certified to be gluten-free. It makes dough stretch and sauces thicken. Gluten is used in most bakery foods as well as everything from ketchup to salad dressing to ice cream. It is found in almost all processed foods in ingredients like maltodextrin (if derived from wheat), seitan, gelatinized starch, hydrolyzed vegetable protein, modified food starch, barley malt syrup, soy sauce, and vegetable starch. Up to 95 percent of meals in restaurants contain wheat in one form or another. It is also found in the inactive ingredients in many medications.

The problem with gluten is the effect it has on our immune system. Ordinarily the immune system recognizes whole food as a non-threat, but the gluten protein triggers an immunological response whether we show symptoms or not. Many studies have documented this fact. The effects of eating gluten are worth looking at because, if we haven't removed it or reduced it in our diet, there is never a time when we don't have it in our bodies, so the immune system is triggered ongoingly.

One study done in Japan, published in December 2005 by the U.S. National Institutes of Health, showed that eating "gluten hydrolysates," or wheat protein processed with enzymes (found in every processed food that uses wheat), significantly increased NK (Natural Killer) cell activity even though there are no other physical symptoms. NK cells are a major component in the immune system, responsible for killing tumors and cells infected with viruses. They are usually tightly regulated because of their potential to turn against our own cells and tissues. They require an activating signal and the gluten protein mimics this signal. The more frequently they are activated, the more of a chance there is they will begin attacking the body they are designed to protect.

The New England Journal of Medicine published a review paper in January 2002 which listed dozens of auto-immune diseases that can be caused by eating gluten: arthritis, asthma, chronic fatigue syndrome, colitis, Crohn's disease, dermatitis, eczema, fibromyalgia, hepatitis, irritable bowel syndrome, Lou Gehrig's disease, lupus, multiple sclerosis, osteoporosis, rheumatoid arthritis, and type-1 diabetes. We aren't recommending that everyone stop eating gluten, but even if we don't take gluten completely out of our diets, it's worth making an informed decision about how much we consume.

It's becoming more common for people to eat "gluten-free," and there are many gluten-free products available. But they are also highly processed, so again, those with as few ingredients as possible are best. Watch out for artificial ingredients and sweeteners. We've included some gluten-free recipes for baked goods in the Recipes section of this book.

If processed foods aren't labeled as "certified gluten-free," they may contain gluten even though it isn't listed on the label. For instance, wheat flour can be added to dried herbs and spices to prevent caking, and it isn't listed. Also, gluten can be present if a food was made in a facility that also makes wheat-based products. Many labels will indicate this.

When a recipe calls for flour, other types can be used—unbleached almond meal or flour, coconut flour, brown or white rice flour, garbanzo bean flour, and teff flour are a few. Usually a couple of these flours need to be combined with each other or with guar or xanthan gum to get a similar texture to wheat flour.

One cup of gluten-free flour does not necessarily replace one cup of wheat flour. Go to http://www.csaceliacs.info for instructions on flour mixes for general and specialty baking. Click on "Recipes" and then "Gluten Free Flour Formulas." Another good website is http://www.gluten-free-diet-help.com. Click on "Recipes" and scroll down to "Miscellaneous." Click on "Gluten Free Flour Blends." For a mini-education on the different gluten-free flours and thickeners used to make blends, go to http://www.theglutenfreelifestyle.com. Scroll down and click on "Ingredient Treasury for Gluten-Free Baking." A good gluten-free cookbook, such as *Gluten-Free Baking with The Culinary Institute of America* by Richard J. Coppedge, is invaluable for experimenting. There are also gluten-free pre-mixed flours in the baking section of the grocery store. Bob's Red Mill,

Arrowhead Mills, and King Arthur's All-Purpose Gluten-Free Flour are recommended brands.

Wheat pastas can be replaced with rice, quinoa, or buckwheat pasta. If you have an Asian market in your town buy rice noodles there.

Food Additives and Prepared Foods

As the natural food movement began to gain momentum in the 1970s, the definition of "natural food" was food in its natural state, such as brown rice, beans, nuts, seeds, and unprocessed oils. Over the last forty years this definition has become distorted, in part, because many of the small companies from the early days of the movement became big companies, and were bought by much larger ones. The end result is that all sorts of synthetic ingredients have been added to "natural foods" that make them not so natural anymore. Just because a food is labeled "natural" (meaning it was originally found in nature) doesn't mean that it is good or safe for us to eat. If we wouldn't be able to pick an ingredient from a field and maybe aren't even able to pronounce it, we should think twice about eating it.

Avoid

Monosodium glutamate (MSG) A neurotoxic food additive. See *Monosodium Glutamate (MSG)* in this list below.

Many other **neurotoxic food additives** such as sodium nitrite and sodium nitrate, artificial colors, and preservatives are found in processed foods. It is best to avoid them all.

Refined sweeteners See *Sweeteners* in this chapter. In addition to being used in food, artificial sweeteners are used in products such as toothpaste and prescription and over-the-counter medications including those for children. Read labels or, in the case of medications, ask your pharmacist or read the product insert, which lists the "other" or "inert" ingredients.

Toxic metals and additives Most baking powders, commercial salt, aluminum cookware and antacids, along with antiperspirants, contain aluminum, which again has been linked to Alzheimer's disease.

Lead is found in some cookware and glazes and is especially dangerous to children when they are still growing. Lead poisoning can lead to brain damage, behavior problems, anemia, and damage to the major organs. Inorganic iron additives, found in processed foods like commercial white flour, are toxic. Cadmium is in the pesticides used on non-organic fruits and vegetables, and is highly toxic and carcinogenic.

Prepared, extruded breakfast cereals When extruded under high temperature and pressure, the proteins in grains are transformed into neurotoxins.

Fluoride Fluoride is in most drinking water that comes out of the tap in the U.S. While many claim fluoride is beneficial, there is much contradictory evidence. One thing is certain: fluoride is listed with the FDA as more toxic than lead. Tom's of Maine has several fluoride-free toothpastes.

Fortified or enriched Vitamins and minerals added to foods are synthetic. We are unable to absorb them. For more information, see Supplementation in this chapter.

Monosodium glutamate (MSG)

Monosodium glutamate (MSG) is the most widely-used flavor enhancer in the world. People commonly associate it with its use in Chinese food but MSG and MSG-containing substances are added to processed food, fast food, and nearly all canned and frozen foods. Prescription and over-the-counter medications may also contain MSG.

There are many claims that MSG occurs naturally and so is not bad for us. What is true is that glutamate, an amino acid, is found naturally in all living cells, especially seafood, which use it to survive in a salty environment. Glutamate is essential for thinking and remembering and is why fish is called "brain food." It is one of the five basic tastes along with sweet, sour, bitter, and salty. We are evolutionarily hard-wired to like how it tastes, which is why the chemically-made form is added to so many products—it makes us crave them.

But the process of making it artificially, no matter what natural source is used, transforms the amino acids into neurotoxins, which interfere with the proper functioning of the brain—the direct opposite of what it does in its naturally-occurring form. Whether a person has adverse reactions depends on their tolerance to MSG and the amount of processed free glutamic acid in the product, but everyone is affected. Reactions can include migraine headaches, upset stomach, diarrhea, heart irregularities, asthma, sleepiness, muscle weakness, impaired thinking ability (fogginess), and mood swings.

When eating in a Chinese restaurant, we suggest that you ask if they use MSG in their cooking and if so, request that they not use it in the dish they are preparing for you.

Because it is a well-known health risk, manufacturers now list MSG under one of its hidden names. Many products list several different forms of it, which can add up to a considerable and dangerous amount in one food product. A few years ago a trusted friend recommended an organic vegetable bouillon-type base that she uses. When I (Theresa) checked the label, I saw that it contained maltodextrin, (MSG is a by-product of its production) natural flavor, and autolyzed yeast extract—all forms of MSG.

All of the following are different names for MSG—autolyzed yeast, calcium caseinate, calcium glutamate, enzyme modified, flavoring, gelatin, glutamate, glutamic acid, hydrolyzed oat flour, hydrolyzed vegetable protein or corn gluten (anything hydrolyzed), magnesium glutamate, monoammonium glutamate, monopotassium glutamate, Natruim Glutamate, olyzed protein, plant protein extract, potassium glutamate, anything protein fortified, sodium caseinate, textured protein, yeast extract, yeast food, and yeast nutrient. This list is not exhaustive.

The U.S. Food and Drug Administration (FDA) only requires MSG to be listed if it's in its salt form. Glutamic acid, which is MSG not in its salt form and which can either be added or produced during processing (as is the case with maltodextrin), does not need to be listed. A product can contain this equally toxic acid and still legally say "No MSG."

The following ingredients may contain glutamic acid—any fermented flavors or flavorings, barley malt, bouillon, broth, carrageenan, citrate, citric acid, corn syrup, corn syrup solids, high fructose corn syrup, disodium inosinate, dried whey, dry milk solids, anything enriched or vitamin enriched, anything with modified enzymes, anything containing enzymes, fermented proteins, flowing agents, hydrolyzed soy protein, "low" and "no fat" foods, malt extract, malt flavoring, maltodextrin, natural flavors and flavorings (e.g. pork, beef, chicken), modified food starch, pectin, protease, protease enzymes, anything protein fortified, protein powders (oat, rice, soy, whey—used in protein bars, shakes, and body building drinks), anything with the word "seasonings," soy protein, soy protein isolate or concentrate, soy sauce, soy sauce extract, stock, anything ultra-pasteurized, whey protein, whey protein concentrate, and whey protein isolate.

Because it is difficult to carry a list of all of these ingredients in order to check to see if a product contains them, we suggest that you purchase products with simple ingredient lists.

New names for MSG and glutamic acid are created every year. One good source for lists is www.truthinlabeling.org/hiddensources.html.

Other sources to learn more about MSG are www.naturodoc.com/library/nutrition/MSG.htm, www.msgmyth.com/hidename.htm, and www.truthinlabeling.org/nomsg.html.

Sweeteners

Most sweeteners are simple sugars which convert instantly to energy and wreak havoc with blood sugar levels, causing mood swings, fatigue, and even immune system malfunction. Many studies show that two of the most highly-processed sweeteners, high fructose corn syrup (HFCS) and refined white sugar, are at the root of a variety of the health issues in the U.S., yet they are found in most of the processed foods sold in grocery stores and served in restaurants.

All sweeteners except raw honey are processed, and processing destroys nutrients. Because there are so many different sweeteners in so many products it is easy to eat too much of them.

We Recommend

Raw honey is best. Brown rice syrup (made from whole rice, not rice flour or starch), date sugar, maple and yakon syrup, stevia, and one brand of agave syrup (see Agave nectar/syrup in this section) are the next best because they are the least processed.

Honey Sold in many forms—the best is **raw** (unprocessed. Folklore says that ingesting local raw honey daily helps allergy sufferers because it contains local pollens.), **comb** (usually raw; contains a piece of the comb) and **strained** (removes impurities, but all the benefits of raw

honey remain). The processed forms are **pasteurized** (which destroys over 200 components, including antioxidants, minerals, vitamins, amino acids, enzymes, carbohydrates, phytonutrients, and anti-bacterial and antiseptic properties), **crystallized** or **granulated** (in which the glucose content has crystallized), **ultrafiltered** (preferred by supermarkets, as it stays very clear and has a longer shelf life, but the filtering process also pasteurizes it), and **whipped** (processed to control crystallization).

Honey is not recommended for infants under one year because it can contain *Clostridium botulinum* spores, which is the cause of botulism. Until they reach a year, an infant's digestive system is not acidic enough to kill these spores.

Brown rice syrup Made by adding sprouted barley or barley malt to rice and cooking until the starch is converted to sugar. The resulting liquid is strained and boiled down. Many commercial brands, however, use brown rice starch or flour instead of whole-grain rice and are to be avoided. Check ingredients.

Date sugar Made by grinding dehydrated dates. The tiny pieces will not dissolve so it is unsuitable for beverages and any cooking that requires the sweetener to melt.

Maple syrup Made from the sap of maple trees. Sap is collected and boiled into syrup. Minimally processed, but boiling destroys many of its nutrients. Use Grade B because Grade A is processed using chemicals.

Yacon syrup Made by pressing the yacon root and boiling the resulting liquid down into syrup. It tastes similar to molasses. Minimally processed, but boiling destroys many of its nutrients.

Stevia Made from the stevia plant. Stevia is one of the best sweeteners because, even though it is processed, it has few negative effects and several benefits—including not raising glycemic levels.

It also helps with candida, a parasitic, yeastlike fungus, which is a normal part of the flora of the mouth, skin, intestinal tract, and vagina. When this fungus grows out of control, it can cause a number of infections. Many say stevia is healthier than sugar because less is needed in cooking. The green-colored kind is made from the whole stevia leaf so contains more nutrients. The white powder, usually called extract or concentrate, is just the sweet part, so is much more processed. Buy green if available.

Agave nectar/syrup The juice of the agave plant is processed either with enzymes or by hydrolyzing it (a water-based process that, when used on plants and their extracts, requires the use of hydrochloric or sulphuric acid) and then heated. This liquid is then filtered and boiled into syrup. The lighter the syrup, the more processed it is. Sunfood Organic Raw Agave Nectar (in either Dark or Amber) is the only one guaranteed to be both raw and enzyme-processed. Order from their website: www.sunfood.com.

We Don't Recommend

Artificial sweeteners Acesulfame potassium (Sunett), alitame (Aclame), aspartame (Equal or Nutrasweet, Spoonful, Equal-Measure, Benevia, and Canderel), cyclamate (Sucaryl and Sugar Twin), saccharin (Sweet'N Low), sucralose (SucraPlus and Splenda), and inulin are the most widely-used.

Much controversy surrounds artificial sweeteners and it is difficult to separate fact from fiction. Many are banned in some countries but not in others. What is uncontested is that all have neuro-toxic effects—they cause an imbalance in neurotransmitters, the chemicals that transmit signals in the brain. Over time, this can manifest as emotional instability, joint pain, fatigue, insomnia, impairment of memory and concentration, loss of vision, and muscle weakness.

They affect health in other ways also. Aspartame turns into formaldehyde and then formic acid when exposed to temperatures over 86°F, which happens during digestion. This causes metabolic acidosis (too much acid in bodily fluids), the symptoms of which can include severe anxiety, chest pain, nausea, vomiting, palpitations, headache, abdominal and bone pain, and muscle weakness.

Evaporated cane juice Made from sugar cane syrup. In fact, the U.S. Food and Drug Administration is now requiring that this ingredient be called "cane syrup." One brand name is Sucanat. While its reputation is as a less-processed, healthier version of refined white sugar, it is still heavily processed. In many studies its effects were identical to those of sugar. See *Refined white sugar* in this section

Fructose This highly-processed sweetener (not to be confused with naturally-occurring fructose in fruits) is chemically derived from sugar beets, sugar cane, and corn. It is used widely because it is inexpensive. It has no nutritional value, and more importantly, fructose is not entirely absorbed in the small intestine. When it moves into the large intestine it ferments, where it can cause bloating, gas, diarrhea, and gastrointestinal pain. It has been scientifically linked to heart disease, insulin resistance, and obesity (especially central body obesity, the most dangerous kind) and can lead to metabolic syndrome, which causes cardiovascular disease and diabetes. It is also linked to liver disease and gout (an inflammatory arthritis). Because it is so widely used as a sweetener it is easy to eat a significant amount without being aware of it.

Golden syrup is a treacle product left over from processing sugar. It can also be made by treating a sugar solution with acid. Unlike molasses, it has no nutritional value.

High fructose corn syrup (HFCS) is a highly refined sweetener made from the cheapest corn, which is genetically modified. It is suspected to be a major cause of childhood obesity in the U.S. and there is also a link between high HFCS intake and adult-onset diabetes.

One of the problems with HFCS[4] is that it does not trigger chemical messengers that tell the brain the stomach is full. This leads to over-ingestion, especially of HFCS-sweetened drinks, which do not have a solid food component. An article in the American Journal of Clinical Nutrition states: "We propose that the introduction of HFCS and the increased intakes of soft drinks and other sweetened beverages have led to increases in total caloric and fructose consumption that are important contributors to the current epidemic of obesity."[5]

HFCS is widely used in everything from commercial salad dressings and tomato sauce, to soda, because it is inexpensive to make. It's in much of the food served in restaurants.

The Corn Refiners Association, aware that HFCS has a negative association, is asking that the U.S. Food and Drug Administration allow them to call it "corn sugar." They are marketing it as a "natural ingredient made from corn" but it is still HFCS.

Corn syrup, which lacks the final processing used on HFCS, is also made from genetically modified corn. Dark corn syrup is made by adding food coloring.

Refined white, brown, raw or Turbinado sugar A highly-refined sweetener made from either sugar cane or sugar beets. White sugar contains phosphoric acid, formic acid, sulphur dioxide, preservatives, and bleaching agents. Brown sugar is white sugar with molasses added back in. The differences between Turbinado and raw sugar are slight—both are less refined than white sugar and the natural molasses is intact.

The list of health hazards associated with all forms of sugar is long and well-documented—colon cancer, adult-onset diabetes, suppression of the immune system, depression, worsened premenstrual symptoms, and depletion of vitamins and minerals as they are pulled to process it during digestion, to name a few. There is evidence that it contributes to osteoporosis in older women by stripping them of magnesium and calcium.

Sugar is an appetite-stimulant and can lead to overeating and obesity. It can be addictive—the more we eat, the more we crave. Eating other sweeteners does not necessarily satisfy the craving. Getting "off" sugar is not easy.

Sugar can also be named dextrose, glucose, or sucrose. A new trend is to use the word "crystals," as in cane juice crystals, dehydrated cane juice crystals, unrefined cane juice crystals, raw cane crystals, washed cane juice crystals, Florida crystals (a trademarked name), unbleached evaporated sugar cane juice crystals, crystallized cane juice, and unbleached crystallized evaporated cane juice, but these are all just other names for sugar.

Sugar alcohols Chemically-derived sugar substitutes. Common names are glycerol, isomalt, lactitol, maltitol (Maltisorb and Maltisweet), sorbitol, and xylitol. They aren't very sweet on their own so are usually combined with high-intensity artificial sweeteners. The simplest one, ethylene glycol, is the sweet and notoriously toxic substance added to anti-freeze. The others are generally classified as "for the most part non-toxic," but some toxicity remains. Sugar alcohols are not absorbed in

[4]www.seattletimes.nwsource.com/html/health/2002658491_healthsyrup04.htmll

[5]www.ajcn.org/content/79/4/537.full

the intestinal tract which can cause bloating, gas, and diarrhea, even with one serving.

Approach With Caution

Barley malt syrup Produced by sprouting and then quickly heating malt. The resulting mash is strained and the liquid is boiled into syrup. Beware of brands which contain corn syrup.

Fruit juice sweetened/concentrate Some are nothing more than highly refined, concentrated white grape juice, apple juice, pineapple juice, etc., and are closer to refined white sugar than the fruits they come from. These cause the same ups and downs as sugar. "Slightly refined" or "unrefined" are still processed, but better choices.

Molasses (Treacle) The other syrup, besides Golden syrup (see Golden syrup in this section), left over from processing sugar. Many brands add sulfur to kill bacteria, which is not healthy. Blackstrap molasses has some vitamins, minerals, and iron.

Microwaves

Research about the effects of microwaves on food and health is controversial but how they work is known. Microwaves bombard the ions (electrically-charged molecules) in food with low-energy electromagnetic waves. This makes the ions switch polarity up to 100 billion times a second. The friction this causes is what heats up the food. This is not a natural way to cook.

We don't recommend the use of microwaves not only because of the above, but because they represent a way of life that is about moving faster and faster. A microwave's reason for existing is to hurry up and give instant gratification.

Plastic

Many plastics originally thought safe have been found not to be. Plastic is made from petroleum, which remains toxic at some level no matter how it's processed.

It is becoming more widely known that minute amounts of plastic and chemicals seep from plastic containers into whatever food or beverage is inside them. We also absorb plastic through the skin when we touch soft and squishy plastic toys, dolls, sandbox and bathtub toys, some lunchboxes, plastic swimming pools, plastic tablecloths, yoga mats, gymnastic balls, plastic plates and cups, and bendable and flexible plastic products in general.

Those of us born in the last thirty years have been ingesting plastic our entire lives. While some of these particles are eliminated through digestion, some of them remain stored in body fat tissue.

The latest plastic to make headlines is Bisphenol-A (BPA). BPA is linked to a variety of health issues. It mimics the hormone estrogen which alters hormone levels in men and has been suspected of causing an increase in the risk of diabetes, heart disease, and cancer. Most metal cans are lined with BPA. The high heat used in commercial canning releases BPA into the food. The highest concentrations of this plastic were found in canned meats, soups, and pastas.

Our recommendations are as follows:

- Never store food in plastic or cans. Never reheat food in plastic or under plastic wrap. You can cover foods with a paper towel instead if they are in a bowl.

- If we must buy water in plastic bottles while in transit, don't use them more than once. They are designed to break down after one or two uses.

- Drink from a stainless steel or glass water bottle.

- Buy as little food as possible that comes in plastic containers and Tetra Paks, which are lined in plastic. Replace plastic food-storage containers with glass ones, especially if they are scratched. Large wholesale stores often offer sets of glass containers with lids at a reasonable price. Another option is to buy canning jars. Most jar lids are lined in plastic so make sure food doesn't touch the lid. Or buy Weck jars, whose glass lids seal with rubber rings (www.weckcanning.com). If price is an issue save the glass containers foods come in.

- To avoid BPA, buy as little canned food and drink as possible. If buying canned foods the following have BPA-free cans—Native Forest/ Native Factor (all cans), Eden Foods (beans), Trader Joe's (corn and beans), and Pomi foods (made by Boschi Food and Beverage of Italy. Pomi can be bought on Amazon.com.) All cans holding acidic foods like tomatoes are lined with BPA. For an extensive list of who offers BPA-free cans as of December 2009, go to www.willystreet.coop/BPA.

- Store bulk foods in reusable cotton or silk bags (www.etsy.com) instead of plastic bags.

- Instead of zip lock bags use stainless steel containers for lunches (www.reuseit.com; also see recommendations in *Ideas for Healthy School Lunches*, Chapter 9).

To completely eliminate plastic from our lives requires a huge commitment of time and attention, but we can make the choice to significantly reduce exposure.

Labeling

Foods come with all sorts of labeling—Fair Trade Certified, Dolphin safe, cage-free, to name a few. It's difficult to know which labels to trust. The most reliable labels are overseen by third-party, independent organizations, which guarantee that the label is meeting the standards it claims.

The most reliable labels internationally are—Bird Friendly (for coffee), Marine Stewardship Council (sustainable seafood—can't deplete fish stocks, harm environment or diversity, or go against local or international laws or standards), Fair Trade Certified (guarantees farmers and farm worker are paid above-market prices and ensures socio-economic development), and Rainforest Alliance Certified (enforces strict guidelines protecting the environment, wildlife, workers and local communities). In the U.S.—Certified Humane Raised and Handled (for humane treatment of farm animals from birth through slaughter), Demeter Certified Biodynamic (a program for organically produced foods and sustainable agriculture), Food Alliance (production, processing, and distribution of sustainable foods), Salmon-Safe (reduces agriculture's impact on endangered salmon and steelhead habitats), and USDA Organic (regulates organic farming standards).

Somewhat reliable, meaning they may or may not be overseen by a third-party, independent source: In the U.S. Dolphin safe (for tuna), Grass-fed or Pastured, No Hormones Administered, Wild-caught.

The least reliable labeling, meaning there is no consistent approved definition, and these definitions are not overseen by a third-party, independent source are: Antibiotic-free, Environmentally Safe, Free-range or Free-roaming, Cage-free, and Natural.

I (Theresa) taught English in a public high school. One of the first things I encountered when I walked onto campus every morning was a row of vending machines. The first were filled with drinks, mostly sodas and energy drinks. Next to them were the machines with chips, cookies, and candy bars, all lined up in neat rows in wire spirals, waiting to drop down behind glass and present themselves to me. Or to the huge line of students crowded in front of them, buying their breakfast. One of my students, knowing my proclivity for healthier foods, held up what she had bought. "I know it's not good to have just sugar in the morning. So I balance it with this." In one hand she had a soda. In the other was a bag of potato chips.

Many of my students also ate lunch in my classroom. I watched them eat fat- and preservative-filled burritos, pizza, French fries, and other nutrition-lacking foods bought from the school cafeteria. One student pointed to my lunch one day and asked, "What's that?" I told him it was an avocado.

"You're going to eat it like that?" he looked incredulous. "Aren't you going to put something on it to make it taste good?"

I asked him what he thought I should add. He held up his burrito. "Refried beans and cheese!"

Obesity: the Norm?

The fact is, our children are bombarded with invitations to form unhealthy eating habits. The effects of these habits can follow them into adulthood. In the U.S., as of 2011, about a third of children aged 2 to 19 are obese. ("Obese" is defined as weighing more than 20 percent higher than the recommended body weight for a particular height, age, build, and gender. It is a measure of body fat, not of how much someone weighs.) To give a perspective, in 2002, only around 10 percent of children in the same age group were obese. In 2009, the American Medical Association listed obesity as the most common medical condition in children. Overweight children are significantly more at risk of high blood pressure, high cholesterol, Type 2 diabetes, sleep apnea, and fatty liver disease, which, if it continues over time, can cause permanent liver damage.

Obesity is considered an epidemic in this country and it's getting worse instead of better. It is "fed" by the proliferation of unhealthy food choices made not only by children but by the adults responsible for them. But even if your child is not obese, there is reason to be concerned about what they are eating, both at and away from school.

Trends

One area of concern is the shift in the American diet. According to a study published in the August 2011 issue of the *Journal of the American Dietetic Association*, instead of eating homemade meals, a third of families now are eating prepared foods for the majority of their meals, whether that be fast food, sit-down restaurant meals, or pre-made foods like frozen dinners, and this trend is growing fast. These foods are of lesser nutritional quality than homemade meals—they contain more fat, salt, and sweeteners than the same foods made at home, not to mention preservatives and other chemical additives. The Caesar salad we order in a restaurant or buy pre-made is no comparison, nutrition-wise, to the one we make with our own hands.

Along with eating out, many families are no longer eating meals together. The children grab something from a fast food restaurant with their friends and busy parents pick up To-Go items on the way home from a long day at work so meals can happen as quickly and conveniently as possible. There is little supervision of what children eat and, given that most children know little about what their growing bodies need, this lack of supervision leads to choices made based on what's easily available in a fast food restaurant or convenience store. It doesn't take long for such eating choices to become a habit— one that can be very difficult to break. After all, without all the excess sodium, sweeteners, and fat, homemade food truly doesn't "taste good" to overstimulated taste buds.

When families fragment this way, the nutritional knowledge the parents hold is not passed down to the children. An uninformed eater is at the mercy of whatever big corporations want to feed them and, as we will see in this section, commercial foods do not in general support a healthy body.

This trend of eating out has another component—portion size. Dr. George Bray, a research professor and former director of the Pennington Center at Louisiana State University (the largest nutritional research center in the world), as well as founding president of the North American Association for the Study of Obesity, states that among other factors, larger portions, less exercise of any kind, irregular sleep patterns, and more high-fat fast foods go a long way toward explaining the obesity epidemic.[1] Restaurants serve portions that go far beyond any nutritionist's recommended serving sizes. Even children's meals are large. It is easy to overeat under such circumstances, and the more a family eats out and is subjected to huge servings, the more

"normal" such servings will feel even when they are eating at home.

Let's take a closer look at one of the most dangerous food trends in this diet shift— namely, fast food, and the link it has to what is served in school lunch programs.

School Lunches: Part of the Problem

In the 2004 American documentary *Super Size Me*, Morgan Spurlock was curious what would happen if someone ate nothing but fast food for a month. His experiment consisted, in part, of eating at McDonald's for every meal. Nutritionists recommend eating fast food no more than once a month. Although initially skeptical that this diet would have any significant impact on his health, by day 21 his supervising doctor asked him to stop because he was having heart palpitations. By day 30 he had gained almost 25 pounds, which took him *14 months* to lose.

According to an article by Alice Waters and Katrina Heron published in 2009 on the *New York Times* Op Ed page, as part of the National School Lunch Program, "schools are entitled to receive commodity foods that are valued at a little over 20 cents per meal. The long list of options includes high-fat, low-grade meats and cheeses and processed foods like chicken nuggets and pizza. Many of the items selected are ready to be thawed, heated or just unwrapped . . . Schools also get periodic, additional 'bonus' commodities from the U.S.D.A. [United States Department of Agriculture], which pays good money for what are essentially leftovers from big American food producers." These bonus foods are no more nutritious than what Mr. Spurlock ate at McDonald's or what we encounter at any other fast food restaurant.

Foods like this are filled with "empty calories"— calories that deliver energy but have little or no accompanying nutritional value, meaning they

[1]www.seattletimes.nwsource.com/html/health/2002658491_healthsyrup04.html

contain little or no vitamins, minerals, amino acids, or anything else the body needs to keep running. These calories are generally converted to fat. The foods that contain the most empty calories are candy, soft drinks, "juice" drinks with a low amount of actual juice, chips, foods with a high sweetener content, and high-fat foods like fast-food and school-lunch hamburgers, hot dogs, fried chicken, chicken nuggets, burritos, pizza, and French fries—the staples of school lunches across America. In essence, children are eating what amounts to fast food once and sometimes twice a day, five out of seven days a week. It is no exaggeration to say this is a health disaster.

However, it isn't as if there is nothing healthy on a school lunch tray. There are standards in place that determine the nutritional requirements for lunches. Cafeterias must offer a protein, a fruit, a vegetable, and a grain. But part of the problem is that the unhealthy foods get eaten and the fruits and vegetables get left behind. Another good example of healthy foods being pushed aside for unhealthy choices is milk. Milk is offered as part of the school nutrition plan, but flavored milks consistently outsell regular milk. Flavored milks are full of sweeteners and artificial flavorings and colorings. In 2011, according to the *Los Angeles Times*, in the L.A. Unified School District, chocolate and strawberry milk accounted for 60 percent of their milk sales. The L.A. Unified School District Board of Education voted to pull flavored milk from all its campuses in a move to make school lunches healthier. Steps like this, which ensure healthy choices are offered for all required food groups, would ensure that children were getting—and eating—good, nutritious food at lunch.

[2]www.ajcn.org/content/79/4/537.full

[3]"Liquid versus solid carbohydrate: effects on food intake and body weight." *International Journal of Obesity and Related Metabolic Disorders.* June 2000, Vol. 24 Issue 6.

Vending Machines, Sugar, and Other Gambles

And now back to those vending machines. The second relevant factor in the obesity explosion and the health crisis facing our children is drinks like sodas, energy drinks, and "fruit" juices. These drinks are full of sugar, high-fructose corn syrup (also called HFCS; it is used in many foods because it's cheap to make), and/or artificial sweeteners, all of which affect health. Artificial sweeteners, for example, are neurotoxins, meaning they cause an imbalance in the chemicals that transmit signals in the brain. Over time, this can manifest as emotional instability, fatigue, insomnia, and impairment of memory and concentration. This has a huge impact on a student's ability to perform in school.

Developed over the last thirty years, sweet corn-based syrups account for fully half of all caloric sweeteners eaten in America today.[2] Dr. Bray is one of many research scientists who have found that HFCS is a contributing factor to childhood obesity in the U.S. A study published by the *International Journal of Obesity and Related Metabolic Disorders* found that when humans are given high amounts of soda, a main vector for HFCS intake, for just four weeks, they gained much more weight than when given only jelly beans for an equal amount of time.[3]

But even if we cut soft drinks from our diet, we are still eating more HFCS that we think. I (Theresa) recently taught a class on sweeteners to a group of fourth- and fifth-graders. I unpacked a bag of groceries and walked them through a typical, "American" food day—processed cereal for breakfast, a popular granola bar and juice drink included with lunch, some gum shared with a friend, soda with their after-school snack, and a barbeque dinner with catsup for French fries. They busily researched the ingredients of each food item and were outraged to find that there were one or more sweeteners in every one of the foods on the table and most had HFCS. The first, meaning biggest percentage, ingredient in the barbeque sauce was high fructose corn syrup!

One of the problems with HFCS is that it does not trigger chemical messengers that tell the brain the stomach is full.[4] This leads to overeating, especially of HFCS-sweetened drinks, which do not have a solid food component. The same AJCN article states:

> We propose that the introduction of HFCS and the increased intakes of soft drinks and other sweetened beverages have led to increases in total caloric and fructose consumption that are important contributors to the current epidemic of obesity.[5]

See *Sweeteners* in *Resources and Recommendations*, Chapter 8, for a fuller discussion of HFCS and other substances.

Soda consumption is also linked to a wide range of other health issues, such as osteoporosis, tooth decay, heart disease, kidney stones, and caffeine and sugar addiction, meaning that people are much more likely to drink more and more soda.

Given the known health risks of drinking soda (and eating empty-calorie snacks), why is that line of vending machines on campus? It is no secret that school districts are struggling for money. For years Pepsi and Coke have been offering money in return for exclusive access for their products. The way the school makes a profit is it receives a commission for every case of soda consumed. To desperate districts scrambling for funds, these deals can seem like a wonderful way to get badly-needed money for any number of projects.

It seems that little thought is given in these deals to the effect easily-available sodas would have on our children, despite the fact that according to an article in *Archives of Pediatrics and Adolescent Medicine*,[6] "sugary drinks are the main source of added sugar in the daily diet of children. The main nutrient in sugary drinks is high-fructose corn syrup; each 12-oz serving of soda has the equivalent of 10 teaspoons of sugar. Between 56% and 85% of children in school have at least 1 can of soda every day."

New Directions

There has been a backlash against these kinds of drinks as well as their accessibility on school campuses. The scientific community is stepping forward with recommendations of its own. An article in the *American Journal of Clinical Nutrition* found such a strong correlation between HFCS intake through sodas and juice drinks and obesity that it recommended "reducing the availability of these beverages by removing soda machines from schools...as [well as] reducing the portion sizes of sodas that are commercially available.[7]" Recently Coca-Cola introduced a new can size—instead of 12 ounces, it's 7.5. This is a move in the right direction, but these cans are sold as an eight-pack instead of a six-pack, and the smaller size doesn't address the actual ingredients or its general availability.

The Alliance for a Healthier Generation, a joint initiative run by the William J. Clinton Foundation and the American Heart Association, has tackled the availability problem. They've brokered a deal with Pepsi, Coca-Cola, and Cadbury Schweppes to get them to stop selling soft drinks on elementary- and middle-school campuses and to replace them with "water, certain fruit juices and low-fat

---

[4]www.seattletimes.nwsource.com/html/health/2002658491_healthsyrup04.html

[5]www.ajcn.org/content/79/4/537.full

[6]"Sugary Drinks and Childhood Obesity." Vol. 163 Issue 4, April 2009

[7]www.ajcn.org/content/79/4/537.full

or fat-free milk." High school students will continue to be offered "diet or low-calorie sodas, teas and sports drinks." While this is a huge step forward, it does not address the fact that the drinks offered at the high school level are still full of artificial sweeteners and other chemicals.

Other organizations are fighting back against the poor quality of school lunches. One is the Edible Schoolyard Project (www.edibleschoolyard.org) formed by Alice Waters, founder of Chez Panisse, a landmark restaurant in Berkeley, California. Chez Panisse's goal has always been to offer meals made from meats and seasonal produce from local, sustainable farms and ranches. According to their website, Ms. Waters "is a national advocate for farmers markets and for bringing organic, local food to the general public." The Edible Schoolyard Project's mission is to "support an educational program that uses food to nurture, educate, and empower youth." Its goal is to "launch an initiative to build and share a national food curriculum."[8] Ms. Waters' program helps schools create Edible Education, where children learn how to grow and cook fresh seasonal foods as part of the school curriculum. "Since 1996, over 3,000 students have graduated from the Edible Schoolyard with the skills and knowledge they need to make lifelong, healthy choices about what they eat."[9] These "school gardens" are catching on across the United States.

Jamie Oliver is another powerhouse in the movement to re-do school lunches. Famous for his many television shows and bestselling cookbooks, including *The Naked Chef*,[10] in 2004 Mr. Oliver,

"motivated by the poor state of school [lunches] in UK schools . . . went back to school with the aim of educating and motivating the kids and [lunch] ladies to enjoy cooking and eating healthy, nutritious lunches rather than the processed foods that they were used to. Jamie launched a national campaign called Feed Me Better and launched an online petition for better school meals. As a result of the 271,677 signatures on the petition . . . the government pledged an extra £280 million to improve the standard of school meals, to provide training for [lunch] ladies and equipment for schools . . . The series prompted a public outcry for change to the school meals system."[11]

He has since started a worldwide petition for better school lunches and is well on his way to having a million signatures. Jamie Oliver's Food Revolution (www.jamieoliver.com:81/us/foundation/jamies-food-revolution/home) is about encouraging people, including school cafeteria workers, to cook healthy, good food from scratch. Mr. Oliver also is working to have cooking lessons be a part of the curriculum at all public schools so children learn how to make healthy meals for themselves.

Michelle Obama's initiative, Let's Move! (www.letsmove.gov), is targeting childhood obesity and family food choices at just about every level. Her program addresses not just school lunches but also getting more accurate food labeling, making sure all communities have good grocery stores, educating children and parents about their food choices, and working toward getting children to be more active. She was a huge advocate for the passing of the "Healthy, Hunger-Free Kids Act," signed into law on December 13, 2010. The bill will, among other things, for the first time establish nutrition standards for school lunches as well as all food sold in schools, including in vending machines. It also covers food offered by schools before, during, and after school and in any federally-funded, school-based feeding

[8]www.edibleschoolyard.org

[9]http://www.chezpanissefoundation.org/edible-schoolyard

[10]Hyperion: New York, New York, 2000

[11]www.jamieoliver.com

programs, even if they occur during summer. It is the "largest investment in child nutrition programs since their inception."[12]

You Can, Too

Even given these facts, we shouldn't expect, or ask, our children never to buy a soda or eat a school lunch. Demonizing foods just makes them more attractive. Instead we can educate our kids and teens about what's in the foods they encounter and the effects of eating them. When we come together as a family to prepare and eat delicious, simple meals, we model our food values. The earlier we begin this modeling the more it will be second nature for our children. Then, even if they buy potato chips, they will not think that is a good counterbalance to a soda.

Packing a lunch for your child is the biggest power you have and a huge step toward healthier food choices. You have control over what goes into that bag. And the more you know about food additives and the other ingredients in the food you put in that lunch, the more truly healthy it will be. Please see *Resources and Recommendations*, Chapter 8, for a more thorough exploration of what we encounter on those grocery shelves, and arm yourself with this knowledge. The more you know, the easier it is to make truly healthy choices, both for yourself and your family. And that is power worth passing on!

IDEAS FOR HEALTHY SCHOOL LUNCHES

Here are five categories to keep in mind as a basis for a healthy school lunch:

- Raw vegetables
- Fresh fruit
- A main dish (could also be soup)
- A snack

- If wanted, a healthy treat

All of our suggestions are easy to prepare and most don't need specific recipes. They are ideas you can mix and match according to the needs and preference of your child, the leftovers in the fridge, and the season.

Children like food that looks interesting in color and shape. Get creative in how you decorate and present! For instance, use a small scoop and serve melon in balls, or fill celery sticks with almond butter and decorate with raisins.

Children in Japan take a "bento box" to school. It is a Japanese lunch box which is fun to open and take apart and has lots of little compartments that make cut vegetables look inviting. Packaging goes a long way, especially for children. You can order good-quality metal bento boxes online at www.justbento.com/bento-boxes-week-stainless-steel or www.lunchbots.com.

If your school permits their use, glass containers are a healthier option than plastic bags and containers: www.locknlockplace.com/ or www.pyrexware.com/index.asp?pageId=14 are good sources.

Raw Vegetable Ideas

- Fennel. Cut into strips. This vegetable tastes sweet and a lot of children like it.
- Celery sticks
- Snap peas
- Kohlrabi. Peel it, cut it in half, and then cut it either in slices or in pieces. It is mild and nicely crunchy so many children like it.
- Carrot sticks. Instead of including the well-known small, peeled carrots that you can buy in the grocery store, send a whole carrot that

[12]National Farmers Union president Roger Johnson

has its green attached. Bringing a vegetable in its natural state (or close to it) can intrigue the other children at school. The child of a friend did this. His classmates were mightily impressed (having never seen such an "original" carrot), asked lots of questions about the carrot, and then actually tried it. He was inspired to bring in lots of vegetables after this, and lunchtime for him became like a show-and-tell opportunity.

- Cucumber sticks
- Red and yellow peppers cut in strips
- Radishes
- Cherry tomatoes

Fruit Ideas

- Apples:

   —Slice apples and lightly sprinkle with cinnamon. Send along a small packet of additional cinnamon, so the child can add more to taste. The cinnamon brings out the sweetness of the apples.

   —Slice apples, sprinkle with lemon juice for freshness, and spread almond butter on the side.
- Cut up different fruit and put on skewers
- Fruit salad in small containers (see *Fruit Salad* in *Recipes*, Chapter 5)
- Orange slices, grapes, berries in small containers
- Banana with a small container of gomasio (see *Gomasio* in *Recipes*, Chapter 5). The banana can be dipped into the gomasio or sliced and sprinkled with gomasio.

Thermos Smoothies

You can switch up the ingredients of this smoothie in many ways. Our favorites include combinations of:

- Frozen banana
- Frozen berries
- Fresh apple
- Plain yogurt
- Almond or other nut milk (see *Grain and Nut Milks* in *Recipes*, Chapter 5)
- A dash of honey, cinnamon, vanilla

For extra punch:

- 1 teaspoon ground flax seed
- 1 teaspoon ground sesame seed
- a dash of Udo's or fish oil (beware—fish oil can taste or smell "fishy")
- 1 teaspoon dried kelp
- 1 teaspoon green powder

You can also use any of the recipes from the Smoothies section.

Main Dish Ideas

- Brown rice, roasted sunflower seeds, and tahini sauce (see *Roasted Sunflower Seeds* and *Tahini Sauce* in *Recipes*, Chapter 5)
- Tzaziki sauce and whole-wheat pita bread cut into triangles (see *Tzaziki Sauce* in *Recipes*, Chapter 5)
- Hummus and whole-wheat pita bread cut into triangles (see *Hummus* or *Fluffy Hummus* in *Recipes*, Chapter 5)
- Organic soft goat cheese and cucumbers sticks rolled up in a whole-wheat or rice tortilla
- Cornbread and pesto (see *Cornbread* and *Pesto* in *Recipes*, Chapter 5)

- Potato salad—cubed boiled potatoes, chopped pickles and celery, and Simple Vinaigrette (see *Simple Vinaigrette* in *Salads in Recipes*, Chapter 5)

- Nori "burritos"—strips of nori with the following rolled in: nut butter, tahini, or refried beans. To seal the roll, run wet fingers down the last bit of unrolled edge and press against body of roll.

- Peas with olive oil and sea salt

- Sautéed soft parsnips and/or carrots with parsley, sea salt, and garlic

- Crispy shallots—shallots sautéed in oil and salt until they get crispy. They go over surprisingly well.

- Hand-cut sweet potato fries or sweet potato chips fried in palm oil. This turns a junk food into a healthier food.

- Brown rice pasta with Marinara Sauce (see *Marinara Sauce*, in *Sauces, Spreads, and Dips* in *Recipes*, Chapter 5)

- Confetti Rice: In a food processor, chop raw broccoli, carrot, onion, cabbage, and a handful of greens. Sauté this mixture in oil or organic butter. Add seasonings (salt, pepper, tamari, and/or any others your child may enjoy) to taste. Toss with cooked brown rice, adjust seasonings. Serve warm in thermos or cold.

Soups

In general when making soup for children, puree vegetables into a smooth soup either in a blender or with a stick blender.

Some options:

- Vegetable Broth (puree the vegetables) with small whole-wheat noodles (see *Vegetable Broth* in *Recipes*, Chapter 5)

- Carrot Almond Soup (see *Soups* in *Recipes*, Chapter 5)

- German Hokkaido Pumpkin Soup, well pureed (see *Soups* in *Recipes*, Chapter 5)

- Miso Soup with Udon Noodles. Cook Udon noodles according to instruction on the package and add to soup (see *Miso Soup* in *Recipes*, Chapter 5)

- Tomato Coconut Soup (see *Soups* in *Recipes*, Chapter 5)

- Green Soup: Coarsely chop one head of cauliflower and the same amount of broccoli (heads and stems). Put in a soup pot with 2–3 inches of water. Steam until tender.

  When soft, add two cups vegetable broth. Puree vegetables and vegetable broth, adding more liquid as desired. Add seasonings to taste.

  Keep warm in a thermos.

Sandwiches/Wraps

Sushi Sandwich

Prepare sushi rice according to instructions on package—generally one cup water to one cup rice. Lay out a sheet of nori seaweed (the kind used for sushi), fill the middle of it with a small amount of rice. Hollow out a bit of room in the middle of the rice and place raw vegetables inside, topped with umeboshi plum paste or with some other sauce, if you like. Then wrap the nori around the rice, creating a square brick-like sandwich.

Pinwheels

Fill a tortilla with colorful foods your child likes, then roll it, slice it, and place it in a container so you can see the spiraled contents. Fillings can include:

Soft goat cheese, cucumbers, sun-dried tomatoes, shredded carrots (slice with peeler so carrots are thin and flexible), thin-sliced olives, hummus (see *Sauces, Spreads, and Dips* in *Recipes*, Chapter 5) or Olive tapenade (see *Tapenade* in *Sauces, Spreads, and Dips* in *Recipes*, Chapter 5)

Cookie Cutter Sandwich

Children like interesting shapes. Use cookie cutters to cut sandwiches into different shapes! Sprouted bread is the healthiest choice. Use ingredients that can be cut easily such as:

Hummus or soft goat cheese with chopped fresh herbs (see *Hummus* or *Fluffy Hummus* in *Sauces, Spreads, and Dips* in *Recipes*, Chapter 5), cucumber slices, lettuce leaves, sliced tomatoes, almond butter and honey (see Roasted Almond Butter in *Nuts and Seeds* in *Recipes*, Chapter 5) or avocado

Snack Ideas

- Olives
- Pickles
- Nori sheets
- Organic corn tortilla chips and salsa (see *Fresh Tomato Salsa* in *Sauces, Spreads, and Dips* in *Recipes*, Chapter 5)
- Kefir
- Homemade Granola and yogurt (pack separately in a small jar) (see *Above the Line Granola and Yogurt* in *Fermented Foods* in *Recipes*, Chapter 5)
- Pretzel sticks and almond butter (see *Roasted Almond Butter* in *Nuts and Seeds* in *Recipes*, Chapter 5)
- Slices of goat cheese and brown rice or whole-grain crackers
- Hummus and brown rice crackers (see *Hummus* or *Fluffy Hummus* in *Sauces, Spreads*, and Dips in *Recipes*, Chapter 5)

- Guacamole and brown rice or whole-grain crackers (see *Guacamole in Sauces, Spreads, and Dips* in *Recipes*, Chapter 5)
- Rice cakes and goat cheese or almond butter (see *Roasted Almond Butter* in *Nuts and Seeds* in *Recipes*, Chapter 5)
- Kale Chips (see *Kale Chips* in *Vegetables* in *Recipes*, Chapter 5)
- Sliced cucumbers or cucumber salad (see *Cucumber Salad* in *Salads and Dressings* in *Recipes*, Chapter 5)
- Cucumber Tomato Salad (see *Salads and Dressings* in *Recipes*, Chapter 5)
- Raisins and almonds
- Roasted Sunflower Seeds (see *Nuts and Seeds* in *Recipes*, Chapter 5)
- Mochi. Mochi is a Japanese rice cake made of glutinous rice—not to be confused with gluten; this is a gluten-free food—that was pounded into paste and molded into shape. It can be bought frozen. Cut into bite-sized strips, bake, and serve with butter and honey.
- Popcorn

Perfect Popcorn

In these days of microwaves, making popcorn "the old-fashioned way" is an opportunity to include your children, so they get to see the process! Make plenty of it, because bowls of fresh popcorn get emptied surprisingly fast.

Serves 2, prep time 10 minutes. Ingredients: 3 tablespoons grapeseed oil, 1/3 cup organic popcorn kernels, 2 tablespoons butter or to taste, Salt to taste.

Heat oil in a 3-quart covered saucepan on medium-high heat.

Put 4 popcorn kernels in and cover. When kernels pop, add all popcorn kernels in an even layer.

Cover, remove from heat, and count 30 seconds. (Count out loud; it's fun to do this with children.)

Return pan to the heat. The popcorn should begin popping soon and all at once. Once the popping really starts, gently shake the pan by moving it back and forth over the burner. Keep the lid slightly ajar to let steam from the popcorn release (this makes it drier and crisper). Once the popping slows to several seconds between pops, remove the pan from the heat, remove the lid, and dump the popcorn immediately into a big bowl.

With this technique the oil is heated to the right temperature. Waiting 30 seconds brings the kernels to a near-popping temperature so when they are returned to the heat, they all pop at about the same time, resulting in nearly all of the kernels popping and nothing burning.

If you are adding butter, you can easily melt it by placing the butter in the now-empty but hot pan.

Salt to taste.

Tips:

Add salt to the oil in the pan before popping. When the popcorn pops, the salt will be distributed throughout the popcorn.

Fun toppings—Spanish smoked paprika, nutritional yeast, cayenne powder, chili pepper, curry powder, cumin, Braggs.

Healthy Treat Ideas

- Dried fruits: mango, banana, papaya, apricots (make sure they are sulphur-free), dates, figs, pineapple
- Freeze-dried strawberries
- Date Nut Balls (see *Desserts* in *Recipes, Chapter 5*)
- "Parfait"

In a small mason jar, layer plain yogurt, frozen or fresh berries or other cut-up fruit, homemade granola, and whatever else suits. Drizzle with honey. (See *Yogurt* in *Fermented Foods* in *Recipes*, Chapter 5, and *Above the Line Granola* in *Breakfast* in *Recipes*, Chapter 5)

APPENDIX

Food Rotation Chart

Varying food choices helps guarantee nutritional needs are met. This guide lists similar foods so we can be sure of variation.

Eat foods of all colors (orange, yellow, red, green, etc.) and from all five tastes (salty, sweet, pungent, sour, and bitter) and remember to follow combining guidelines (see *Food Combinations* in *The Basics*, Chapter 3).

DARK LEAFY	CRUCIFEROUS	SQUASH	ROOTS AND TUBERS	BULBS
Kale	Broccoli	Acorn	Parsnips	Garlic
Dandelion Greens	Cauliflower	Butternut	Rutabagas	Leeks
Collards	Bok Choy	Kabocha	Turnips	Onions
Mustard Greens	Cabbage	Pumpkin	Ginger	Scallions
Romaine Lettuce	Brussels Sprouts	Delicata	Beets	Shallots
Chard	Daikon		Sweet Potatoes	
	Radishes		Potatoes	
			Yams	
			Carrots	
			Celery	
			Parsley	
			Fennel	

These are genetically identical:

ALGAE	APPLE	BANANA	BIRCH	BUCKWHEAT	CASHEW
Agar	Apple	Banana	Filbert	Buckwheat	Cashew
Dulse	Pear	Plantain	Hazelnut	Rhubarb	Mango
Kelp	Quince				Pistacio

CITRUS	COMPOSITE	FUNGUS	GINGER	GOOSEBERRY	GOOSEFOOT
Mandarin	Artichoke	Cheese (all)	Gardamon	Currant	Beets
Grapefruit	Chamomile	Mushrooms	Ginger	Gooseberry	Beet Sugar
Kumquat	Chicory	Sourdough	Turmeric		Swiss Chard
Lemon		Vinegars			Spinach
Lime		All Yeasts			
Orange					
Tangerine					

GOURD	CEREAL A	CEREAL B	CEREAL C	CEREAL D	CEREAL E
Cantaloupe	Barley	Oats	Corn	Rice	Bamboo Shoot
Casada	Bulgur		Millet	Wild Rice	Sugar Cane
Cucumber	Gluten				Molasses
Honeydew	Malt				Sorghum
Melon (all)	Rye				
Pumpkin (incl. seeds)	Triticale				
Squash (all)	Wheat				
Veg. Marrow	Bran				
Watermelon	Germ				
Zucchini	Graham				

GRAPE	HEATH	LAUREL	LEGUMES	LILY	MALLOW
Cream of Tartar	Blueberry	Avocado	Alfalfa	Asparagus	Okra
Grape	Cranberry	Bay Leaves	Carob	Chive	Cottonseed
Raisin		Cinnamon	Chick Pea	Garlic	
			Snow Peas	Leek	
			Kidney	Onion	
			Lecithin	Shallot	
			Lentils		
			Licorice		
			Lima Bean		
			Mung		
			Navy		
			Split Pea		
			Peanuts (+ butter)		
			Pinto Bean		
			All Dried Peas		
			Tofu		
			String Bean		
			Tamarind		

MAPLE	MULBERRY	MYRTLE	NUTMEG	OLIVE	PALM
Syrup	Fig	Allspice	Mace	Black	Coconut
Sugar	Hop	Clover	Nutmeg	Green	Date
	Mulberry	Cloves		Olive Oil	
		Guava			

(groupings from *Infant Nutrition,* Health Coach Systems Int'l, Inc. Canada, 3rd Ed., 1995)

MINT	MUSTARD	PARSLEY	PLUM	POTATO	SPURGE
Basil	Bok Choy	Anise	Almond	Cayenne	Cassave
Marjoram	Broccoli	Caraway	Apricot	Chili Pepper	Tapioca
Mint	Brussels Sprouts	Carrot	Cherry	Eggplant	
Oregano	Cabbage	Celery	Nectarine	Green Pepper	
Peppermint	Cauliflower	Coriander	Peach	Paprika	
Sage	Collard	Cumin	Plum	Pimento	
Savory	Horseradish	Dill	Prune	Potato	
Spearmint	Kale	Fennel		Red Pepper	
Thyme	Kohlrabi	Parsley		Tobacco	
	Mustard	Parsnip		Tomato	
	Radish				
	Rutabaga				
	Turnip				
	Watercress				

ROSE	STERCULE	SUNFLOWER	TEA	WALNUT
All Berries	Cocoa	Jerusalem Artichoke	Green	Butternut
Rosehip	Cola	Sunflower Oil	Pekoe	Hickory Nut
	Chocolate	Sunflower Seeds		Pecan
				Walnuts
				Pineapple
				Pine Nut
				Pomegranate
				Poppy Seed
				Quinoa
				Saffron
				Sesame (oil + seeds)
				Sweet Potato
				Yam
				Taro Root
				Vanilla

RECOMMENDED COOKBOOKS

Brown, Simon G. *Modern-Day Macrobiotics: Transform Your Diet and Feed Your Mind, Body, and Spirit* (Berkeley, California: North Atlantic Books, 2007).

Chesman, Andrea. *Serving Up the Harvest: Celebrating the Goodness of Fresh Vegetables* (North Adams, Massachusetts: Storey Publishing, 2007).

Colbin, Annemarie. *The Book of Whole Meals: A Seasonal Guide to Assembling Balanced Vegetarian Breakfasts, Lunches and Dinners* (New York: Ballantine Books, 1985).

Coppedge, Richard J., Jr., C.M.B. *Gluten-Free Baking with The Culinary Institute of America: 150 Flavorful Recipes from the World's Premier Culinary College* (Avon, Massachusetts: Adams Media, 2008).

Dragonwagon, Crescent. *Passionate Vegetarian* (New York: Workman Publishing Company, 2002).

Fenster, Carol Ph.D. *Wheat-Free Recipes & Menus: Delicious, Healthful Eating for People with Food Sensitivities* (New York: Avery Trade, 2004).

Katzen, Mollie. *The New Moosewood Cookbook* (Berkeley, California: Ten Speed Press, Revised Edition, 2000). —All her cookbooks are excellent.

Levitt, Atma Jo Ann. *The Kripalu Cookbook: Gourmet Vegetarian Recipes* (Woodstock, Vermont: Countryman Press, 2005).

Patenaude, Frederic. *Raw Soups, Salads, and Smoothies* (Ojai, California: Raw Vegan, 2003). This book is out of print but copies can be found online.

Patenaude, Frederic. *Sunfood Cuisine: A Practical Guide to Raw Vegetarian Cuisine* (Nature's First Law, 2002).

Phyo, Ani. Ani's *Raw Food Kitchen: Easy, Delectable Living Foods Recipes* (Jackson, Tennessee: Da Capo Press, 2007).

Pierson, Joy, Bart Potenza and Barbara Scott-Goodman. *The Candle Café Cookbook: More Than 150 Enlightened Recipes from New York's Renowned Vegan Restaurant* (New York: Clarkson Potter, 2003).

Santillo, Humbart "Smokey," N.D. *Intuitive Eating* (Prescott, Arizona: Hohm Press, 1993). This book is out of print but copies can be found online.

Walters, Terry. *Clean Start: Inspiring You to Eat Clean and Live Well* (New York: Sterling Epicure, 2010).

Walters. Terry. *Clean Food: A Seasonal Guide to Eating Close to the Source* (New York: Sterling Epicure, 2009).

RECOMMENDED READING

Anderson, Richard. *Cleanse and Purify Thyself: The Definitive Guide to Internal Cleansing, Book 1: The Cleanse* (Medford, Oregon: Christobe Publishing, 2000). An explanation of the health benefits of cleansing and a guide for doing an excellent one called the Arise and Shine Cleanse.

Batmanghelidj, F., M.D. *Your Body's Many Cries for Water* (Falls Church, Virginia: Global Health Solutions, 1995). Explains why water is essential to the functioning of the body and the many symptoms and diseases that can arise from a chronic state of dehydration.

Bourdain, Anthony. *Kitchen Confidential: Adventures in the Culinary Underbelly, A Cook's Tour* (New York: Harper Perennial, 2001).

Bourdain, Anthony. *The Nasty Bits* (New York: Bloomsbury USA, 2006).

Bourdain, Anthony. *Medium Raw: A Bloody Valentine to the World of Food and the People Who Cook* (New York: Ecco, 2011). These books by Bourdain will open your eyes to what is happening on the world stage with food and in the restaurants you eat in.

Brooklyn Botanic Garden. *Salad Gardens: Gourmet Greens and Beyond* (New York: Brooklyn Botanic Garden, 1995). A guide to growing vegetables, herbs, and salad greens no matter where we live or how much room we have.

Campbell, T. Colin, Ph.D. and Thomas M. Campbell II. *The China Study: The Most Comprehensive Study of Nutrition Ever Conducted* (Dallas, Texas: BenBella Books, 2006). An accessible scientific argument for how and why animal-based diets are at the base of Western diseases.

Explains why the diet we recommend is the best possible diet.

Dogen, Eihei. *How to Cook Your Life: From the Zen Kitchen to Enlightenment* (Boston: Shambhala, 2005). Translated by Kosho Uchiyama. Draws parallels between cooking and spiritual work and shows how to use being in the kitchen as a vehicle for transformation.

Howell, Dr. Edward. *Enzyme Nutrition: The Food Enzyme Concept* (New York: Avery Publishing Group, 1995). The definitive guide to what enzymes are and how to eat so that you are not constantly pulling enzymes from your immune system in order to digest.

Kingsolver, Barbara. *Animal, Vegetable, Miracle: A Year of Food Life* (New York: Harper Perennial, 2008). Kingsolver, a well-respected author in the fields of both science and fiction, and her family lived for a year on what they could grow or buy in local farmers markets. They wrote about their experiences and ways in which we, too, can eat more locally.

Kushi, Michio and Aveline Kushi. *Macrobiotic Diet* (Tokyo: Japan Publications, 1993). Still the standard for explaining the macrobiotic diet.

Morse, Robert, N.D. *The Detox Miracle Sourcebook: Raw Foods and Herbs for Complete Cellular Regeneration* (Prescott, Arizona, Kalindi Press, 2004). A comprehensive guide on detoxifying the body and why this is essential.

Pollan, Michael. *In Defense of Food* (New York: Penguin Group USA, 2008). Explains how (and where) to buy, cook, and eat our food and why paying attention to that is a vital part of conscious, intentional eating.

Red Hawk. *Self Observation: The Awakening of Conscience: An Owner's Manual* (Prescott, Arizona: Hohm Press, 2009). A clear guide on how to practice self-observation, which is important in terms of being able to stick with a new diet.

Santillo, Humbart. *Intuitive Eating: Everybody's Guide to Lifelong Health and Vitality Through Food* (Hohm Press: Prescott, Arizona, 1993). How to work with self- awareness and diet to restore an intuitive sense of what, how much, and when to eat. This book is out of print but copies can be found with an Internet search.

Thomas, Lalitha. *10 Essential Foods* (Prescott, Arizona: Kalindi Press: 1997). A list of ten foods essential for optimal health and well-being with explanations for why each food is on the list. Includes food for children.

Wolf, David. *The Sunfood Diet Success System* (Berkeley: North Atlantic Books, 2008). One of the most in-depth explanations and how-tos of the raw food diet available.

RECIPE INDEX*

RECIPE INDEX*

Recipe Index*

RECIPE INDEX*

RECIPE INDEX*

RECIPE INDEX*

Recipe Index*

RECIPE INDEX*

SUBJECT INDEX*

Subject Index*

Subject Index*

ANOTHER TITLE OF INTEREST FOR READERS OF
DHARMA FEAST COOKBOOK

DHARMA FEAST
Eating An Intentional Diet

by Purna Steinitz and Theresa Rogers

With an in-depth consideration of both processed and natural food, this adjunct or companion volume to the *Dharma Feast Cookbook* addresses the enormous role that the consumption and preparation of food play in our lives. Right diet is a gateway to clear and unconflicted relationship with ourselves, others, and all of life. This book details the many ways that diet functions as a building block—or a stumbling block—on the spiritual path. It is a guide to using diet as part of the process of human maturation. (Contains some material from *Dharma Feast Cookbook*.)

Published privately by Aspen Grove Press

Paper, 233 pages, $30.00   ISBN: 1-978-0-983564-50-8

To Order: contact Tika@Dharmafeast.com

10 ESSENTIAL FOODS

by Lalitha thomas

Carrots, broccoli, almonds, grapefruit and six other miracle foods will enhance your health when used regularly and wisely. Lalitha gives in-depth nutritional information plus flamboyant and good-humored stories about these foods, based on her years of health and nutrition counseling. Each chapter contains easy and delicious recipes, tips for feeding kids and helpful hints for managing your food dollar. A bonus section supports the use of 10 Essential Snacks.

Paper, 324 pages, $16.95   ISBN: 978-0-934252-74-4

A VEGETARIAN DOCTOR SPEAKS OUT

by Charles Attwood, M.D., F.A.A.P.

By the famed author of *Dr. Attwood's Low-Fat Prescription for Kids* (Viking, 1995), this new book proclaims the life-saving benefits of a plant-based diet. Twenty-six powerful essays speak out against the myths, the prejudices and the ignorance surrounding the subject of nutrition in the U.S. today. Read about the link between high-fat consumption and heart disease, cancer and other killers; the natural and non-dairy way to increase calcium intake; obesity and our children—more than a matter of genes!; controlling food allergies, for the rest of your life, and many more topics of interest and necessity.

Paper, 216 pages, $14.95   ISBN: 978-0-934252-85-0

To order: Visit our website at www.kalindipress.com

BEYOND ASPIRIN

Nature's Challenge To Arthritis, Cancer & Alzheimer's Disease

by Thomas A. Newmark and Paul Schulick

A reader-friendly guide to one of the most remarkable medical breakthroughs of our times. Research shows that inhibition of the COX-2 enzyme significantly reduces the inflammation that is currently linked with arthritis, colon and other cancers, and Alzheimer's disease. Challenging the conventional pharmaceutical "silver-bullet" approach, this book pleads a convincing case for the safe and effective use of the COX-2-inhibiting herbs, including green tea, rosemary, basil, ginger, turmeric and others.

Paper, 340 pages, $14.95   ISBN: 978-0-934252-82-9

Cloth, 340 pages, $24.95   ISBN: 978-1-890772-01-7

FACIAL DIAGNOSIS OF CELL SALT DEFICIENCIES

A User's Guide

by David R. Card

The condition of facial skin is a primary indicator of overall bodily health. Deficiencies in diet and metabolism, together with disease conditions, are easily observed in the face, if one knows what to look for. This book is about how to "read the face" to determine which essential cell salts (also known as tissue salts) are lacking in the body. When a diagnosis is determined, the patient can then remedy that condition by supplementing with the proper cell-salt. Cell salts (tissue salts) exist in every human body. These are the inorganic biochemical elements found in the blood and tissues. They are the builders and the catalysts for many essential processes. Contains 24 full-color photos of facial conditions.

Paper, 176 pages, $24.95   ISBN: 978-1-935826-18-7

To order: Visit our website at www.kalindipress.com

TRAVEL HEALTHY

A Guidebook for Health-Conscious Travelers

by Lalitha Thomas

This book will "go" anywhere, whether your itinerary calls for a day trip to your local state park or an odyssey around the world. Lalitha Thomas, author of the highly-acclaimed books *Ten Essential Herbs* and *Ten Essential Foods*, will show you how to prepare a Health-Smart Travel Kit, and how to use it! You'll learn how to apply natural and healthy means to prevent and to remedy dozens of minor emergencies¬ and major inconveniences, like: Indigestion . . . food poisoning . . . jet lag . . . poor water . . . poor air . . . colds and flu . . . toothache . . . diarrhea . . . constipation . . . pesky insects, including bedbugs . . . sunburn . . . and more.

Lalitha has traveled extensively, and with children, throughout Mexico, India and Europe. Each chapter contains a section of *Tips for Kids*—simple ways to make their trip more enjoyable and to help them stay healthy on the road, in the air, or on the water.

Paper, 120 pages, ~~$9.95*~~ only available as publishers' "seconds" $5.00   ISBN: 978-1-890772-25-3

YOUR BODY CAN TALK

How to Use Simple Muscle Testing to Learn What Your Body Knows and Needs

by Susan L. Levy, D.C. and Carol Lehr, M.A.

Clear instructions in *simple muscle testing,* together with over 25 simple tests for how to use it for specific problems or disease conditions. Special chapters deal with health problems specific to women (especially PMS and Menopause) and problems specific to men (like stress, heart disease, and prostate difficulties). Contains over 30 diagrams, plus a complete Index and Resource Guide.

Paper, 350 pages, $19.95   ISBN: 978-0-934252-68-3

To order: Visit our website at www.kalindipress.com

BOOKS FOR CHILDREN AND PARENTS FROM **KALINDI PRESS**

WE LIKE TO HELP COOK

by Marcus Allsop

Illustrations by Diane Iverson

All the young children in these brightly-colored picture books (available in both English and Spanish) are helping adults to prepare healthy and delicious foods — all in accordance with the Healthy Diet Guidelines approved by USFDA. Simple text, plus some rhymes, make the books easy to read, and appealing to both kids and parents. Children help themselves or assist the adults by performing many age-related tasks, like pouring, shaking, washing, mashing and mixing—actions that most young children love to do.

Paper, 32 pages, $9.95   ISBN: 978-1-935826-05-7 (English)

ISBN: 978-1-935826-00-2 (Bilingual - Spanish / English)

WE LIKE TO EAT WELL

by Elyse April

Illustrations by Lewis Agrell

What we eat is vitally important for good health ... but so is *how* we eat ... *where* and *when* we eat ... and *how* much we eat ... especially in reducing obesity and diabetes II, which have reached epidemic proportions in the U.S. This book encourages young children and parents to develop the healthy eating habits that can last for a lifetime.

Paper, 32 pages; $9.95   ISBN: 978-1-890772-69-7 (English)

ISBN: 978-1-935826-01-9 (Bilingual - Spanish/English)

To order: Visit our website at www.kalindipress.com

WE LIKE TO MOVE

by Elyse April

Illustrations by Diane Iverson

Obesity prevention for children is one of the nation's prime objectives. The children in these brightly-colored picture books (available in English or Spanish) are engaged in many different forms of physical activity. The book also presents multicultural characters—including African, Hispanic, Caucasian and Asian children and adults, along with varied locales from a busy city street scene to a country landscape.

32 pages, paperback, $9.95   ISBN: 978-1-935826-02-6 (English)

ISBN: 1-935826-08-8 (Bilingual - Spanish/English)

WE LIKE TO LIVE GREEN

By Mary Young

Design by Zachary Parker

This Earth-friendly book provides an introduction to vital environmental themes in ways that will appeal to both young children and adults. We can all recycle and reuse, conserve water or grow a garden! Lively full-color photo montages demonstrate how to make a difference in a world threatened by pollution and ecological imbalance.

Paper, 32 pages, $9.95   ISBN: 978-1-935387-00-8 (English)

ISBN: 978-1-935387-01-5 (Bilingual- Spanish/English)

To order: Visit our website at www.kalindipress.com

NOTES

NOTES

CONTACT INFORMATION

Theresa Rogers has extensively researched and experimented with natural food and nutrition for 20 years. She has used her knowledge of healthy eating to work with several chronic conditions and loves helping others create and maintain an intentional diet. Theresa has a B.A. in Philosophy from U.C. Berkeley and a teaching credential in English. Several of her cookbook reviews, and some fiction, have been published in newspapers and an anthology. She lives in Northern California with her family, where she writes and helps run a restaurant with her husband. Contact: Theresa@Dharmafeast.com

Tika Altemöller has served as head cook and kitchen manager in an intentional spiritual community for 5 years. Born in Germany, she has an M.A. degree in German literature, sociology and linguistics. Over the past 20 years she has worked in several catering companies and restaurants. Many of the recipes in Dharma Feast Cookbook are favorites of those she has cooked for. Tika has always had a great love and passion for food preparation and its connection to conscious life and spiritual practice. That passion is expressed here for the inspiration and motivation of others. She lives in Bozeman, Montana. Contact: Tika@Dharmafeast.com

Visit their website/blog: www.dharmafeast.com

www.twitter.com/DharmaFeast

www.facebook.com/DharmaFeast

ABOUT KALINDI PRESS

KALINDI PRESS, an affiliate of HOHM PRESS, proudly offers books in natural health and nutrition, as well as the acclaimed Family Health and World Health Series for children and parents, covering such themes as nutrition, dental health, reading, and environmental education. Contact: hppublisher@cableone.net

Visit our website at: www.kalindipress.com